ECONOMICS
AND MAKING DECISIONS

ECONOMICS
AND MAKING DECISIONS

Marilyn Kourilsky
University of California, Los Angeles

William Dickneider
Chapman College

with

David Kaplan
Santa Monica College

Victor Tabbush
University of California, Los Angeles

WEST PUBLISHING COMPANY
St. Paul   New York   Los Angeles   San Francisco

Copyediting Sherry Goldbecker
Design Janet Bollow
Illustrations Rolin Graphics
Typesetting Parkwood Composition Service, Inc.
Cover Design and Part-opening Art Delor Erickson, Studio West

Library of Congress Cataloging-in-Publication Data

Economics and making decisions / Marilyn Kourilsky . . . [et al.].
    p.   cm.
Includes index.

    ISBN 0-314-65247-7
    1. Economics.   2. Economics—Decision making.   I. Kourilsky,
Marilyn L.
HB171.5.E3353 1988
330—dc 19   87-29514
                                                                                            CIP
                                                                                             AC

Photo Credits

2 Erik Simonsen/The Image Bank; 5 Bob Daemmrich/Stock, Boston; 7 *(left)* Jim Caccavo/Stock, Boston; 7 *(right)* Don Johnson/The Stock Market; 8 David Farr/Imagesmythe, Inc.; 9 Bob Daemmrich/Stock, Boston; 10 Mike Mazzaschi/Stock, Boston; 11 Courtesy of Hewlett-Packard; 12 Martin Rogers/Stock, Boston; 14 Erik Simonsen/The Image Bank; 26 Jeff Albertson/Stock, Boston; 29 Brent Petersen/The Stock Market; 30 Fredrik D. Bodin/Stock, Boston; 32 Howard Sockurek/Woodfin Camp & Associates; 33 Jeff Albertson/Stock, Boston; 34 Mike Maple/Woodfin Camp & Associates; 37 Kim Newton/Woodfin Camp & Associates; 43 Courtesy of Chevron; 44 Craig Hammell/The Stock Market; 45 G. Colliva/The Image Bank; 48 Abigail Heyman/Archive Pictures Inc.; 49 Courtesy of W. R. Grace & Company; 50 Rob Nelson/Picture Group; 52 Mike Mazzaschi/Stock, Boston; 58 Gary Crallé/The Image Bank; 61 Bob Daemmrich/Stock, Boston; 62 Susan Greenwood/Gamma Liaison; 63 Gary Crallé/The Image Bank; 66 Elizabeth Crews/Stock, Boston; 67 David Woo/Stock, Boston; 68 Dave Schaefer/The Picture Cube; 69 Jeff Jacobson/Archive Pictures Inc.; 70 Jon Feingersh/Stock, Boston; 71 Chris Jones/The Stock Market; 73 Melchior Di Giacomo/The Image Bank; 84 Doug Handel/The Stock Market; 87 Jeff Adamo/The Stock Market; 90 Doug Handel/The Stock Market; 91 Chris Jones/The Stock Market; 92 David W. Hamilton/The Image Bank; 94 Courtesy of the Coca-Cola Company; 96 Gary Gladstone/The Im-

 (continued following index)

Marilyn Kourilsky, an economist, is a professor at UCLA Graduate School of Education and Assistant Dean of Teacher Education. She has conducted extensive research in economics and education. In October 1987 she received the *National Leadership in Education Award* given by the Joint Council on Economic Education and the National Association of Economic Educators.

David Kaplan is a professor of economics at Santa Monica College, where he has taught for thirty years. He has written for numerous publications and is the coauthor with William Dickneider of two books on economics. Kaplan and Dickneider are also coauthors of a weekly newspaper column.

William Dickneider has taught introductory economics for twenty years. He writes for the syndicated radio program "Midnight Economist," affiliated with the Institute for Contemporary Studies. He has written for high school teachers of economics, has coauthored two books, and has been published in various newspapers, including *The Wall Street Journal.*

Victor Tabbush is Associate Dean of the UCLA Graduate School of management and lecturer in economics at UCLA. He serves as Vice President of the Foundation for Research in Economics and Education, and as an economic education consultant to the Beverly Hills Unified School District.

Contents in Brief

Contents

Preface

High in the Peruvian Andes, five young Aymara women have gathered in an adobe hut to learn double-entry bookkeeping. Their teacher, a U.S. Peace Corps volunteer, had reached the community on foot. The young ladies have had little schooling, but they are bright, motivated, and able to read and write. After four meetings, they have mastered the unfamiliar elements of debits and credits and have begun keeping accounting records for their community's arts and crafts business.

Although this event occurred some years ago, it remains a highlight in the teaching career of one of the authors. It stands out because it illustrates successful, interesting, and rewarding education. We have found similar highlights while teaching introductory economics over the years, and we think that many more can occur in economics classes throughout our nation. But that is unlikely unless teachers and students have the right tools to promote learning. With care and patience we have crafted this textbook and its supplements. We have tried to write clearly, simply, and concisely, keeping in mind the wisdom of E. B. White, who advised that good writing is a clear window to an author's thoughts.

Our objective is to provide teachers and students with comprehensible tools that will enable them to enjoy successful economic education. That objective will not be attained, however, if economics is presented as a list of disconnected facts and principles without the essence of economics. That essence is critical thinking. As John Maynard Keynes eloquently stated some years ago, "The Theory of Economics does not furnish a body of settled conclusions immediately applicable to policy. It is a method rather than a doctrine, an apparatus of the mind, a technique of thinking which helps its possessor to draw correct conclusions."

Economic thinking means using economic principles to analyze events and decisions. In order to promote this objective, we present only sound, generally accepted economic principles. **Unit I** introduces economics by examining scarcity, opportunity cost, and resource ownership. It provides an overview of the book by presenting the circular flow of a market economy. **Unit II** focuses on markets for goods and services by developing demand, supply, and equilibrium price. **Unit III** summarizes the important functions of market prices and also presents the vital role of government in a market economy. **Unit IV** discusses resource markets by focusing on labor markets and unions. And by looking at unemployment, it moves logically to **Unit V,** which presents an aggregate view of the economy. That unit discusses aggregate demand and aggregate supply, money and banks, and monetary and fiscal policies. The last unit, **Unit VI,** further expands the horizon by looking at international trade and the Soviet economy.

In addition to sound economic principles, we have also used up-to-date learning theory. For example, the book motivates the reader to learn economics by showing how it can help understand interesting events. Each chapter begins with a familiar event that serves as a hook on which the reader can hang the chapter's unfamiliar concepts. Some of the issues we use are as follows: How does the controversy about raising the speed limit on our nation's highways illustrate scarcity and opportunity cost? Why does our government store enormous surpluses of dairy products? Could a higher tax on beer reduce highway fatalities among young drivers? Would our eating less meat mean more food for the world's hungry people? And why did Kent cigarettes become Romania's smokable money?

Each chapter also contains two sections entitled *The Economic Way of Thinking.* These brief sections present interesting questions and compare how one would answer them by using the economic way of thinking and the noneconomic way of thinking. Some of the questions analyzed are as follows: Is a concert free if we do not have to pay any money to see it? Would an increased supply of apartments reduce an apartment shortage? Do higher meat prices result from the greed of grocers? Do consumers benefit from government price ceilings? Does automation reduce employment?

Motivation is further encouraged by other chapter sections entitled *Now and Then.* These lengthier sections apply economic thinking to current issues by examining their historical roots. For example, immigration illustrates scarcity and opportunity cost in Chapter 1, and "The Visible Jeans of Adam Smith" illustrates resource ownership in Chapter 2 by tracing the development of Levis 501 jeans. Examples of other *Now and Then* sections are, "A Whale of a Crisis," "A Long Drive to the Quarter-Pound Patty," "Phone Rates and Government Regulation," "Skateboards, Karl Marx, and The Law of Motion," "Economic Pains and John Maynard Keynes," and "Reports About American Manufacturing."

In addition to its emphasis on motivation, the book also uses up-to-date learning theory by carefully explaining all concepts verbally before presenting them graphically. We use this method because evidence confirms that learning is promoted when economic concepts are presented in the verbal-graphic sequence. That is why we do not introduce graphic analysis until Chapter 4. Before presenting the carefully crafted introduction to graphic analysis in that chapter, we first introduce demand through a verbal presentation in Chapter 3.

Effective teaching and learning also require practice in order to develop critical economic thinking. We offer some practice by presenting a few additional questions in each *Economic Way of Thinking* section. We also present many questions and activities at the end of the chapter. There, review questions are keyed to the chapter's learning objectives, and discussion questions range from simple ones based on the text to complex, open-ended questions designed for class discussion or essays. The various activities suggested at the end of the chapter provide additional practice with economic thinking.

Besides the many questions and activities at the end of the chapter, we have also provided a thorough teacher's manual and student's workbook. Considerable effort and care were spent creating these supplements in order to provide a wide range of useful activities and tests. The teacher's manual reviews each chapter by emphasizing lessons we have learned from years of teaching economics. It answers all questions found in both the textbook and the student's workbook, and it suggests many classroom opportunities and activities. The manual also presents two complete tests, consisting of vocabulary questions, true-false questions, multiple choice questions, and essay questions. The student's workbook contains a chapter review, vocabulary exercises, and a sample test. It also contains worksheets for building thinking skills and for developing graphing and computational skills.

Many people assisted us while we developed this book over the last few years. While we cannot list all of them here, we would like to express our gratitude. We thank all the teachers who made many valuable suggestions while experimenting with portions of the book in their classes. We are especially grateful to William R. Allen, professor of economics at UCLA, for reading the entire manuscript and making many worthwhile suggestions. We also thank the following reviewers whose valuable comments and suggestions steered us in the right direction:

Dorothy A. Barrett
Independent School District No. 77
Mankato, Minnesota

John Bowen
Hillsborough Senior High School
Tampa, Florida

Max F. Chandler
A. L. Brown High School
Kannapolis, North Carolina

LaFuan Humphreys
Eldorado High School
Albuquerque, New Mexico

David W. Miller
Pennsbury High School
Fairless Hills, Pennsylvania

Sharry Murschall
Grants Pass High School
Grants Pass, Oregon

Kay Raap
McCullough High School
The Woodlands, Texas

George Wright
North Monterey County High School
Castroville, California

Not least to thank are the people at West Publishing Company. Without the encouragement and direction of our editor, Carole Grumney, we would still be doodling on computers and dreaming about the light at the end of the tunnel. Production editor Mark Jacobsen also helped push us through this dark tunnel with his tireless efforts in design, graphics, and scheduling. We also thank production editor Barbara Fuller, who tenaciously tracked down our suggested photographs while also recommending many of her own.

Despite our persistent efforts to eradicate them, some errors have surely remained. We accept full responsibility for these imperfections, and we solicit corrections and suggested changes from you, the reader and user of our book. Though learning economics requires hard work, we know it can be a road filled with challenge, excitement, and reward. And by improving critical thinking, it can make much difference in one's perception of the world. As Robert Frost put it some years ago: *I shall be telling this with a sigh/Somewhere ages and ages hence:/Two roads diverged in a wood, and I—I took the one less traveled by,/And that has made all the difference.*

ECONOMICS

AND MAKING DECISIONS

Introduction to Economics

Unit

I

How does purchasing gasoline illustrate scarcity and opportunity cost?

Scarcity and Opportunity Cost

Chapter 1

■ Student's Goals ■

1. Define and give examples of *scarcity*.

2. Define and give examples of *resources*.

3. Explain the importance of *opportunity cost* when making choices.

4. Analyze a decision in terms of its *marginal costs* and *marginal benefits*.

5. Distinguish between *marginal cost* and *sunk cost*.

The Economics of Speed Limits

Statistics show that many highway accidents occur because motorists drive at different speeds on the same road. This suggests that we could reduce the number of accidents if vehicles on a particular highway moved at a uniform speed. Because a lower speed limit not only slows traffic but also produces a more uniform driving speed, it is strongly supported as a way of reducing highway injuries and fatalities. For example, the National Research Council estimated that each year the federal 55-miles-per-hour speed limit saved between 2,000 and 4,000 lives.[1]

These benefits cannot be obtained without sacrifice, however. As an extreme example, consider the sacrifice if *all* motor vehicles were banned in order to reduce the maximum driving speed to *zero* miles per hour. Although such a ban would eliminate all highway injuries and deaths, it would severely restrict mobility and vastly increase the time it takes us to get from one place to another. Even if driving were not banned, a lower speed limit would still mean we would have to spend more time driving. A study of the 55-miles-per-hour speed limit concluded that the extra time everyone spent on the highway in a given year added up to more than 400,000 years.[2]

Because of the additional driving time required, many drivers in rural areas have strongly opposed the "double nickel" speed limit. As a result, legislators changed the maximum permissible driving speed in 1987. In that year, Congress passed a law that allows states to raise the speed limit to 65 miles per hour on rural stretches of interstate highways. Although many drivers applauded the change, others opposed it because they predicted it would result in more highway deaths and injuries.

Proposals to raise or lower the speed limit illustrate two important economic principles presented in this chapter. The first principle is *scarcity*. Time is scarce because there are not enough hours in a day to do everything we would like to do. When you must choose between doing homework and visiting friends, you know your time is scarce. Similarly, income is

[1]Damon Darlin, "Does 55-MPH Speed Limit Save Lives? More Drivers Are Doubtful," *The Wall Street Journal*, April 28, 1986, p. 25.
[2]Thomas H. Forester, Robert F. McNown, and Larry D. Singell, "A Cost-Benefit Analysis of the 55 MPH Speed Limit," *Southern Economic Journal* (January 1984): 631–41.

Scarcity is the reason why people disagree about raising the speed limit on our nation's highways. The scarcity of time requires us to choose between spending more time driving at slower speeds in order to reduce accidents and driving faster in order to have more time for other activities we enjoy. This motorist would probably agree that the 55-miles-per-hour speed limit should be raised.

scarce because you don't have enough to purchase everything you want; you must often choose between one item and another. The scarcity of both time and highway safety also makes us choose between slower speeds that cut automobile accidents and faster speeds that reduce driving time.

The second principle explained in this chapter is *cost*. Because your time and your income are scarce, you must decide how to use them. When you use them to do one thing, you sacrifice something else. This sacrifice is your cost. If we want a lower speed limit in order to reduce traffic injuries and fatalities, then we must pay the cost of spending more time on the highway. On the other hand, if we want a higher speed limit in order to cut driving time, then we must pay the cost of having more traffic injuries and deaths. We bear a cost no matter what we do.

Is Anything Really Free?

Whether it is promoting highway safety, sleeping later in the morning, or purchasing new clothes, everything we enjoy seems to be scarce. **Scarcity** is the inability of limited means to satisfy all of everyone's wants. It means that all of us want more than we have. Although a selfish person and a generous person may want different things for different reasons, they both seek to satisfy additional wants. No matter what we want, however, we cannot be satisfied without the use of something limited. If we spend money for new clothes, we have less money to spend for food, gasoline, and other items. Even watching a sunset or meditating requires the use of our limited time. So, too, do we use limited time to produce more kindness and friendship. These items are scarce, even though they are not material goods.

> **Scarcity:** The inability of limited means to satisfy all of everyone's wants.

Since you cannot have everything you want, you must choose among various opportunities. You can't be in two places at once, for example, so you must choose how to use your limited time. If you watch television, then you have made a choice not to do other things with your time, such as visiting friends or doing homework. When you choose to do one thing rather than another or to buy one item instead of another, you bear an unavoidable cost: You give up something in order to get something else. Because your cost is the most valuable *opportunity* you give up, the cost of any choice is called an opportunity cost. **Opportunity cost** is the best opportunity given up when a choice is made.

> **Opportunity cost:** The best opportunity given up when a choice is made.

You make choices and pay opportunity costs every day when you spend your money. As an illustration, suppose you spend $5 to buy gasoline for your car. When you make that choice, you sacrifice the opportunity to spend your $5 on other things you want. Perhaps you also want a cassette that is on sale, a lunch, and a new hairbrush, each of which costs $5. If *you* value the cassette more than the other two items sacrificed when

Scarcity means that no matter what we want, we cannot be satisfied without the use of something limited. In order to purchase these sunglasses, this teen-ager must give up some of her limited income which could have been used to buy something else.

Scarcity also means that we must choose how to spend our limited time. By choosing to spend time talking and eating pizza, these individuals sacrifice other uses of their limited time.

buying the gasoline, then the cassette is your cost of buying the gas.

Since $5 will not purchase the cassette, the food, *and* the hairbrush—which together are worth $15—all three of these cannot be considered the opportunities you sacrifice. Only the option you most value among those given up—in this example, the cassette—is your cost.

The Costs We Bear

A cassette, a lunch, and a hairbrush are only a few of the possible alternatives sacrificed when buying $5 worth of gasoline. You might think there are other, more important opportunities you would sacrifice, and your friends might see other possible opportunities they would give up if they were to purchase the gasoline. People have different likes and dislikes, so they do

What is the opportunity cost of spending $5 to buy gasoline? Suppose you could have used the $5 to purchase either a new hairbrush, a blank cassette, or a lunch. Since each of these items would have required an expenditure of $5, all three are not your opportunity cost. Instead, your opportunity cost is whichever one you value the most.

not all identify the cost of a particular choice in the same way. But if you spend $5, you can't avoid giving up $5 of something. Whatever *you* think is the most valuable opportunity given up is the cost of your choice.

However, $5 is not necessarily the total cost of the gasoline. You might also spend time waiting in line at the gas station. Since time is scarce, you must consider the most valuable option sacrificed when you take time to obtain the gas. Perhaps your next best use of this time would have been walking your dog. If so, walking your dog is also part of your cost of purchasing the gasoline.

If you have ever waited in a long line to buy gasoline, tickets, groceries, or some other item, you know that some costs, like your time, might not have money price tags. Lacking money price tags, these costs are sometimes ignored. Other costs are ignored because someone else besides the person making the choice bears them. Take this illustration. A writer who works at home was bothered by the noise of her neighbors' barking dogs. Although her neighbors made the choice to have dogs, they ignored the cost suffered by the woman when her scarce peace and concentration were sacrificed.

You can think of other examples that show how individuals involuntarily bear the costs of someone else's choice. In fact,

The people waiting in this line would agree that some costs do not have money price tags. In addition to the ticket's money price, these people bear an opportunity cost by waiting in line. This cost is the best use of the time they give up while standing in line. Would you prefer to pay a higher ticket price if doing so decreased your waiting time?

the shifting of costs to others who bear them unwillingly is the economic definition of pollution, as explained in Chapter 8. But even if individuals shift the costs they create to others and even if individuals ignore the costs that lack money price tags, costs are still all around us. We find costs everywhere because wherever we look, we see scarcity.

Scarcity For All

Just as you must make choices because of scarcity, so, too, must business managers make decisions. A good illustration relates to the scarcity of shelf space in a supermarket. Supermarket managers must decide how to use their limited shelf space in the same way that consumers must decide how to use their limited money income and time. The wise use of scarce shelf space is important because store managers want to display the products shoppers are most likely to buy. By carefully comparing the estimated sales of different products, store managers can use their scarce shelf space to display those items that earn

Scarcity and decision making are also confronted by businesses. Because the space in this shop's window is scarce, the store's manager must decide which items to display and how to arrange them.

the most profit. Similarly, by carefully comparing different opportunities, individuals can use their scarce time and money to their best advantage.

In all nations, individuals confront scarcity and make choices because no country has the means to satisfy all the wants of every citizen. The United States is a wealthy country, but we still make choices: Should we use our land to build more houses or to grow more food? Should we use our scarce time to provide more health care or more hamburgers? Should we make more tanks or more tank tops? Should we use a particular river for rafting or for generating hydroelectric power?

We face these choices because our resources are scarce. **Resources** are the basic ingredients used to produce what we want. They are often called *inputs* or *factors of production.* Resources are *land* (our soil, water, minerals, and other natural resources), *labor*, and *capital* (our buildings, machines, and tools). *Management* is the ability to organize the factors of production, and it, too, is a resource.[3] As wealthy as our nation is compared to

[3]Instead of management, some prefer the term **entrepreneurship.** Entrepreneurship is the willingness and ability to innovate, to take risks, and to organize the other factors of production.

other countries, we still do not have enough resources to provide everything we want. We must choose how to use our scarce resources, just as all other nations must decide how to use theirs.

Resources: The four basic ingredients used to produce what we want: land, labor, capital, and management.

These choices are often much harder for those who live in poorer countries. The choice of starving African peasants to eat crops set aside for next year's seed is certainly different from the choice of shoppers in U.S. supermarkets to purchase a particular brand of cereal. No matter how painful or pleasant choices are, they still arise because people want more than can be produced with the resources they have available.

Scarcity is the fundamental economic problem people have always faced. If we were to pass laws against it, it would not go away. Nor would scarcity disappear if we all worked harder to produce more of what we want. Even as a nation becomes richer, scarcity is not eliminated, for no matter how hard we try, scarcity will remain.

Capital goods are also found in the provision of medical services. Here, equipment produced by Hewlett Packard measures an infant's heart and lung functions.

Scarcity refuses to go away because people's wants always exceed the ability of limited resources to satisfy them. Economic growth enables a nation to produce more, but people's changing and expanding wants race continually ahead of their ability to satisfy these desires. For example, your wants are very different and probably much greater than those of someone your age living in a less developed country. One of the reasons for this difference is the fact that our expectations about our living standards are continually expanding.

Owning a television is not even a dream for many people around the world, but for most of us in the United States, it is taken for granted. Even electricity and plumbing, once thought to be rare blessings, are now considered essential. And only 20 years ago who would have thought that today so many families would have computers and videocassette recorders?

Scarcity thrives as the unknowns of yesterday become the wants of today. Making a nation richer does not eliminate scarcity, nor does redistributing the nation's income. Even if we would want only to satisfy others' wants, scarcity would still exist because resources would be insufficient. No matter how wealthy or poor they are, individuals must still make choices

Sometimes scarcity presents difficult choices. In the Peruvian Andes, cold, dry weather often destroys crops of potatoes, a staple in the diet of Quechua Indians. Imagine a poor family selling some of its meager potato crop in order to obtain money for other staples. The family would then have fewer seed potatoes when planting time arrives.

and pay costs—a fact that confirms the existence of scarcity, not abundance. Scarcity is everywhere, in rich nations and in poor ones because people everywhere want more than can be produced with the limited resources available.

Thinking About Choice

Because scarcity exists in all societies, nations as well as individuals must make decisions carefully about the use of their limited resources if they are to satisfy their most important desires. **Economics** is the study of how scarce resources are allocated among alternative uses in order to accomplish this goal.

> **Economics:** The study of how scarce resources are allocated among alternative uses.

Economics is a way of thinking about the choices we make about the use of our scarce resources. By enabling us to think more clearly about the alternative uses of resources, economics helps us compare the costs and benefits of our choices. To help us make this comparison, economics emphasizes **thinking at the margin.** The easiest way to understand what this term means is to consider an example. Assume that you must decide how many hours to study for a particular course. Yours is not an all-or-none decision in which you must choose at the beginning of the course either to study all the time or not to study at all. Instead, as the term progresses, you must choose each day whether or not to use another hour of your scarce time for studying.

At the beginning of the term, before you have studied at all for the class, you must decide whether or not to use one hour of your time for studying. This first hour of study time is the one at the margin. At some time during the term, when you've already spent 50 hours studying for the course, the next, or 51st, hour is the one at the margin. A margin is a border or an edge, such as the margin on this page. At the beginning of the term, the first hour of studying is the one at the border or edge,

The fact that this woman has decided to purchase gasoline does not mean that she will spend all her money on this product. Instead, she chooses to spend an additional dollar on gasoline only when the marginal benefit compensates her for the marginal cost.

and it is the one about which you must make a decision. Later in the term, after you have already studied 50 hours for the class, the next, or 51st, hour is now the one at the margin. It is the hour about which you must make a decision. The extra benefit you think you will obtain by spending this additional hour studying is called the *marginal benefit*. Similarly, the extra opportunity cost you will bear if you use this hour for studying is called the *marginal cost*.

Thinking at the margin: Comparing the additional (marginal) benefit of a choice with its additional (marginal) cost.

Marginal benefit and marginal cost are also illustrated by the purchase of goods and services. We do not usually choose between spending all our money or none of it on a particular product, such as gasoline. Instead, we decide between using an *additional* dollar to buy gas and using the dollar to buy something else. The benefit of spending one more dollar on gas is the marginal benefit. Similarly, the opportunity given up by spending one more dollar on gas is the marginal cost.

(text continues on page 19)

Choosing to Immigrate

Despite telephones, television, and other modern means of communication, you still can't be in two places at the same time. You can't simultaneously sit in a classroom, ski down a mountainside, and sack groceries at a supermarket. Nor can you be in two countries at the same time. Because your time is scarce, you must choose to be in one place or another, just as you choose to spend your money on one item or another. We make choices about our geographical locations, just as we make decisions about the goods and services we buy.

Consider immigration to the United States. Immigrants of various nationalities have come to America. However, Table A shows that in recent years the proportion of immigrants coming from Asia has increased and the proportion coming from Europe has decreased.

We can understand some of the reasons for this change by examining why people choose to immigrate. Like any other choice, the decision to migrate from one nation to another depends on the expected benefits and expected opportunity costs. Some costs, such as transportation expenses, and some benefits, such as increased earnings in the new nation, are monetary. Others are personal. Personal costs are illustrated by the friends and relatives and the particular way of life that would be lost if

one chooses to move to another nation. On the other hand, an immigrant often expects personal gains in the form of greater political, religious, and economic freedom. Individuals choose to immigrate, therefore, because they expect their gains to exceed their costs.

When the costs or benefits of immigration suddenly change, there can be an increase or a decrease in the rate of immigration. For example, between 1960 and 1984, political and economic instability in Vietnam, Iran, Iraq, and the Philippines reduced the opportunities that people from these nations would have to give up by moving to another country. As a result, the opportunity costs of their moving to the United States were reduced. The resulting rise in immigration from these four nations accounted for more than half of the increase in Asia's share of immigration shown in Table A.

Rapid changes in immigration are not new in our country. Figure A shows how legal immigration to the United States has varied since records were first kept in 1820. In order to allow for the rising population of our nation, immigration is presented as the number of immigrants per 1,000 members of the U.S. population.

Notice the big jump in immigration around 1850. One of the reasons

Table A Immigrants' Place of Birth

Place of Birth	Percentage of Total Immigrants	
	1961–70	1985
Europe	37%	11%
Asia	13	46
Canada	9	2
Mexico	13	11
Caribbean and Central America	19	19
South America	7	7
Africa	1	3
Other	1	1
	100%	100%

Source: Statistical Abstract of the United States (1987), 8.

for this was the Irish potato famine. As food in Ireland became increasingly scarce, the opportunity cost of migrating to the United States was reduced. At about the same time, revolution in Austria meant that many people would give up less security or wealth by leaving that country. Once again, the opportunity cost of migrating to the United States lessened. A third factor responsible for the increased immigration during that time was the discovery of gold in California. By increasing the expected benefits of moving to the United States, the discovery of gold encouraged greater immigration.

Figure A also shows that immigration peaked in the 1870s, in the 1880s, and again in the early 1900s. During this time laws prohibiting emigration were repealed in Italy, the Austro-Hungarian empire, and the Slavic nations. Moreover, the persecution of Jews in Russia encouraged migration to the United States.

In addition to increases and decreases in the rate of immigration to the United States, Figure A also reflects our government's policies on immigration. With the exception of the Chinese Exclusion Act of 1882, which blocked the migration of Chinese to our country, immigration was virtually unrestricted by the government until 1921. In that year, a national quota system was inaugurated which allowed immigration from nations in the Eastern Hemisphere according to the fraction of the U.S. population already composed of immigrants from each of those nations. Since most prior immigrants had come from Europe, the quota had the effect of favoring immigration from European nations.

In 1965, the national origin system of limiting immigration from the Eastern Hemisphere was abolished.

Instead, the government enacted a numerical ceiling for immigration from both the Eastern and Western Hemispheres. In 1985, the yearly worldwide ceiling was 270,000, with a ceiling of 20,000 on immigrants from any one particular country. Preference is given for family reunification and for employment considerations. Moreover, spouses, children, political refugees, and individuals seeking political asylum are exempted from the numerical quota.

This change in the immigration law allowed immigration to shift

Figure A U.S. Immigration, 1820–1985

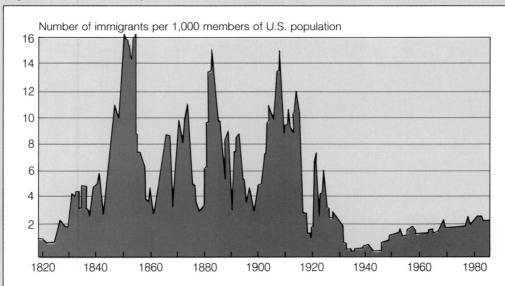

Source: *Historical Statistics of the United States, 1820–1970; Economic Report of the President, 1986; Statistical Abstract of the United States (1987), p. 11.*

away from Europe to Asia. While the major source of new immigrants has shifted from Europe to Asia, however, the proportion of legal immigrants coming from Mexico has remained between 10 and 15 percent of total immigration for the last few decades.

Illegal immigration is a different story. Although an accurate measure of the increase of illegal immigrants in the United States is not available, the U.S. Bureau of the Census estimates that between 100,000 to 300,000 undocumented individuals illegally settle in the United States each year. Although most of these illegal immigrants are thought to enter the United States from Mexico, only about half are estimated to *enter* our country illegally. The other half come to the United States on legal visas but then remain illegally by violating the terms of their visas.

References

Economic Report of the President. Washington, D.C.: U.S. Government Printing Office, 1986. Chapter 7.

Vedder, Richard K., *The American Economy in Historical Perspective.* Belmont, Calif.: Wadsworth Publishing Co., 1976. 124–32, 350–61.

Because we suffer when we make foolish decisions in a world of scarcity, we want to make the best choices we can. If we think the marginal benefit of a choice exceeds its marginal cost, we will probably call the decision a wise one. But if we think the marginal cost is greater, we will probably call it a foolish decision.

Marginal benefits and marginal costs are not always easy to identify. Take the example of the high school students who purchased tickets to a professional football game. On the morning of the game, it was raining cats and dogs, so one of the students suggested they miss the game and do something else instead. "We can't do that," remarked another student. "It's too late to resell the tickets or return them for a refund, so we'll waste all that money if we don't go to the game."

The students were incorrectly thinking the money they had already spent for the tickets was a cost of choosing on this rainy day to do something else besides going to the game. This thought was incorrect because the students could no longer avoid the cost of the tickets. The cost of the tickets was not a marginal cost because it was not an *additional* cost of choosing to skip the football game. This cost had already been incurred in the past and could no longer be avoided, so it is an example of a **sunk cost.**

> **Sunk cost:**   A cost that was incurred in the past and can no longer be avoided.

Being unavoidable, sunk costs should be ignored if we want to make wise choices. Because the money spent on the tickets was a sunk cost, not a marginal cost, the students should have ignored it on that rainy morning as they decided whether or not to attend the football game. Instead, the students should have compared the marginal benefits and marginal costs of attending the game in order to choose how to spend their day.

Without training, we would have difficulty learning to think in terms of marginal benefits and marginal costs. Indeed, economic thinking as a skill, like driving a car or playing a sport, so it takes practice to learn it. In order to provide practice for you, each chapter of the book presents sections entitled "The Economic Way of Thinking." These sections demonstrate economic thinking by applying it to many different topics.

Costs

One of the authors of this book spent some time in Kenya, Africa. When he arrived at the Kenyan airport to travel back to the United States, he had the equivalent of $20 in Kenyan currency. He was told he could not convert his money into U.S. dollars and he was not allowed to take the money out of the country. The gift shop was closed, so he decided to use the Kenyan currency to purchase refreshments for strangers waiting to depart. What was his cost of purchasing these refreshments?

Noneconomic Way of Thinking

The cost of the refreshments is measured by the amount of Kenyan currency spent on them. In this case, the cost to the author of providing the refreshments was $20 worth of Kenyan currency.

Economic Way of Thinking

Other than the author's time, there was no cost for the refreshments. Since he could not convert the money into U.S. dollars or spend it at the gift shop, he had no alternative uses for the money. Because he gave up nothing when he chose to spend the money on refreshments, he incurred no opportunity cost. Remember that the cost of a choice is the most valuable opportunity you give up, not the dollars you spend.

Questions

1. If he could have exchanged the Kenyan currency for U.S. dollars at the airport, would the author have bought refreshments for strangers?

2. If the author had had the option of spending the money on newspapers and magazines at the airport, what effect would this have had on the cost of buying the refreshments?

Implicit Costs

Sometimes we encounter things we can enjoy without having to pay for them. For example, we might go to a "free" concert in the park or we might put our money in a "free" checking account at a bank that does not charge us a monthly service fee. Are these things really free?

Noneconomic Way of Thinking

A checking account or a concert ticket costs us nothing if no dollars are required to obtain them. For a cost to be incurred, money must change hands. Otherwise, the items are free.

Economic Way of Thinking

If we give up alternatives when we make a choice, then we incur a cost. This cost may be implicit, meaning it does not require an explicit payment of money. For example, a bank might not charge you a monthly service fee, but you still sacrifice the interest that you could otherwise have earned by depositing the money in a savings account. Consequently, you bear an implicit cost, which is the interest the money could have earned somewhere else. Similarly, when you attend a concert without an explicit charge, you still incur an implicit cost. The cost is the value of the next best use of the time you sacrifice by attending the concert.

Questions

1. Suppose you were given a record as a present. Would there be a cost involved in using it as a Frisbee? If so, what would that cost be?

2. What is the cost of being in the school band if you must quit a part-time job in order to attend afternoon practices?

3. Because some older people completely own their homes, they make no house payments. Does this mean they do not incur any costs (besides maintenance, taxes, etc.) by living there? (*Hint:* Could they rent their house to someone else?)

Chapter Summary

1. *Scarcity* occurs because our wants exceed the resources available to satisfy them. Scarcity, which is illustrated by our limited time and money, does not apply only to material goods. Friendship, kindness, and beautiful sunsets are valuable—and also scarce.

2. Scarcity forces us to choose among alternatives. *Opportunity cost* is defined as the most valuable opportunity sacrificed when you make a choice.

3. Costs do not always involve money prices. An example is the additional time you might spend waiting to buy gas, time that you could have used to do something else. In addition, costs associated with choices are often borne by someone other than those persons who are making the choices, such as when a neighbor's dog disturbs a person trying to work.

4. No nation has enough resources to satisfy all of everyone's wants. *Resources*—the basic ingredients or tools used to produce what we want—are *land*, *labor*, *capital*, and *management*. Management is the ability to organize the basic tools of production.

5. Scarcity exists because our limited resources cannot satisfy all of our wants. As a result, neither economic growth nor greater national wealth nor a redistribution of existing national income will eliminate scarcity.

6. *Economics* is the study of how scarce resources are allocated among alternative uses. Economics is a way of thinking that allows us to make better decisions by carefully considering the costs and benefits of our choices.

7. *Thinking at the margin* enables us to think more clearly about the choices we make. Thinking at the margin means comparing the additional benefit, or *marginal benefit*, of a choice with its additional cost, or *marginal cost*. Unlike marginal costs, which can be avoided, other costs have been incurred and can no longer be avoided. Because these costs, called *sunk costs*, have already been borne, they are irrelevant when making current choices.

1. What is *scarcity?* Do all people, including the rich, experience scarcity?

2. If individuals were always unselfish, would scarcity be eliminated? Why or why not?

3. What is *economics?*

4. What is meant by the term *resources?* Is management considered a resource? Why or why not?

5. What is meant by the statement "Every decision involves a cost"?

6. Do individuals sometimes bear the costs of someone else's decision? Explain.

7. What is meant by the phrase *thinking at the margin?* Give an example.

8. In economics, what is the difference between a wise decision and a foolish one?

9. What is meant by the term *sunk costs?* Give an example, and explain the role of sunk costs in making decisions.

Discussion Questions

1. Why does scarcity force you to give up some things in order to get other things? Explain and give examples.

2. Explain why limited resources force individuals and nations to make choices.

3. What costs should be ignored if you are going to make wise choices? Why?

4. Some people advocate the military draft because they believe it is less costly than a volunteer army. Explain why the cost of the army is or is not the amount of money the government spends on it. Which do you think is a wiser choice for the nation—the draft or the volunteer army? Why?

Activities

1. Using your knowledge of opportunity cost, make a case for reducing the lunch period for high school seniors in your school by twenty minutes.

2. Describe a decision you have made that involved the concept of sunk cost. Did you correctly apply the concept? Why or why not?

3. Using your knowledge of marginal costs and marginal benefits, write a paragraph analyzing the following statement: "The school day should be increased by fifteen minutes."

4. Before purchasing a new car, most people decide how much time to spend shopping in order to find the best deal. More time spent shopping often means more money saved, as the hypothetical numbers in the following table show. Calculate the marginal benefit (additional money saved) for each extra day spent shopping. If each day of a shopper's time is worth $30, how many days should an individual who wants to make a wise economic choice spend shopping?

Total Days Spent Shopping	Total Money Saved	Marginal Benefit
0	$ 0	0
1	$200	_____
2	$300	_____
3	$350	_____
4	$375	_____
5	$385	_____

Additional Readings

Albrecht, William P., Jr. *Economics*. 4th ed. Englewood Cliffs, N.J.: Prentice-Hall, 1986. 3–11.

Dickneider, William, and Kaplan, David. *Choice and Change: An Introduction to Economics*. St. Paul: West Publishing Co., 1978. 2–7.

Waud, Roger N., *Economics*. 3d ed. New York: Harper and Row, 1986. 24–28.

How are resource owners coordinated so the pizza you enjoy is produced?

Resource Ownership

■ Student's Goals ■

1. Explain the three basic economic decisions that all societies must make: *what*, *how*, and *for whom* to produce.

2. Define a *command economy*, and describe how it makes the what, how, and for whom decisions.

3. Explain how a market economy decides what to produce on the basis of consumer demand.

4. Explain how a market economy decides how to produce based on comparisons of the prices and productivities of resources.

5. Explain how a market economy decides for whom to produce based on how much individuals contribute to production.

6. Draw a circular flow map that shows the interrelationships among the decisions about what, how, and for whom to produce.

Calendars and Dances

Many high school and college students have started their own businesses. Take the case of Dan Bienenfeld, who began producing calendars while he was a student at the University of California.[1] Bienenfeld used $2,000 he borrowed from his father to produce calendars featuring photographs of good-looking men on the campus. Spurred on by his initial success in selling $20,000 worth of calendars, Bienenfeld added two partners, persuaded an investor to put up $80,000, hired a few employees, and then spent the summer convincing card shops, beauty parlors, boutiques, bookstores, and other small businesses around the country to carry the calendars. After more than one thousand stores agreed to display the product, sales jumped to $200,000 for the year. Bienenfeld then added other products, such as posters, gift wrap, and a teddy bear that sings "Love Me Tender." As a result, annual sales rocketed to more than a million dollars.

Other student businesses have not been as successful. Consider the two college freshmen who hoped to develop a profitable business catering to people who enjoyed dancing but were too young to attend many of the local nightclubs. They spent more than a thousand dollars to rent a roller-skating rink, print up thousands of invitations, and purchase hundreds of roses. When only 350 people showed up for the first dance, however, the partners were saddled with a big loss and a bundle of roses. They cut costs for the next dance by eliminating the printed invitations and roses. For a third dance they cut expenses again, but even with lower costs; the business was not profitable. The partners closed up shop as a result.

What, How, and For Whom?

Not one of the 12 million businesses in our economy can take survival for granted. Nor can the more than 100 million people who work at these businesses take their jobs for granted. In-

[1]Karen Blumenthal, "On Campuses, Making Dean's List Comes Second to Making a Profit," *The Wall Street Journal*, April 4, 1985.

When two students opened a business providing dances for people too young to attend nightclubs, they illustrated the three basic economic decisions: They decided whether or not to produce dances; they decided how to produce the dances; and many others decided for whom the dances would be produced when they made choices about earning the incomes necessary to buy this service. If this many customers had shown up, the students would not have gone out of business.

stead, the survival of both businesses and jobs depends on how well they satisfy the wants of consumers.

But who tells businesses and workers what to produce in order to satisfy these wants? Who tells them how many of each item they should produce? Who tells them what combination of resources they should use to produce each item? And who tells them how to distribute each scarce item among all those consumers who want more items than are available?

These are the kinds of choices that had to be made about calendars and dances:

1. **What** *should be produced?* Should campus photo calendars or dances for young people be produced, and, if so, in what quantity?

2. **How** *should each item be produced?* What combination of resources, such as labor time, raw materials, and equipment, should be used? Should the calendars be produced on printing presses or xeroxed and assembled by hand? Should the dances be held in a large roller-skating rink with

The activities and resources of many individuals had to be coordinated so that these products would be available. What caused all these individuals to decide to produce these products? What guided them in determining the combination of resources to use in their production? How are these products distributed among all the consumers who want more items than are available?

a live band and roses or in a small room with recorded music and no flowers?

3. *For whom* *should the items be produced?* How will individuals obtain the income that enables them to pay for the calendars or dances?

Because of scarcity, these three questions must be answered in every nation. There are not enough resources to satisfy all of everyone's wants, so nations must choose *what* goods and services to produce with their scarce resources, *how* to combine existing resources in order to produce these goods and services, and *for whom* to produce these scarce goods and services. Although all nations must make these three basic choices, they do not have to make them in the same way. Instead, the method a nation uses to make the what, how, and for whom choices depends on the way its resources are owned.

Collective Ownership and the Command Economy

Scarcity forces a nation to choose how its resources will be used, so someone must have the authority to make these choices.

The authority or right to determine how resources are used is called **ownership.**

Ownership: The authority or right to determine how resources are used.

If a nation has collective ownership, then the rights to choose how resources are used are held by the government. The government can be democratically elected, or it can use force to maintain its authority over the use of resources. In either case, private citizens of the nation do not have ownership. They do not have the rights to decide how to use land, labor, capital, and management.

Because it centralizes authority over resources with the government, collective ownership results in a command economy. **A command economy** is one in which the government owns the nation's resources and decides what, how, and for whom to produce.

Command economy: An economy in which the government owns the nation's resources and decides what, how, and for whom to produce.

When a government owns an economy's resources, it commands that those resources be used to produce the goods that its planners want. Government planners decide which goods and services to produce, how many of them to produce, and how to produce them. The government also determines who will be able to consume these goods and services.

The last chapter of this book explains more fully how government planners in the Soviet Union have made economic plans that favor the production of capital goods over the production of consumer goods. As a result, government planners have directed that more scarce resources be used for the production of trucks, machines, and other capital goods and fewer resources for the production of clothes, restaurant food, and other consumer goods.

This truck plant in the Soviet Union illustrates a command economy. Because the Soviet government owns most resources, government planners decide what, how, and for whom to produce.

Private Ownership and the Market Economy

Instead of having collective ownership, a nation can allow resources to be privately owned. In this case, private individuals have the authority to determine how particular resources are used. Because Bienenfeld and his two partners owned their labor time, materials, and other resources, they were able to decide to produce calendars for consumers.

In an economy in which resources are privately owned, no individual or group of central planners commands how resources will be used. Instead, many individual owners independently determine how their resources will be used. How, then, can all these private owners be made to work together, so that their resources are used to produce the goods and services people want?

Think about all the labor and other resources that must be brought together to prepare a pizza. The restaurant's employees are only the tip of the iceberg. Who makes the tomato sauce, and what tools and machinery do they use? Who makes these tools and machines, and how are the metals obtained for their manufacture? What land is used to grow fresh tomatoes, and how do the thirsty tomato plants get enough water? Who manufactures the cheese, grows the wheat for the flour in the crust, and raises the herbs that make each bite so tasty?

When we own resources privately, the desire to do what is best for ourselves can also lead us to cooperate with other people in order to produce the goods and services that consumers want. For example, people who go into business for themselves own their time and other resources, so they receive the benefits and bear the costs of using those resources. Consequently, business owners have an incentive to use their resources carefully to produce something that consumers want. Similarly, corporations and other producers who pay private owners for the use of their resources also receive the benefits and bear the costs of using the resources they purchase. They, too, have an incentive to use resources carefully by providing something that consumers want. As a result, producers make exchanges with consumers. They produce calendars and other goods and services for consumers, and in return, consumers pay them money.

In an economy with private ownership, therefore, individuals can freely exchange with one another. These exchanges are

A pizza cannot be enjoyed without the coordinated activities of many individuals who don't know each other. Someone must grow tomatoes for sauce, someone must mill flour for the crust, another must prepare spices, another must produce ovens, and someone must assure the availability of cheese. How are these people and activities coordinated in a market economy?

called markets. A **market** exists whenever buyers and sellers trade with one another. Indeed, a market might or might not have a particular physical location. For example, many of us now shop using cable television and telephones. We can purchase furniture, power tools, jewelry, and other products over the telephone when we see these products displayed and demonstrated on special TV channels. This market, called the *electronic shopping market*, exists wherever people have televisions and telephones.

> **Market:** A market exists whenever buyers and sellers trade with one another. A market might or might not have a particular physical location.

Markets create *market prices*, which then show producers how much value consumers put on the various things that the resources can produce. Those of us who produce what consumers value most will obtain the most in exchange. In markets, therefore, we as individuals have an incentive to work with one

A market might not have a particular physical location. This woman is using her television and computer in order to shop at home. Although there is no particular store, a market still exists because a buyer and seller are trading with one another.

another in order to use our resources to produce what consumers want most.

You will see later in the book that there are times when producers are guided by self-interest, at the consumer's expense. But in the marketplace this harm is the exception, not the rule. Markets usually guide producers to provide the most benefit for others by doing what is in the owners' self-interest. That is because market prices accomplish two important tasks: (1) they tell producers which goods and services consumers want produced, and (2) they give producers an incentive to provide the most desired goods and services.

Both of these tasks are illustrated by the experiences of the student businesses described at the beginning of this chapter. The price that consumers were willing to pay for calendars showed that they wanted this product. Moreover, the fact that consumers were willing to pay a price above the company's production costs provided the incentive to increase the production of calendars. On the other hand, consumers revealed that they placed a low value on the other business's products by refusing to buy its dances and roses. By not paying a price that enabled the business to cover its costs, consumers denied the business the incentive to continue production.

The effects of market prices on these two businesses demonstrate why prices are often compared to an *"invisible hand."* Unlike the commands of central planners in an economy of collective ownership, the overall guidance of an economy by market prices often remains unnoticed in a system of private ownership. Even if most people do not understand how their entire economy can be guided by market prices, these prices still direct private resource owners to cooperate with one another in order to produce the goods and services that consumers value most.

The Invisible Hand and VCRs

The development of videocassettes and videocassette recorders (VCRs) illustrates the role of market prices in an economy of private ownership. Although both of these products were rare before the 1980s, millions of homes now have VCRs, and tens of thousands of video stores offer a wide selection of cassettes. How did the production of these products come about?

Thinking About Self-interest

Market economies are often criticized because producers are allowed to make decisions on the basis of what is good for them. These critics argue that self-interest results in conflict and confusion. Does it?

Noneconomic Way of Thinking

How can an economic system produce the right goods in the right quantities when it is based on greed, self-interest, and competition? The market system leads to incorrect decisions because individuals are out for themselves and do not consider the broader social good.

Economic Way of Thinking

It is questionable whether individuals act only out of self-interest. But even if they do, the interest of the community will be furthered. Take, for example, a physician. He or she aids the sick and injured not necessarily out of concern for their well-being, but because patients pay for the medical services. It pays producers to supply what consumers want. By so doing, producers increase their own wealth. Under capitalism, economic decisions are generally wise, and they are made in an orderly, rather than a chaotic, manner. These decisions further the interests of both consumers and producers, and so they serve the best interest of the community.

Questions

1. Are individuals always out to promote their self-interest, or do they sometimes harm themselves in order to benefit others?
2. Do owners of grocery stores keep their shelves stocked with food because they are concerned about the health of their customers? Is there another reason?

In order to produce these products, producers had to choose to divert scarce resources from the production of other things that consumers wanted. So too, did they have to make choices so that the right amount of each product would be available. There was no point in making videocassettes if VCRs were not widely available, and there was no point in making VCRs if cassettes were not widely available. In order to produce these products, therefore, the resources and efforts of many individuals had to be combined, like so many pieces of a jigsaw puzzle. Who made these choices? Why did so many different resource owners who had never met one another cooperate by using their resources to make these products?

The answers would not be difficult to understand in a command economy based on collective ownership. Because the government would own the available resources, planners would first decide whether or not such products should be produced. If they were to decide in favor of their production, the planners would then decide how to produce them by commanding resources to produce the numbers and kinds of these new products the planners thought appropriate.

The "invisible hand" of market prices has directed land, labor, capital, and management to produce these VCRs. Private owners are using their resources to make these products because they benefit by providing what consumers want. Similarly, market prices have directed others to produce the videocassettes necessary for these VCRs.

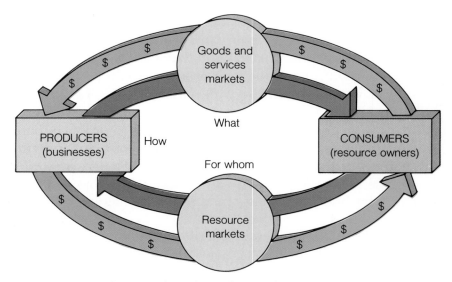

Figure 2–1   The Circular Flow of a Market Economy

Resource owners sell land, labor, capital, and management to businesses in the resource markets shown at the bottom of the diagram. The dark loop at the bottom shows this flow of resources from owners to businesses. In return, resource owners receive money from businesses in the resource markets, a flow shown by the bottom loop containing the dollar signs. As consumers, resource owners use their money earnings to demand goods and services from businesses in the markets shown at the top of the diagram. Money flows from consumers to businesses in the top loop containing the dollar signs, and goods and services flow from businesses to consumers through the blue loop at the top

Not as apparent, however, is the way the "invisible hand" of market prices coordinates an economy based on the private ownership of resources. In a market economy, no central economic authority directs individuals and resources to produce products, such as videocassettes and VCRs. Instead, individual owners use their resources in ways that most benefit them. Just as market prices directed student business owners to produce more calendars and fewer dances, so, too, have market prices directed and coordinated the individual businesses that produced videocassettes and VCRs in our economy.

The Circular Flow of a Market Economy

This brief description cannot completely explain how a market economy chooses what, how, and for whom to produce. That is one of the tasks of the chapters ahead. As an introduction, however, the "map" in Figure 2–1 illustrates some of this book's

(text continues on page 43)

The Visible Jeans of Adam Smith

What shrinks, has rivets, and is displayed in the Louvre in France and the Smithsonian Institution in Washington, D.C.? The *Random House Dictionary* defines the answer as "close-fitting, heavy trousers made of denim or denimlike material that have a low waistline and are reinforced with copper rivets at the strain points." More commonly, we know them as Levis.

Levis are produced by the Levi Strauss Company, headquartered in San Francisco, California. According to *Fortune* magazine, it is one of the 200 largest industrial corporations in the United States. Indeed, it sells more than $2 billion worth of products a year and employs about 37,000 people.

Not long ago the company had many more workers. In 1980, Levi Strauss employed almost 50,000 people as it tried to expand its product line to include new items, such as hats, leather goods, and designer apparel. Although the company offered these new items in the goods and services markets, consumers were not interested. After losing money on these ventures, Levi Strauss abandoned the new lines, closed forty factories in three years, and cut its work force by more than 10,000 people. Consumers had spoken clearly to Levi Strauss, so the company concentrated its efforts on the products

consumers *were* willing to buy, such as shirts, slacks, women's tops, jeans, and, in particular, the classic 501 Levis.

The change made the company more profitable, which must have pleased its owners, who are primarily the descendants of the company's founder, Levi Strauss. Strauss was a twenty-year-old Bavarian immigrant who joined the California Gold Rush in the 1850s. But his objective was not to dig for gold. In fact, if he had pursued his original plan, Levis might have been tents, not jeans.

Levi Strauss's original idea was to sell dry goods to miners in California. When he came to America, he brought supplies of silk, broadcloth, and canvas for tents and covered wagons. Then he met a miner who remarked, "Pants don't wear worth a hoot up in the diggin's. You can't get a pair strong enough to last no time."

The young immigrant didn't waste any time. Taking his rolls of canvas to a tailor, he asked that they be made into pants. Consumers loved the new durable pants, so they demanded more. Strauss supplied more and referred to them according to their lot number, 501. On that day Levis 501s were born.

Strauss, in partnership with his brothers, founded Levi Strauss Company in San Francisco in 1853. Sales soon depleted the original supply of canvas, so the brothers looked for a substitute. They found it in a durable cotton fabric from France known as *Serge-de-Nimes,* from which we get the word *denim*. A similar fabric had been used to make pants for Italian sailors from Genoa. Because the French word for *Genoa* is *Gênes,* Levis also became known as *jeans*.

Rivets were added some years later when Levi Strauss heard about a joke played on an old prospector. The prospector, who usually stuffed his pockets with mining tools, continually complained to a tailor that the pockets were always falling off. As a joke, the tailor took the miner's pants to a harnessmaker and had the pockets riveted on the pants. When the pockets stayed on, however, the prospector praised the tailor. Upon hearing the story, Strauss began using rivets to secure the pockets on his jeans. In 1873, he patented the idea.

The history of jeans illustrates how a market economy makes the what, how, and for whom choices that inevitably result from scarcity. No government authority commanded that Levis be produced or that they be manufactured with denim and rivets. Nor did a government authority determine who would wear them. Instead, the Levi Strauss Company

has produced Levis over the years because the company's owners have profited from doing so. But they have profited only because consumers have also benefited. As consumers have used their dollars to vote for Levis in the goods and services markets, consumers and the company both have benefited.

The story of Levis illustrates how the marketplace can harness self-interest and make it work for the benefit of the community. This point was thoroughly and systematically explained more than 200 years ago by a shy, absent-minded professor of moral philosophy at the University of Glasgow in Scotland.

After observing and contemplating the growing market economy in Great Britain, Adam Smith wrote an extraordinary book about it entitled *The Wealth of Nations*. The book's publication date, 1776, marks another important event: the writing of the American Declaration of Independence.

Smith saw a market economy as a beneficial system that would operate best without strong government guidance. He pictured an economy in which individuals would have private rights to the use of property. Although government would be essential, its role in the economy

Figure A Value of Clothing Production

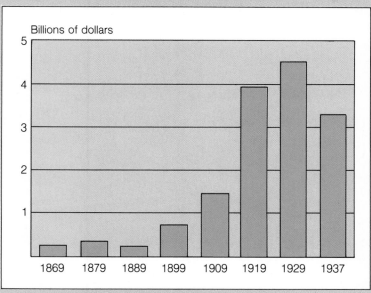

Source: *Historical Statistics of the United States, Colonial Times to 1970.* p. 699.

would be minimal. Instead of following government directives, individuals would be free to use their resources as they thought best, receiving the benefits and also bearing the costs of their own decisions. But in the marketplace, thought Smith, the motivation of self-interest would benefit others as well. By doing what was best for themselves, therefore, individuals would create more wealth for the nation. In fact, Figure A shows that the Levi Strauss Company was not alone in producing the clothing demanded by U.S. consumers.

As Adam Smith stated, "It is not from the benevolence of the butcher, the brewer, or the baker, that we expect our diner, but from their regard to their own interest." But Adam Smith was not advocating selfishness, by which the rights of others would be abused. Instead, he was advocating what might better be called *autonomy*, which is the freedom to pursue one's self-interest without harming others. Indeed, Smith argued that a market economy, like an *"invisible hand,"* would lead autonomous individuals to promote the interests of others. Would you say the story of Levis supports his judgment?

References

Beauchamp, Marc. "Tight Fit." *Forbes*, 138 (August 11, 1986): 94–95.

Berendt, John. "Classic Blue Jeans." *Esquire*, 106 (September 1986): 24–26.

Clawson, Elmer U. *Our Economy: How It Works*. Reading, Mass.: (Addison-Wesley, 1980) 53–57.

Smith, Adam. *The Wealth of Nations*. (New York: The Modern Library, 1937). 14.

Service stations must decide what services to produce. Here the station's attendants pump gas and check the oil and tires. By employing fewer people, however, the station could choose not to offer these services. Customers would then perform the services themselves.

important ideas. Like the simple maps you draw to direct friends to a particular place, this map leaves out many details in order to emphasize the important ideas we will be examining.

What to Produce   Figure 2–1 illustrates how a market economy chooses the kinds and quantities of goods and services to produce. As consumers, we use our money to *demand* goods and services from producers. Demand does not mean that we try to force producers to supply what we want. As Chapter 3 explains, demand means that as consumers we are willing and able to buy goods and services from producers. When we demand goods and services, therefore, we send money to producers by way of the goods and services markets. Our money flows from right to left through the white loop at the top of the map.

As consumers, we are free to demand whatever goods and services are not prohibited. We use our money as dollar votes to tell businesses what we want produced. And we don't just pick what we want from a big menu of goods and services; we also help to determine the kinds and amounts of items that will be included on this menu. As a result, in a market economy

By making a purchase, a consumer sends her dollar votes to the producer through the market for goods and services. These dollar votes help determine the kinds and quantities of clothing and other goods and services a market economy will produce.

we have both consumer freedom and consumer sovereignty. **Consumer freedom** is the ability of consumers to spend their money on whatever goods and services they choose. **Consumer sovereignty** is the ability of consumers to influence the kinds and quantities of goods and services produced.

> **Consumer freedom:**   The ability of consumers to spend their money on whatever goods and services they chose.
>
> **Consumer sovereignty:**   The ability of consumers to influence the kinds and quantities of goods and services produced.

Consumer sovereignty exists when consumers decide which goods and services to buy. According to the circular flow map in Figure 2–1, consumers decide which producers to send their money to in the top loop that contains the dollar signs. Producers respond to the dollar votes of consumers by producing what consumers want and sending these goods and services to consumers through the dark loop at the top of the map.

As an illustration, consider the calendar business described at the beginning of this chapter. Consumers willingly sent their dollars to the calendar company through the top loop of the goods and services markets because they chose to purchase the company's product. In turn, the company produced calendars and sent them to consumers through the dark loop of the goods and services markets. Consumers used their dollars to vote in favor of the company's product, so the business prospered and continued to produce calendars.

On the other hand, consumers did not cast enough dollar votes in favor of the dances offered by the dance business. As a result, the business stopped offering its product to consumers. The failure of the dance business and the success of the calendar business demonstrate consumer sovereignty. They both show how consumers influence the kinds and quantities of items produced.

Our ability as consumers to control production does not mean that we are the ones who first suggest a particular item. The owners of both the calendar business and the dance business first thought up their products and then offered them to consumers. By using their dollars to vote for or against these products, however, consumers determined which items would survive. Similarly, we choose which of the many products offered by businesses will survive. But we consumers are picky, so it

Sellers advertise in order to inform buyers of their products and to persuade consumers to buy them. But unless consumers willingly spend their money on a particular item, producers will not continue to offer it. In this picture, Nike is trying to persuade consumers to buy its basketball shoes.

is not surprising that many businesses spend much time and money on market research and advertising. Through market research, businesses try to discover what items we are willing to buy before they make substantial outlays of time and money to produce particular products. Through advertising, businesses also try to persuade us to buy what they offer. Despite market research and advertising, however, success is not guaranteed. The fact that two out of every three new products fail shows that businesses will not continue to produce particular products unless we choose to buy them.

By deciding how to spend our money in the goods and services markets, we consumers affect the kinds and quantities of things that producers offer. Because the goods and services markets determine what to produce, the word *What* appears just beneath the circle depicting these markets at the top of the circular flow map. In these markets, the flow of money from consumers and the flow of goods and services from producers show the process of choosing what to produce.

For Whom to Produce   As consumers, we are powerful when we choose how to spend our money in a market economy. But how do we get the money to make these choices? One way is to earn the money by selling our labor services or other resources to producers. We might also have borrowed the money or have been given the money by families, friends, or the government. We might also have stolen the money.

Although we can obtain money from each of these four sources, we cannot beg, borrow, or steal the money unless someone else has earned it in the first place. The only permanent, dependable source of money is a money-paying job, which is why your ability to consume depends mostly on how much money you can earn. These earnings depend, in turn, on the resources you own. Because of the connection between earning money and owning resources, the box on the right of the map shows consumers and resource owners as the same people.

Chapter 1 explained that productive resources are land, labor, capital, and management. As a consumer you earn your money by selling resources to producers. If you pack groceries at a supermarket, for example, you are selling labor to the supermarket. According to the circular flow map, you send labor services to the grocery store through the dark loop at the bottom of the map.

Thinking About Consumer Sovereignty

Consumer sovereignty means that as buyers we have the power to influence the kinds and quantities of products made available for sale. Do we really have this power in the United States?

Noneconomic Way of Thinking

In the United States big businesses tell us what to buy. They place products in stores whether we desire them or not. If the products sell poorly, then they are heavily advertised. The products that big businesses push are those that involve big profits. Often, businesses will deliberately make products that break down quickly, knowing we will have to replace them more frequently.

Economic Way of Thinking

The self-interest of big businesses lies in providing us with products that we demand. The products that big businesses push *are* those that involve big profits, but profits are big only if we desire these products and are willing to pay for them. And companies do not make products that break down prematurely. If they did, we would avoid them and turn instead to competitors' products. But by catering to our demands as consumers, sellers receive increased dollar votes.

Questions

1. Why do businesses advertise their products? Is all advertising designed to persuade, or is some designed to inform?

2. If a tire company introduces a tire that lasts twice as long as other tires, would you tend to favor that seller with your dollar votes? Would that seller benefit from the introduction of this product?

This picture illustrates how a market economy decides for whom to produce. The clerk packing the groceries is earning income by selling labor services in the resource markets. This income will then allow the clerk to demand products in the goods and services markets. By contributing more to the economy's production, one will earn more income and thus obtain more of what the economy produces.

In a market economy, money income depends not only on the quantity of productive resources you own but also on the amount that producers will spend to obtain your resources. The more resources you own or the more valuable those resources are to businesses, the more money you will earn. With more income, you will then be able to consume more by spending more money in the goods and services markets.

As a result, resource markets distribute a nation's income and thereby enable individuals to purchase goods and services. For whom a market economy produces is, therefore, decided in the resource markets shown at the bottom of the map. That is why the words *For whom* appear just above the circle depicting these markets.

How to Produce   When you own a resource, its selling price is important to you because a higher price enables you to earn more money. The price of a resource is also important to a business because it shows what the business must pay to use a resource when producing for consumers. Higher prices encourage businesses to use less of a particular resource, and lower prices encourage them to use more. In this way, market prices help to determine how resources are used.

When producing a given item, a supplier must usually choose among various combinations of resources. In order to mow lawns, for example, a gardener can substitute power equipment for labor. In order to determine the *best* combination of resources, businesses look at the productivity, as well as the price, of each resource. **Productivity** is the amount of a good or service that a resource can add to production during a given time.

> **Productivity:** The amount of a good or service that a resource can add to production during a given time.

Take the case of some teen-agers who started a part-time business delivering birthday cakes for a few bakeries in their city. The business became so successful that the students decided to hire a delivery person. One applicant, who was willing to work for $2 per hour, was able to deliver two cakes per hour. Another applicant could be hired for $4 per hour but could

A chemist at W. R. Grace & Co. decides how to combine chemicals. Similarly, producers decide how to combine resources when deciding how to produce.

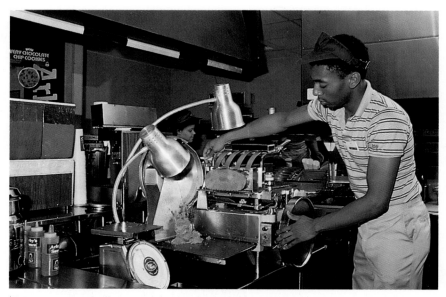

This photograph illustrates the basic economic decision of how to produce. Different combinations of resources can be used to provide food for restaurant customers. The meat in this picture could be sliced by hand or by machine. When the restaurant decided to use more capital and less labor, it looked at the prices and productivities of these resources.

deliver eight cakes per hour. Although the price they would pay per hour was higher for the second applicant, the students wisely decided to hire this person. Figure 2–2 shows why: Although the second applicant's price (wage) was twice as high, that person's productivity was *four times* greater than that of the first person. That's why the delivery cost *per cake* was lower ($.50 compared to $1) with the second applicant, even though that person's time cost twice as much.

When deciding how to produce, other businesses also compare the prices and productivities of the various resources they could employ. In terms of the circular flow map, businesses look at the prices they have to pay in the resource markets at the bottom of the map. They also look at the productivity of those resources when producing the items they will sell to consumers in the goods and services markets at the top. Thus, businesses use information from both the resource markets and the goods and services markets to determine the kinds and quantities of productive resources to use. Because businesses look to both markets when deciding how to produce the goods and services consumers demand, the word *How* is shown next to the producers box.

$4 per hour

$2 per hour

2 cakes per hour = $1 per cake   8 cakes per hour = $.50 per cake

Figure 2—2 Productivity Takes the Cake

Applicant A is willing to work for $2 per hour but can deliver only two cakes per hour. As a result, the business would pay $1 for each cake delivered if it hired this person. Applicant B is willing to work for $4 per hour but can deliver eight cakes per hour. As a result, the business would pay only $.50 per cake if it hired this more productive person.

What's Ahead

The circular flow map summarizes the way in which a market economy decides what, how, and for whom to produce. Two circular flows move in opposite directions. The outer loop containing the dollar signs, shows a counterclockwise flow of money. The inner, black loop shows a clockwise flow of goods, services, and resources. Together, these two flows show the process a market economy goes through when deciding what, how, and for whom to produce.

Many things have been left out of this economic map. The government's role in the circular flow has been ignored, even though this role is enormous. Some goods and services, such as national defense and education, would probably not be provided in sufficient quantity unless the government spends money for them. Chapter 8 shows that government purchases now account for a substantial portion of all the goods and services produced in our economy. That chapter also explains how the government taxes citizens in order to obtain the money required to make these purchases.

Figure 2–1 also ignores the government's role in altering the distribution of income among citizens. The circular flow shows that in a market economy, the ability to get what we want in the goods and services markets depends on the amounts and productivities of our resources. Those of us who have few resources, or resources with little productivity, will earn little income and receive few goods and services. In order to give more goods and services to these citizens, the government can tax the incomes of some of us and transfer this money to those of us who have lower incomes. The task of income redistribution is yet another topic to be examined later in this book.

Although the circular flow map is an incomplete diagram of a market economy, it does show that markets arise whenever buyers and sellers make exchanges. In other words, markets exist when buyers demand something and sellers supply it. A humorous television skit once presented the idea of a five-minute university. In that short time students would take all the classes necessary for a college degree. One of the university's classes was economics, and the only task the students were given was to memorize the words *supply* and *demand*. A parrot could also learn to repeat these two words, but the parrot wouldn't un-

The ability to get what we want in the goods and services markets depends on the amounts and productivities of our resources. Because this individual has few resources or has resources with low productivity, he earns little income and thus obtains few goods and services. Through taxes or private charity, however, income can be transferred to the poor.

derstand their meaning. The next few chapters will explain and illustrate the meaning of these two important principles.

Chapter Summary

1. Since there are not enough resources to satisfy all of everyone's wants, individuals in all nations must choose *what* goods and services to produce with those scarce resources, *how* to use those resources in order to make the goods and services, and *for whom* to make the goods and services.

2. The authority to make choices about the use of scarce resources is called *ownership*. Under collective ownership, the rights to decide how resources are used are held by the government, not by private individuals. *Collective ownership* results in a *command economy*, in which the government decides what, how, and for whom to produce.

3. In nations in which the productive resources are privately owned, private individuals determine how to use their own resources and the resources they purchase from others. Producers find it profitable to use resources to make the goods and services people want.

4. *Markets* exist whenever buyers and sellers trade with one another. Makets create *market prices*, which reflect how much value we as consumers put on the goods and services that are produced with privately owned resources. We give our money to the producers in exchange for their goods and services. By producing what we consumers want most, the producers maximize their gains from this exchange. Not only do market prices tell producers what we want produced, but also they give producers the motivation to produce these goods and services. Consequently, market prices are like an invisible hand that directs private resource owners to produce what consumers want.

5. A map of a market economy's circular flow shows how this kind of economy decides what, how, and for whom to produce. We consumers direct production by indicating, through our spending, a willingness and ability to purchase various items in the goods and services markets. We are free to spend our money on whatever goods and services we choose,

which is *consumer freedom*. We also have the ability to influence the kinds and quantities of goods and services produced, which is *consumer sovereignty*.

6. As consumers, we earn the money to buy goods and services by selling the resources we own to producers. That is why consumers and resource owners are the same people. Our earnings as resource owners depend on how many resources we own and how productive these resources are to the businesses that use them. The more money income we receive for our resources, the more goods and services we can consume. For whom a market economy produces is decided in the resource markets, where those resources are sold to producers and income is thereby distributed.

7. The selling prices of resources are important to both businesses and resource owners. A higher price allows owners to earn more money, but it also dictates that businesses will use less of these resources than if they were being sold at a lower price. *Market prices* for resources thus help to determine how much of them will be used and in what ways they will be used. *Productivity* is the amount of a good or service that a resource can add to production during a given time; it helps to determine the *best* combination of resources to use to produce various goods and services. Businesses use information from both the resource and the goods and services markets to determine the kinds and quantities of productive resources to use. Accordingly, producers (businesses) determine how to produce the goods and services we consumers want.

Review Questions

1. What three choices must every nation make as a result of scarcity? Do all nations make these choices in the same way?

2. What is meant by the term *ownership*? Who has the right to choose how resources are used in a command economy? Who has the right to choose how resources are used in a market economy? Explain.

3. Explain how the term *market* is used in economics.

4. Why do individuals in a market economy have an incentive to work together and to combine their resources to produce what consumers want most?

5. What is meant by the term *invisible hand*? Give an example.

6. How does a market economy decide *what* to produce?

7. What is the difference between *consumer freedom* and *consumer sovereignty*?

8. How does a market economy decide *for whom* to produce?

9. Explain why the *productivity* of a resource, as well as its price, is important in deciding *how* to produce in a market economy.

Discussion Questions

1. What are the basic differences between a *command economy* and a *market economy*?

2. What tasks do market prices accomplish? How do they accomplish these tasks?

3. What does a circular flow map of a market economy show us? Explain.

4. Do you think a centrally planned economy satisfies the preferences of consumers better than a market economy does? Explain.

5. Do you think self-interest and selfishness are the same? If so, why? If not, why not? Provide examples to illustrate your answer.

Activities

1. Write a paragraph attacking or defending the following statement: The three basic economic decisions—what, how, and for whom to produce—would not need to be made if a society were really rich.

2. Draw a circular flow map and then write an essay describing how a market economy makes the what, how, and for whom decisions.

3. You are a world-renowned hamster trainer, but no one is casting dollar votes for the production of trained hamsters. Describe in a short paragraph what will happen to your power to cast dollar votes.

4. Research how a nation other than the United States decides what, how, and for whom to produce. Then write a short essay describing your findings.

5. Worker A receives $6 per hour and can sew twelve pairs of mittens per hour. Worker B receives $3 per hour and can sew six pairs of mittens per hour. What is the labor cost per pair of mittens for each worker? Do you think an employer would want to hire one worker instead of the other? Why or why not?

Additional Readings

Browne, M. Neil, and Haas, Paul F. *Modern Economics: Principles, Goals, and Trade-Offs.* Englewood Cliffs, N.J.: Prentice-Hall, 1987. 40–47.

Mansfield, Edwin. *Economics: Principles, Problems, Decisions.* 5th ed. New York: W. W. Norton, 1986. 30–35.

Reynolds, Lloyd G. *Macroeconomics: Analysis and Policy.* 5th ed. Homewood, Ill.: Richard D. Irwin, 1985. 3–12.

Markets for Goods and Services

Unit

II

Why does the price of ice cream determine the number of scoops you buy?

Demand

■ Student's Goals ■

1. Define the concept of *demand* as it is used in economics.

2. Describe the *price effect* as it applies to demand.

3. Explain at least two reasons for the existence of the price effect.

4. Explain at least three of the factors that affect demand.

The Economics of Drinking and Driving

In 1984 the U.S. Congress passed a law to cut federal highway funds for states in which the legal drinking age is under 21. The purpose of this law was to encourage states to raise the drinking age and thereby reduce the number of alcohol-related highway fatalities among young drivers. Although persons under the age of 21 represented only about 10 percent of all licensed drivers, they accounted for nearly 25 percent of all alcohol-related traffic fatalities between 1977 and 1984.[1]

Some people believe the higher drinking age is unfair. If an 18-year-old can vote for the President of the United States, they argue, isn't he or she also old enough to make a decision about drinking? Fairness, like beauty, is in the eye of the beholder, so it is not surprising that different people have different views about the higher drinking age. While we debate the fairness of the issue, some economists have proposed an alternative to raising the minimum drinking age. Their solution is to increase the federal excise tax on alcohol.

The tax on beer, wine, and liquor has remained virtually unchanged since 1951. A study by the National Bureau of Economic Research concludes that if the tax on beer were increased to compensate for the inflation that has occurred since 1951, the consumption of beer would fall. According to the study, decreasing beer consumption in this manner would reduce fatalities about twice as much as would raising the drinking age.[2]

Whether you agree or disagree with the proposal, it certainly illustrates demand, which is one of the most important concepts in economics. In its ordinary, day-to-day use, the word *demand* often means that you make a command or an urgent request, such as when you demand that a friend return something that was borrowed. In economics, however, demand re-

[1]Drivers under 21 years of age also accounted for the same high proportion of **non**alcohol-related highway fatalities. Driving inexperience has been cited as a possible reason why this group had a high proportion of fatalities for both alcohol- and nonalcohol-related traffic deaths. For a discussion of this point, see Jack P. Desario and Fredric N. Bolotin, "A Sober Look at a Drunken Driving Cure-All," *The Wall Street Journal*, December 31, 1985.

[2]See, for example, the following two articles: Gary S. Becker, "Don't Raise the Drinking Age, Raise Taxes," *Business Week* (November 25, 1985): 21; Martin Feldstein and Kathleen Feldstein, "Raising the Tax on Beer Would Curb Drunk Drivers," *Los Angeles Times*, October 28, 1986.

Traffic accidents involving young, intoxicated drivers can be reduced by raising the drinking age or by increasing the tax on alcoholic beverages. The higher tax would reduce accidents because of the economic principle of demand: the higher tax would raise the price of alcoholic beverages and decrease the quantity of them consumed by young drivers.

fers to the way an item's price affects the amount that consumers want to buy.

Scarcity and Demand

As the first step in understanding the economic meaning of demand, you must recognize its relationship to scarcity. Because scarcity prevents the satisfaction of all wants, we do not satisfy one want completely before beginning to satisfy others. Instead, we use our limited incomes to satisfy one want until its continued satisfaction becomes less important than the satisfaction of other wants.

As an illustration, assume you have $7.00 in your pocket and your stomach is sending out SOS signals for hamburgers. You know you will get enough satisfaction if you spend $1.50 on one hamburger, but you have to decide whether or not you should buy more than one. Even though you would like more hamburgers, you realize you have a stronger desire to see a new movie that all your friends are talking about. As a result,

SANDWICHES			SANDWICHES		
CHICKEN McNUGGETS.. 6 PIECES		1.29	McNUGGETS de POLLO. 6 PEDAZOS		1.29
9 PIECES		1.95	9 PEDAZOS		1.95
20 PIECES		3.95	20 PEDAZOS		3.95
BIG MAC.		1.35	BIG MAC.		1.35
QUARTER POUNDER.		1.25	CUARTO de LIBRA.		1.25
with cheese		1.39	CUARTO de LIBRA.con queso		1.39
FILET-O-FISH.		.95	FILETE de PESCADO		.95
CHEESEBURGER		.60	HAMBURGUESA Con Queso		.60
HAMBURGER		.50	HAMBURGUESA		.50
FRENCH FRIES	.55	.74	PAPAS FRITAS	.55	.74
HAPPY MEAL. - CHEESEBURGER		2.25	CAJITA FELIZ ™ HAMBURGUESA con queso		2.25

If you were to purchase something from this menu, you would not only want the item but you would also demand it. In economics, demand and wants are not the same. Demand means that you are willing and able to pay an opportunity cost to get what you want. What would your opportunity cost be if you purchased a Big Mac?

you spend the remainder of your money at the movies, even though you are giving up the additional hamburgers you still want.

In order to have more of something, you have to accept less of something else. No one can avoid *opportunity cost*, as was explained in Chapter 1. If you spend $5 for a new cassette, you must do without $5 worth of something else. The amount you must give up to buy more of an item determines how much of that item you will purchase during a given time. When the price of something falls, you will buy more of it. When its price rises, you will buy less. This behavior illustrates the economic meaning of demand. **Demand** is a list of the various quantities of an item that someone is willing and able to buy at different possible prices.

> **Demand:**   A list of the various quantities of an item that some-one is willing and able to buy at different possible prices.

Think about the definition for a minute. It says *various quantities* and *different possible prices* because demand is not a particular quantity that someone will purchase at a given price and time. If John buys an average of twenty scoops of ice cream per week at a price of fifty cents per scoop, this quantity is not John's demand. You can call it the quantity purchased or the amount bought, but you would be incorrect if you say that twenty scoops per week is John's demand. You would be incorrect because demand refers to *all* the different quantities that John would purchase per time period at various possible prices. If you knew how many scoops of ice cream John would buy per week at many possible prices, not just at fifty cents, then you would know John's demand for ice cream.

The Price Effect

Our demands can be very different. Someone with a strong demand for an item might purchase large quantities at high prices. Someone else with a weak demand for that same item might purchase small quantities even at low prices.

Despite these differences, all demands share a common characteristic. This characteristic is the fact that you purchase less

This individual's demand for ice cream cones is not the number of cones he buys at a particular price. Instead, his demand refers to a list of all the different quantities that he would purchase per time period at various possible prices.

of an item when its price is high and more when its price is low. How many hamburgers would you buy per week if each one cost one cent? How about fifty cents? What about two dollars? Ten dollars? Five hundred dollars? In other words, what is *your* individual demand for hamburgers? The quantity you would buy at each possible price would probably differ from those of other people. Although our demands for hamburgers vary enormously, each one of us buys fewer hamburgers at higher prices and more hamburgers at lower prices. This characteristic that higher prices cause people to buy less of an item and lower prices cause them to buy more is called the **price effect.** Because the price effect is shared by all demands for goods and services, it is the universal characteristic of demand.

> **Price effect:**   Higher prices cause people to buy less of an item, and lower prices cause them to buy more.

The fact that all our demands have this feature doesn't mean that *every* price increase will *always* cause *every* person to reduce consumption of a particular product. A higher price might cause you to cut down on your purchases of hamburgers, while someone else, facing the same price increase, might continue to buy the same quantity as before. But if the price continues to rise, even this person will eventually purchase fewer hamburgers. There is some price increase that will cause any individual to purchase less of an item.

There are three reasons why people respond in this way to price changes. These reasons, which have to do with the psychology of individual decision making, explain the price effect.

Reason 1: Uses of Different Value

Hamburgers, like all other goods and services, have uses that each of us values differently. For example, you can eat hamburgers for breakfast, for lunch, or for dinner. You can use hamburgers to feed other people who are hungry or to feed your pets. By buying gift certificates, you can even use hamburgers as presents.

Although each of these uses has value, some uses are more valuable to you than others. Hamburgers for lunch are often

Thinking About the Price Effect

Economists are often criticized for focusing only on the price of an item when evaluating individuals' purchases. Is this criticism correct?

Noneconomic Way of Thinking

Price is not an important factor in determining whether or not someone will buy a product. Other factors are much more important. For example, in comparison with price, tastes have a more powerful influence on what we will buy. That is why we can safely ignore the role of price and concentrate instead on people's tastes and preferences.

Economic Way of Thinking

Economists recognize that tastes are an important determinant of the amounts that we want to buy at any given price. But little is known about why we like what we do or why our preferences change. Economists do know, however, that price changes have predictable effects on our behavior. Although these effects may be strong in one instance and weak in another, they are always present. By concentrating on prices, economists are focusing on one of the important, and often ignored, factors that determines individuals' behavior.

Questions

1. Americans prefer coffee to tea, but the English prefer tea to coffee. Do economists have anything to say about this difference?

2. What would an economist predict if the price of tea rose in England and the price of coffee rose in the United States?

3. In the 1970s, people bought less gasoline for their automobiles. What factors could have influenced this change?

more valuable than hamburgers for breakfast. Filling your empty stomach might have more value than feeding your pets. Eating the tenth hamburger at dinner has less value than eating the first one.

The fact that an item's alternative uses have different values helps explain why people buy more or less of something when its price changes. If hamburgers cost $1.50 each, for instance, no one will buy them for uses that they value at less than $1.50. If the price rises to $3.00, people will purchase fewer hamburgers and only put them to those uses that are worth at least $3.00 to them. On the other hand, if the price of hamburgers falls, people will purchase them for more, but less valuable, uses. If hamburgers cost only a penny each, for example, many people would use them for pet food or plant fertilizer.

Other goods are no different. If a gallon of water were to cost as much as a gallon of gasoline, people would no longer use it to satisfy as many of their lower-valued uses as they do now at the lower price. Wouldn't you expect, for example, that the higher water price would cause more people to sweep their driveways instead of washing them down with a hose? On the

This dog does not know about the price effect, but its meal certainly depends on it. If the price of hamburger dropped as low to the ground as the dog's ears, some people would begin using it as pet food. All goods and services have uses that consumers value at different levels. This fact is one reason for the price effect.

If the price of water increased dramatically, more people would choose to sweep their driveways instead of hosing them off. This behavior would occur because water, like all other goods and services, has uses that people value at different levels. If the price of water rises, people use less water by excluding the uses they value less than the higher price.

other hand, suppose the price of gasoline fell to ten cents a gallon. Wouldn't you expect to see your friends using gasoline for everything from cruising to playing chauffeur for their younger sisters and brothers? If the price of gasoline suddenly rose to $10 a gallon, however, we would all give up our lower-valued uses of gas and drive our cars only when we thought it was "absolutely necessary."

The fact that each good or service has alternative uses of different value is an important reason for the price effect. Because an item does have alternative uses, higher prices influence us to buy less of it. The smaller quantity is then used only for its more valuable uses. On the other hand, lower prices encourage us to apply the item to less valuable uses, too. That is one reason why we buy more at lower prices.

Reason 2:
Substitutes Here, Substitutes There

Another related reason for the price effect is the existence of substitutes. A higher price causes us to purchase less of a good

Buses are substitutes for private automobiles. If the price of buying an automobile soared, people would use fewer automobiles and take the bus more often.

or service and to use substitutes in its place. On the other hand, a lower price stimulates us to use that item as a substitute for other things. If the price of buying an automobile for basic transportation rose to $30,000, we would use more substitutes; we would ride buses, bicycles, trains, and airplanes, and walk. So, too, would we seek ways to live closer to our work and schools. Similarly, if the price of steak rose to $20 a pound, we would substitute more hamburger, chicken, fish, and vegetables for steak.

If the prices of cars and steaks tumbled, however, we would buy more of them as substitutes for other goods. We would use more automobiles and less public transportation, and we would consume more steak and less hamburger, chicken, fish, and vegetables.

Reason 3: Buying Power That Expands and Contracts

The third and last reason for the price effect relates to a buyer's limited money income. When the price of a particular item falls, your limited income has more buying power than before. This means you can afford to purchase more of something when its price falls. When a price increases, the effect is just the opposite. Your income loses some of its buying power, so you buy less of the higher-priced item.

Here, then, are three reasons that explain why the price effect is the universal trait of demand: (1) each item we buy has uses of different value; (2) each item also has substitutes; (3) changes in an item's price increase or decrease the buying power of our money. Accordingly, the amount of a good or service that we buy during a given time is less when prices are higher and more when they are lower. The extent to which price changes affect purchases depends on the particular item and the particular buyer. Even so, during a given time, everyone purchases less at higher prices and more at lower prices. That's the price effect.

The Determinants of Demand

The price we pay for something can have a powerful influence on the amounts of it we buy. But what are the factors that

Just as this balloon can expand and contract, so also can the buying power of your limited money income expand and contract. If the price of a product falls, for example, a given amount of money has more buying power. As a result, you will be able to buy more of the product. The change in the buying power of money income caused by a higher or lower price is one of the reasons for the price effect.

Income is one of the determinants of demand. If your income increases, you will want to buy more of a product at all possible prices.

determine how much of something we will buy at each and every possible price? These factors—called the *determinants of demand*—fall into the following four categories:

1. *The amount of income we have to spend.* When our incomes go up, our abilities to buy increase, and we usually purchase more of a particular good or service at any given price. (There are a few things, however, such as ground beef and city bus services, that people often buy in smaller quantities as their incomes rise. As they become wealthier, people eat more steak and less hamburger, and they buy their own cars instead of using public transportation.)

2. *Tastes or preferences.* Demand is influenced not only by our *ability* to buy, but also by our *willingness* to buy. Changes in our tastes or preferences can alter the amounts of something we will buy at all possible prices. When evidence showed a more definite link between smoking and cancer, many people reduced or even eliminated their demands for cigarettes.

   Tastes and preferences can be influenced by almost anything—family background, religion, education, social status, political beliefs, and advertising. If you think a new style of clothing will make you more popular, you will be more likely to purchase it at any given price.

3. *Expectations.* Our demands depend on the future events we expect. If we expect the price or the availability of a product to change in the future, we will buy different amounts of it at various prices today. If we expect the price of peanut butter to increase tomorrow, we will probably buy more today than we would otherwise purchase. That expectations determine demand was illustrated by the behavior of U.S. consumers after a severe drought in Brazil altered their expectations. It was reported that one man tried to order $6,000 worth of Maxwell House coffee from a supermarket because he expected the price to jump in the near future.

4. *The prices of other goods and services.* Changes in the current prices of other goods and services can alter the amounts of something we will buy at any given price. If the price of hamburgers doubles, people will demand more pizza because pizza is a good *substitute* for hamburgers. But other goods, such as pickles and tomatoes, are *complements* because they are consumed along with hamburgers, not instead of them. The higher price of hamburgers will increase

Another determinant of demand is expectations. If a consumer suddenly expected the price of coffee to rise in the near future, he or she would want to purchase more coffee now at all possible prices.

Thinking About Price Expectations

Economists believe there are no exceptions to the price effect. When the price of an item rises, the quantities that consumers want to buy *always* fall. Does the price effect hold in cases in which a price goes up but people expect it to continue rising in the future?

Noneconomic Way of Thinking

Past events certainly disprove the price effect. Not long ago the rising price of coffee caused people to expect a shortage. Buyers then rushed to their supermarkets to buy more, not less, coffee. This event shows that economists are wrong to think that there are no exceptions to the price effect.

Economic Way of Thinking

There are no exceptions to the price effect. In the example above, the higher price of coffee caused people to expect a shortage and, thus, even higher coffee prices in the future. In order to avoid the higher price expected tomorrow, people bought more coffee today. Although today's price had risen, it had actually fallen in relation to the price expected tomorrow. Being relatively lower, today's price caused people to buy more coffee, just as the price effect predicts.

Questions

1. How would buyers behave if they expected the price of a product to decrease?

2. In 1986, the price of oil began to fall as OPEC (Organization of Petroleum Exporting Countries) increased its production of oil. Yet, at first petroleum buyers bought less, not more, petroleum. Why? What belief would eventually cause purchasers to buy more petroleum at the lower price?

The prices of other goods and services are an important determinant of demand. If the price of renting a tennis court or the price of tennis rackets went way up, the demand for complementary goods, such as tennis balls, would decrease. Consumers would then want to buy fewer tennis balls at all possible prices. (Would this event affect the demand for running shoes?)

the demand for substitutes but also decrease the demand for complements. Other examples of substitutes include Morton Salt and Leslie Salt, saccharin and NutraSweet, and butter and margarine. Goods that are often thought of as complements include toothpaste and toothbrushes, tennis rackets and tennis balls, and peanut butter and jelly.

You can see that the amount of something you purchase depends on many things besides its price. When economists speak of a particular demand, however, they are referring to the effects that price changes have on purchases when all these other nonprice determinants are unchanged. For example, your demand for hamburgers shows the various amounts you would buy at different prices, *if the determinants of demand—your income, your tastes, your expectations, and the prices of other goods and services—are unchanged.*

Anna List

This last section explains why the price of an item is **not** one of the determinants of its demand. This point is often a source

(text continues on page 78)

A Whale of a Crisis

A crisis is not necessarily bad; it can be a turning point for better as well as for worse. Take the energy crisis of the 1970s. When the Organization of Petroleum Exporting Countries (OPEC) suddenly cut the availability of oil around the world, the U.S. economy confronted a crisis. Would it make the best of this painful circumstance by responding quickly and effectively, or would it collapse in chaos?

At the time, may people thought our economy would be unable to cope on its own with the sudden decrease in the availability of oil. Believing the United States lacked enough oil to meet its needs, they advocated new laws to restrict the use of oil. Government standards were developed to specify the energy use of appliances and automobiles. The maximum legal speed limit was cut to save gasoline, and builders were required to meet tougher standards in order to save energy in homes and factories.

This was not the first energy crisis the United States had faced; another had occurred much earlier in our nation's history. The crisis began long before the first U.S. oil well was drilled in 1859 at Titusville, Pennsylvania. Indeed, it began years before people in Pennsylvania first produced petroleum by throwing blankets in oil-covered creeks and then wringing

the oil into small bottles. The bottles of oil, known as "Seneca Oil," were then sold as a cure for illnesses, such as corns, cholera, and colds.

Before petroleum was produced in our nation, we used considerable quantities of whale oil in our homes and factories. In the early 1800s, America was lit and lubricated thanks to her mariners, who had begun hunting whales out of Nantucket a hundred years before. But as the population grew, the demand for whale oil soared. This increasing demand alarmed those people who believed that the total destruction of whales would deny their need for whale oil.

It was soon discovered, however, that the amount of whale oil people consumed depended on its price. As whale oil became more scarce, its price increased. Because of the higher price, consumers used it more sparingly. Indeed, over a period of 30 to 40 years, the price of whale oil increased to more than five times its original cost. At higher prices, consumers "needed" less whale oil than they "needed" at lower prices. Not only did the higher price cause consumers to conserve whale oil for its most valuable uses, but also it caused them to use substitutes. Early substitutes were lard oil, vegetable oils, and coal gas, but by the mid-1800s kerosene, made from coal (coal oil), was widely used. When petroleum became available in the late 1800s, it offered a new source of kerosene.

As the United States moved rapidly into the new age of petroleum in the late 1800s, whale oil dropped in importance faster than a whale diving to the dark depths of the ocean. After the invention of the internal combustion engine in 1860 and the development of motor vehicles in the early 1900s, petroleum production spurted (see Figure A).

During the twentieth century, many changes occurred that made consumers want to buy more oil at each and every price. One important event was the growth of the economy, a growth that increased consumers' incomes. But the demand for oil did not rise just because Ameri-

Figure A Yearly Production of Oil and Natural Gas, 1880–1920

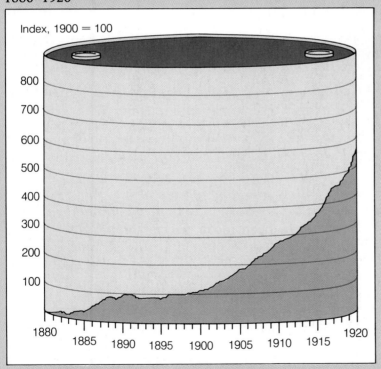

Source: Historical Statistics of the United States, Colonial Times to 1970, p. 586.

cans had more money in their purses and pockets. In addition, automobiles, appliances, record players, and other new consumer products altered Americans' tastes. As a result, they demanded more petroleum in order to enjoy and to manufacture these new goods and services. No longer were homes and factories lit by whale oil. Instead, electric wires, like a weaver's fine threads, began forming a complex pattern across the land.

About a hundred years after oil began trickling into America's homes and factories, OPEC suddenly reduced the availability of oil in the 1970s. At first, the U.S. government kept the price of oil from rising. When the price of oil was finally allowed to rise, however, consumers reduced the amount of oil they wanted to use. Just as the quantity of whale oil consumers wanted to use depended on its price, so, too, did the amount of petroleum consumers wanted to use depend on its price.

Figure B shows the changes in total consumption of petroleum in our country during the late 1970s and early 1980s. The four major classes of oil consumers are households, industries, drivers, and electric utilities. In the years following the first price increase in 1973, oil consumption continued to grow. This occurred

Figure B   U.S. Oil Consumption, 1970–1983

In billions of barrels

Legend:
- Households
- Electrical
- Transportation
- Industrial

Source: Statistical Abstract of the United States, 1986, p. 702.

because the price effect was not strong enough to offset the increase in demand caused by rising incomes and other changes in the determinants of demand. This was not true after the second price increase in 1979, however, because Figure B shows that consumption dropped.

The quantity of petroleum we want to consume depends on many things. But one important factor is the price we pay.

References

Alchian, Armen A. "Energy Policy: An Introduction to Confusion." In A. Lawrence Chickering, ed., *Readings in Public Policy*. San Francisco: Institute for Contemporary Studies, 1984. Chapter 2.

Gramm, Philip W. "The Energy Crisis in Perspective." *Wall Street Journal*, November 30, 1973.

La Force, Clayburn J. *The Energy Crisis: The Moral Equivalent of Bamboozle*. Los Angeles: International Institute for Economic Research, 1978.

Lebergott, Stanley. *The Americans: An Economic Record*. New York: W.W. Norton, 1984. Chapter 25.

of confusion, so students usually have many questions about it. They also raise questions about other aspects of demand. The following fictional interview presents some of these typical questions. In the interview, conducted by a high school student, an economist named Anna List explains some of the most common sources of confusion about demand.

Student: Professor List, a lot of us are confused by the meaning of demand. Is demand the same thing as wants or desires?

Anna List: No, they're very different. There are probably no limits to what people want or desire, but their demands are limited. When you demand something, you must give up something else to get it. Demand shows your willingness and ability to give up money that you could have spent on something else. You may *want* a new car, but that doesn't mean you *demand* it enough to buy it. A hungry person with no money can want food but still not demand it. Demand is desire backed by the ability and willingness to pay.

Student: Does the demand for a good or service depend on its availability or its current price?

Anna List: No, it doesn't. Demand is a list of the various amounts that you are willing and, with your income, able to buy at different possible prices. If the price goes up or down, therefore, demand doesn't change because your list doesn't change.

Let me go back to the new car example to make this point clear. You might not purchase a new car at an existing price of $20,000, but at some lower price, say $1,000, you might be more than happy to buy it. If the price went much lower, you might buy one for your family or friends, too. Your demand for a new car is an entire list showing the number you would buy at many different prices. Because the amount you buy at the current price is only *one* of many possible amounts on that list, it does not show your demand. The current price affects how many cars you actually purchase, but it doesn't change the list of how many you would buy at different possible prices. That's why the demand for a good or service doesn't depend upon its current price.

In the same way, demand doesn't depend on the quantities that are actually available. The availability of something certainly determines how much, if any, you can actually obtain. But the list of how much you would *like* to buy at different prices doesn't depend on how much is actually available.

Student: Suppose we took the average price of gasoline in each of the last 15 years and then found out how much gas people bought at those prices. Would this comparison of gas prices and consumption show the demand for gasoline during this period?

Anna List: No. The demand for gasoline refers to the various amounts people would buy at different possible prices *if* incomes, tastes, and the prices of other things are unchanged. The statistics you're talking about would reflect changes in incomes and other determinants of demand, not just changes in the price of gasoline. Remember, demand means how much you would purchase at different possible prices when the determinants of demand are unchanged.

Student: Is it necessary to state the time period when referring to demand?

Anna List: Yes, it is. Demand refers to the quantity of purchases per time period. It's like the electric meter on your home, which measures how much electricity you use each month. If someone told you how many kilowatts of electricity you used, they wouldn't be telling you much unless you knew the time period during which you consumed them. Similarly, the market demand for a good or service indicates that at various prices consumers would buy different quantities during a period of time, such as a day, month, or year.

Student: Does the price effect apply to things that people call "necessities?"

Anna List: That's a good question. Many people believe that some goods have no substitutes. Food and water are often cited as examples. They say we *need* these things, so the price effect doesn't apply to them. But food and water are seldom used for survival. Using water to wash the car, clean off the driveway, water the lawn, or fill a swimming pool is probably valued differently by most people than is drinking water to stay alive. Similarly, eating the twentieth piece of pizza, snacking after school, and eating restaurant food could be eliminated, and we would still survive. In fact, simple diets of rice, beans, vegetables, and other things would keep us alive, even though we might prefer to eat substitutes, such as hamburgers, french fries, and ice cream. At very high prices, we would buy only enough food and water for survival, eliminating all other uses of these things that have less value to us.

Chapter Summary

1. Because of scarcity, we do not completely satisfy one want before beginning to satisfy others. Instead, we use our limited incomes to satisfy a want until further satisfaction of that want becomes less important than the satisfaction of other wants.

2. *Demand* is a list of the various quantities of an item that someone is willing and able to buy at different possible prices during a given time period. Demand is *not* a specific quantity that an individual will buy at a specific price and time.

3. All our demands have a common characteristic—we will buy more of any good or service at lower prices and less at higher prices. This characteristic is called the *price effect*.

4. There are three reasons for the price effect: (1) Goods and services have various uses that individuals value at different levels. For example, at higher prices most of us would not use hamburger for pet food or fertilizer; at lower prices, however, we would use hamburger for these lower-valued uses. (2) Substitutes exist. If the price of meat increases, we will buy more fish and chicken. (3) Any buyer's income is limited. When the price of a good or service falls, a specific amount of income can be used to buy more of it; when the price increases, this same amount of income can be used to purchase less of it.

5. How much of any good or service we will purchase at various prices depends on four factors, called the *determinants of demand:* the amount of income we have, our tastes and preferences, our expectations, and the prices of other goods and services. When economists refer to the effects that price changes have on how much we want to buy, they assume that the determinants of demand remain unchanged.

6. Demand is not the same thing as wants or desires; rather, it is a want or desire for a good or service supported by both the ability and the willingness to pay to satisfy that want or desire. Demand for a good or service does not depend on an item's availability or its current price. Demand is a list of the amounts a person will purchase at various possible prices. This list does not change because the price changes,

and the availability of the good does not change the amount of it a person would like to buy.

7. Historical comparisons of gas consumption at average prices do not show the demand for gasoline because nonprice determinants of demand, such as income, have also changed over the years, and they affect how much gasoline will be purchased. Demand tells us how much will be purchased at various prices if those determinants remain unchanged. It is necessary to state the time period when referring to demand. The price effect applies even to those goods designated as "necessities," by which we mean goods or services that we believe have no substitutes.

Review Questions

1. What is the economic meaning of *demand?*
2. What is the difference between *desire* and *demand?*
3. What is a characteristic that the demands of all individuals have in common?
4. Explain the three reasons for the price effect.
5. Does the price effect apply to all goods? To water? To insulin?
6. The determinants of demand are those factors that can change our willingness to buy something at each and every price. Describe these determinants.
7. Explain the following statement: A higher price of hot dogs increases the demand for substitutes but decreases the demand for complements.
8. Explain why the price of an item is *not* one of the determinants of its demand.

Discussion Questions

1. Explain how *scarcity* is related to *demand.*
2. If you purchase a pair of jeans for $30, can you call this your demand for jeans? Why or why not?
3. Many people argue that the price effect does not apply to luxury goods, such as fur coats and very expensive auto-

mobiles. They claim that people buy these goods *because* their prices are high. Consequently, if their prices were lower, people would buy fewer, not more, luxury goods. Do you agree with this reasoning? Explain.

4. Explain why you agree or disagree with this statement: The price effect does not apply to water because there is no substitute for water.

Activities

1. Assume you are an economist writing a book for high school students. Which of the following would you use to illustrate the economic meaning of demand? Why?
   (a) Demand is when your younger sister wants some of your dessert and says she will cry until you give her some.
   (b) Demand is when you want a compact disc player and are willing to work at the local gym to get the money to buy it.
   (c) Demand is when the school bully says he will beat you up unless you give him your lunch money.

2. Write three short paragraphs using economic terms to describe your reactions to each of the following situations:
   (a) You find out that your favorite pizza causes bad breath.
   (b) Because your income is limited, you order a tiny portion of your favorite pasta dish at a restaurant. Then you discover your date is paying the bill.
   (c) You like hamburgers and hot dogs almost equally, but you discover that the price of hot dogs has doubled.

3. Write an essay supporting the following argument: A complementary good goes *with* or is used *with* another good. A substitute is used *in place of* another good. If the price of a good goes up, the demand for its substitute goes up, but the demand for its complement goes down. (Be sure to give concrete examples.)

4. The following table shows how much value Carol puts on having an additional gallon of gas in a week. How many gallons must Carol consume in a week in order to satisfy all her wants for gasoline? Suppose the price of gasoline is $1.25 per gallon. At this price, how many gallons would

Carol want to buy in a week? Why would she choose not to satisfy all her wants for gasoline at this price? Suppose the price of gas rises to $2.25 per gallon. How many gallons would she then want to buy? How does Carol's behavior illustrate the relationship between scarcity and demand?

Amount	Carol's Value of a Gallon of Gas
First gallon per week	$3.00
Second gallon per week	2.50
Third gallon per week	2.00
Fourth gallon per week	1.50
Fifth gallon per week	1.00
Sixth gallon per week	0.50
Seventh gallon per week	0.00

Additional Readings

Amacher, Ryan C., and Ulbrich, Holley H. *Principles of Microeconomics*. 3d ed. Cincinnati: South-Western, 1986. 46–54.

Barron, John M. and Lynch, Gerald J. *Economics*. St. Louis: Times Mirror/Mosby, 1986. 46–56.

McKenzie, Richard B. *Economics*. Dallas: Houghton Mifflin, 1986. 47–51.

How is a football field similar to a graph of demand?

Graphing Demand

■ Student's Goals ■

1. Graph a demand curve from a given demand schedule.

2. Explain why the demand curve slopes downward to the right.

3. Explain and illustrate how the price elasticity of demand might affect the shape of the demand curve.

4. Use a graph to illustrate an increase in demand.

5. Use a graph to illustrate a decrease in demand.

An Economic Riddle

More hamburgers are sold at higher prices today than were sold at lower prices ten years ago. Doesn't this fact disprove the principle of demand, which states that we buy less at higher prices and more at lower prices? In seeking a solution to this riddle, remember that price is only one of many factors that determine how much of something we buy. If these other factors change, the demand for an item might not be *visibly* affected when its price goes up or down. Although the new price alters the amount we buy, its effect on purchases can remain hidden.

This explanation probably sounds unconvincing because it is not easy to explain in a few sentences. Many people asked a similar question right after the price of gasoline soared in the early 1970s. Even though gasoline prices jumped, at first people bought more, not less.

Market Demand

The riddle can be explained more clearly if we first present demand visually in the form of a graph. The purpose of this chapter is show you how to construct and interpret such graphs. After accomplishing this objective, we will return to the riddle and use a graph to solve it.

The graph we are about to construct shows the combined demands of various individuals. When their demands are added together, the total is called the market demand. **Market demand** is a list of the *total* quantities of a good or service that *all* consumers will buy at different possible prices.

> **Market demand:** A list of the *total* quantities of a good or service that *all* consumers will buy at different possible prices.

In Table 4–1 we calculate the market demand for hamburgers by adding the individual demands of all consumers in a particular market for a given time period. Since there are many consumers in the market, the table cannot show each individ-

The economic principle of demand says that people buy more of something at lower prices and less at higher prices. But hamburger prices are higher today than they were ten years ago, and consumers are buying and eating more hamburgers than ever before. Why doesn't this fact violate the principle of demand?

ual's demand. Instead, it presents the demands of four individuals and then combines all other consumers' demands in the column labeled *All Other Demands per Day*. By adding the amounts each individual will purchase at each possible price,

Table 4–1   Computing Market Demand

Price	Mary's Demand per Day		Joe's Demand per Day		Jennifer's Demand per Day		David's Demand per Day		All Other Demands per Day		Total
$2.50	0	+	4	+	2	+	4	+	90	=	100
2.00	1	+	5	+	3	+	6	+	135	=	150
1.50	2	+	6	+	4	+	8	+	180	=	200
1.00	3	+	8	+	7	+	12	+	270	=	300
.50	6	+	14	+	10	+	20	+	450	=	500

This table shows the daily hamburger demands of four individuals in a particular market. It also shows the combined demands of all other individuals in the column labeled *All Other Demands per Day*. The total demands are found by adding the quantities that would be purchased at every price. When the price is $2.50, for instance, 100 hamburgers are purchased per day. As the price falls, however, the total purchased increases as shown in the last column. The first column labeled *Price* and the last column labeled *Total* show the *total* quantities of hamburgers that *all* consumers will buy at different possible prices. Therefore, they give us the market demand for hamburgers per day.

we calculate the total number of hamburgers that all consumers will buy at each price. As a result, the first column labeled *Price* and the last column labeled *Total* show the total quantities of hamburgers that all individuals will buy at different possible prices. These two columns give us the market demand for hamburgers per day.

Table 4–1 shows us that demand is the relationship between the price of a product and the amount of the product purchased per time period. When we present this relationship numerically as in Table 4–1, it is called a *demand schedule*. We can also show this same relationship visually on a graph. In Figure 4–1 the numbers representing market demand (the first and last columns of Table 4–1) have been plotted in order to show the *market demand curve*.

The prices that could be charged per hamburger are put on the graph's vertical line, and the quantities demanded per day are put on the horizontal line. (Each of these lines is called an *axis*.) Table 4–1 shows that at $2.50 only 100 hamburgers will be demanded during a day. This relationship can be presented

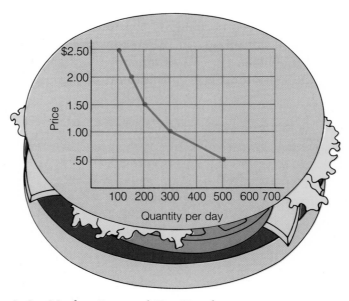

Figure 4–1 Market Demand For Hamburgers

The prices that could be charged for a hamburger are shown on the vertical axis of the graph. The quantities demanded at each of these prices are shown on the horizontal axis. The demand curve slopes downward to the right because consumers buy more hamburgers at lower prices than they buy at higher prices. At $2.50, for example, consumers want to buy 100 hamburgers per day. At $.50, however, they want to buy 500 hamburgers per day.

on the graph by placing a dot in a position that lines up with $2.50 on the vertical axis and 100 hamburgers on the horizontal axis. You can place this first dot easily by going up the vertical axis and locating the grid line marked $2.50. Then, move to the right along this line until you come to the grid line that comes up from the quantity of 100. Here is where you place the first dot. Similarly, at a price of $2.00, 150 hamburgers will be demanded. This point is plotted by marking a dot in a position that lines up with $2.00 on the vertical axis and 150 on the horizontal axis. After you have plotted the remaining three points and then connected all the dots with lines, you will have drawn a graph of the daily market demand for hamburgers.

Rules of the Game

Notice that as you move up the vertical axis, the numbers on the grid lines *increase* by equal amounts. Each time you move to a higher grid mark on the graph, the price increases by fifty cents. You see something similar whenever you watch a football game because the heavy white lines across a football field all measure exactly five yards apart. In fact, a football field is composed of many grid lines, just like a demand graph. No wonder a football field is often called a gridiron.

Now, look at the graph's horizontal axis, which measures the quantity of hamburgers. Here, the numbers on the grid lines increase by equal amounts as you move from left to right. In this case, a quantity is increased by 100 each time you move from one line to the next.

The grid lines in Figure 4–1 suggest two rules to follow whenever you draw a graph of demand:

Rule 1: Always put the prices per unit on the vertical axis and the quantities per time period on the horizontal axis.

Rule 2: Always make the price per unit increase by equal amounts as you move up the grid lines on the vertical axis, and always make the quantity per time period increase by equal amounts as you move from left to right on the grid lines of the horizontal axis. It's up to you to decide what these equal amounts should be, but you will probably want to choose them carefully, so your graph isn't too big or too small.

The white horizontal lines on this football field measure exactly five yards apart. Because a football field contains many of these grid lines, it is often called a gridiron. Similarly, a graph of demand consists of many horizontal grid lines that measure equal distances. These distances represent the quantities of a good that consumers want to purchase. Unlike a football field, however, a demand graph contains many vertical lines, which also measure equal distances. These distances represent the price of the good.

Following these rules permits us to use and interpret all demand curves in the same way. For example, by following these rules for graphing demand, we can conclude that demand curves always slope downward to the right. This fact is a visual image of the price effect (the universal characteristic of demand). The price effect tells us that during a given time period, we will purchase more at lower prices than we will at higher prices.

The Price Elasticity of Demand

Just because all demand curves slope downward to the right doesn't mean they are all identical. The price effect of one good might be strong, while that of another might be weak. One important reason why the strength of the price effect can differ from one demand to another is that substitutes are available. The more substitutes there are for a particular good or service, the greater the effect of a change in price will be.

Consider fresh tomatoes and water. If the price of tomatoes rises, we will readily substitute more lettuce, cucumbers, carrots, and other vegetables for some of the tomatoes in our salads. So, too, will we substitute more canned tomatoes for fresh tomatoes in casseroles and other dishes. If the price of water rises, we will also make substitutions and use less water. However, these substitutions are not as easily made. We can wash our cars less frequently, sweep our driveways instead of hosing them off, replace lawns with rock or cactus gardens, repair leaky faucets, and keep water in the refrigerator instead of running the tap for a cold drink. Although we must have some water to survive, we do not drink most of the water we use. If the price of water increases, we will still use less of it, a fact that confirms the price effect. Because the substitutions for water are not made as easily as those for fresh tomatoes are, the price effect is weaker for water than it is for fresh tomatoes.

In order to measure the price effect, economists use the price elasticity of demand. The **price elasticity of demand** shows the strength or weakness of the price effect: it measures how responsive the quantity we want to buy is to changes in price. If a lower price causes a substantial "stretch" in the amount individuals want to purchase, then the price effect is strong

The availability of substitutes determines a product's price elasticity of demand. Fresh tomatoes have many substitutes, so their demand is relatively elastic. What are some of the possible substitutes that consumers would use if the price of fresh tomatoes increased?

Because water has many uses besides drinking, consumers will use substitutes if the price of water increases. But these substitutions are usually not as easy to make as they are for fresh tomatoes. Consequently, the demand for water is relatively inelastic. What are some of the possible substitutions that consumers would use if the price of water increased?

and demand is elastic. In order to determine the strength or weakness of the price effect, the price elasticity of demand compares the *percentage* change in quantity purchased with the *percentage* change in price. If the percentage change in quantity purchased is greater than the percentage change in price, the price effect is strong and demand is *elastic*. On the other hand, if the percentage change in quantity is less than the percentage change in price, the price effect is weak and demand is *inelastic*. For example, suppose a 20 percent increase in the price of gasoline causes us to decrease the number of gallons purchased by 10 percent. Our demand for gasoline would be *inelastic* because the percentage change in price is greater than the percentage change in quantity purchased.

> **Price elasticity of demand:** A measure of the price effect. When the price effect is strong, demand is *elastic*. When the price effect is weak, demand is *inelastic*.

Changes in Demand

Substitutes are an important determinant of the price effect. But the price effect is also caused by two other reasons mentioned in the previous chapter. One is the fact that we place different values on the various uses of goods or services. If the price of a good rises, we eliminate the uses we value at less than the new higher price. Another reason is the fact that price changes increase or decrease the buying power of our money incomes. If the price of gasoline falls, we have more buying power—almost as if we had received more money. Because of our increased buying power, we can then buy more of the lower-priced gasoline.

The price effect refers to the effect of price changes on the amount purchased, *given the demand for the product.* The last part of this sentence is emphasized because the price effect is easily confused with a change in demand.[1] Indeed, the key to solving the hamburger riddle presented at the beginning of the chapter is to distinguish between the price effect and a change in demand.

Those Shifty Demand Curves

It will be easy to understand the difference between the price effect and a change in demand if we use an example presented earlier in the chapter. In that example, the market demand for hamburgers is described as a list or schedule of all the hamburgers that individuals in a particular market will buy at different possible prices, given their incomes, tastes, and expectations, and given the prices of substitute and complementary goods. The list does not change when the price of hamburgers changes. The entire list is called demand, and demand does *not* change as prices go up or down. What *does* change in the example is the particular amount that consumers want to purchase.

[1]The price effect is often referred to as a *change in quantity demanded.* Because this term is almost identical to a change in demand, it is easy to confuse the two different concepts. We use the term *price effect* to avoid this confusion.

Consumers differ in many ways, but when they share certain characteristics, such as age or occupation, producers often direct their marketing efforts to this particular market segment. To what market segment is this advertisement for Diet Coke directed? If the advertisement is successful, would its effects illustrate a change in demand or the price effect?

Changes in the amount purchased that are caused by changes in price are examples of the price effect, not a change in demand. A **change in demand** for a particular item is a change in the entire list of amounts that consumers will purchase at all possible prices. This list does not change with a change in the price of hamburgers.

> **Change in demand:**   A change in the entire list of amounts that consumers will purchase at all possible prices.

The only factors that can increase or decrease the demand for something are the four we just reviewed: (1) changes in our incomes, (2) changes in our tastes or preferences, (3) changes in expectations, and (4) changes in the prices of substitutes or complements. For example, let's look again at the daily demand for hamburgers.

A Decrease in Demand

Table 4–2 shows the original market demand for hamburgers during a given day. Now, let's suppose that we suddenly be-

The Economic Way of Thinking

Thinking About Factors Affecting Demand

Sometimes the price of a product rises or falls along with the amount of it bought. Does this fact deny the validity of the price effect?

Noneconomic Way of Thinking

The law of demand says that people buy fewer cars when the prices rise. Yet, in prior years more Japanese cars were sold despite the fact that their prices increased. This is not what economists would predict, so it denies the validity of the price effect.

Economic Way of Thinking

Nothing about the behavior of the Japanese car market invalidates the price effect. The price effect states that, everything else held constant, higher prices reduce the amount that people want to buy. However, if other factors are changing along with the price of Japanese cars, the net result is not predictable. For example, if the prices of American cars, which are substitutes for Japanese cars, are rising at the same time, then we don't know the net effect on the quantity of Japanese cars sold. In this instance, the rising price of American cars would have increased the demand for Japanese vehicles. This might have more than offset any decline in sales resulting from the rising price of Japanese cars.

Questions

1. What would happen to the demand curve for cars if people became wealthier? If the price of gasoline were to rise? If automobile insurance were to become cheaper?
2. Predict the net impact on sales of DAT (digital audio tape) players if their price fell at the same time that the price for blank tapes rose.

Table 4-2 A Decrease in the Demand for Hamburgers

Price	Old Demand	New Demand
$2.50	100	0
2.00	150	50
1.50	200	100
1.00	300	200
.50	500	300

This table shows a decrease in demand because the amounts that we are willing and able to purchase decrease at all possible prices. At $2.50, for example, our original demand was 100 hamburgers each day. After the change in demand, however, we demanded no hamburgers at all at this price.

come more concerned about eating red meat. Our tastes or preferences would then change, and that means a new schedule showing fewer hamburgers purchased at all possible prices. Demand has decreased, and this change is shown by the column on the right labeled *New Demand*.

The market demand has decreased because the amount purchased at each possible price is less than it was before. The graph in Figure 4-2 shows this change visually. Notice that

As the prices of personal computers declined, the demand for ordinary typewriters decreased. Consumers demanded fewer typewriters at all possible prices, so the demand curve shifted. Did it move up to the right or down to the left?

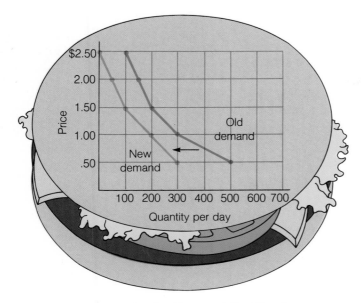

Figure 4–2   A Decrease in the Demand for Hamburgers

A change in our preferences as consumers has caused our demand for hamburgers to decrease. This decrease in demand is shown graphically as the demand curve shifts to the left. The leftward shift from *Old demand* to *New demand* shows that at all possible prices we now want to buy fewer hamburgers than we did before. At $1.00, for example, the amount we want to buy has fallen from 300 to 200 hamburgers per day.

the entire demand curve has shifted to the left, reflecting the fact that fewer hamburgers would now be purchased at each possible price.

An Increase in Demand

Now let's make a different assumption. Go back to the original demand (old demand), and assume there is a big increase in the price of pizza or some other substitute good. The higher price of pizza would cause us to eat less pizza and more hamburgers. The demand for hamburgers would increase, therefore, because we would buy more hamburgers at all possible prices. Table 4–3 shows this increase in demand numerically.

The market demand for hamburgers has increased because we purchase more at each possible price than we did before. Figure 4–3 shows this increase as a shift of the entire demand curve to the right. The quantity we demand at all possible prices is now greater than it was before.

On your mark! Get set! Shift! Because of a greater preference for exercise, the demand curve for running shoes shifted up to the right. Consumers wanted to buy more running shoes at each and every price.

The Price Effect Versus a Change in Demand

A change in demand is shown visually by *shifting the entire demand curve* to the right or the left. This change is very different from the price effect, which is shown graphically by *moving up or down an existing demand curve*. You need to understand this difference in order to avoid confused thinking.

Table 4–3   An Increase in the Demand for Hamburgers

Price	Old Demand	New Demand
$2.50	100	200
2.00	150	250
1.50	200	350
1.00	300	500
.50	500	700

This table shows an increase in demand because the amounts that we will purchase increase at all possible prices. At $2.50, for example, our original demand was 100 hamburgers each day. After the change in demand, however, we demanded 200 hamburgers at this price.

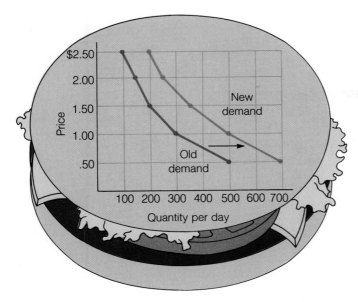

Figure 4–3 An Increase in the Demand for Hamburgers

An increase in the price of pizza or of some other substitute has caused our demand for hamburgers to rise. This increase in demand is shown graphically as the demand curve shifts to the right. The rightward shift from *Old demand* to *New demand* shows that at all possible prices we now want to buy more hamburgers than we did before. At $1.00, for example, the amount that we want to buy has increased from 300 to 500 hamburgers per day.

Take the riddle presented at the beginning of the chapter. Is the price effect denied by the fact that more hamburgers are sold today at higher prices than were sold 10 years ago at lower prices? Look at Figure 4–4, a graph of the market demand for hamburgers, and you can see how important it is to understand the difference between a change in demand and the price effect.

Examine the original demand curve, labeled *Old demand*. At the original price of $1, we purchased 2 thousand hamburgers per day. If the price now rises to $2, the price effect will cause our purchases to fall to 1 thousand per day. But at the same time that the price increases, some of the determinants of demand can also change. For example, our incomes might rise, and this rise would cause the demand curve to shift to the right to *New demand*, which shows we purchase more hamburgers at every possible price.

The increase in our demand means that at the new, higher price of $2 we will purchase 5 thousand hamburgers per day. As a result, the price has increased from $1 to $2, but so, too,

Comparing the Price Effect and a Change in Demand

A politician has made the following comment: "We have an apartment shortage in our city; but if we expand the supply and thereby reduce the cost of rentals, demand will increase." Is the politician correct?

Noneconomic Way of Thinking

If an increased supply of apartments decreases the rent that people have to pay for them, then apartment demand will surely increase. The politician is obviously correct.

Economic Way of Thinking

If the supply is expanded and rents fall as a result, demand will *not* increase. The politician is confusing a change in demand with the price effect. If rents fall, then the quantity of apartments people want to rent will rise, meaning that the community will move *along* its demand curve, say, from point A to point B on the lefthand graph below.

An increase in demand means that the entire demand curve will shift up to the right, so that people want to rent more apartments at all possible prices. The graph on the right shows an increase in the demand for apartments, which might occur, for example, if the price of houses goes up. But a lower rental price caused by an increased supply of apartments does not cause the demand curve to shift. Remember that a change in price does not affect demand because demand is the entire list of different quantities of apartments that people would want to rent at all possible rental rates. The politician is confusing the price effect with a change in demand, so the politician is wrong.

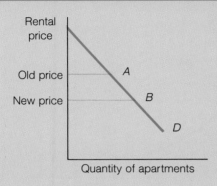

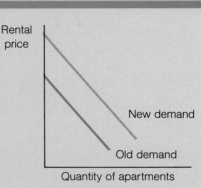

Questions

1. What effect would a fall in the price of bicycles have on the demand for bicycles? On the amount of bicycles sold?

2. What factors would cause an increase in the demand for apartments? Could price be one of these factors?

3. If our demand for gasoline rises, what can you then say about the amount we are willing and able to buy at each price?

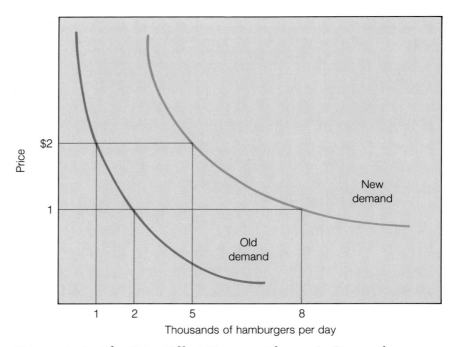

Figure 4–4 The Price Effect Versus a Change in Demand

If the price rises from $1 to $2 per hamburger, the *Old demand* curve shows that the quantity we would consume will fall from 2,000 to 1,000 hamburgers per day. But if higher incomes or other factors cause our demand to increase to *New demand*, the number of hamburgers we would consume will rise from 2,000 to 5,000 per day, *at the same time* that the price increases from $1 to $2. Because an increase in price occurs along with an increase in the number of hamburgers consumed, you might incorrectly conclude that the price effect is absent. Although it is not readily apparent, the price effect still exists. If the price had remained at $1, our consumption would have risen from 2,000 to 8,000 hamburgers per day. But the higher price of $2 caused movement up the *New demand* curve from 8,000 to 5,000 hamburgers per day. As a result, the higher price has prevented our hamburger consumption from rising as much as it would otherwise have risen, a fact that illustrates the price effect.

has the quantity purchased gone up from 2 to 5 thousand hamburgers per day. This fact does not disprove demand (the price effect). The price effect (movement up the *New demand* curve) is still there, but you don't notice it because it is overshadowed by the change in demand as the demand curve shifts to the right. Indeed, if the price had not increased to $2, the quantity we would have purchased would have risen even more—to 8 thousand hamburgers per day. The price effect, caused by the price increase from $1 to $2, prevents our purchases from increasing as they would have otherwise.

1. *Market demand* is a list of the total quantities of a product that all individuals would buy at different possible prices. A numerical presentation of market demand is called a *demand schedule.* You can graph a demand schedule by putting the money prices on the vertical line and the quantities demanded per time period on the horizontal line. Each of these lines is called an *axis.* You can construct a graph, first by plotting the points that show the amounts of a good that would be purchased at different prices and, then, by connecting these dots. The result is called a *demand curve.*

2. It is important to follow two rules when you are graphing demand: (1) Always put the prices per unit on the vertical axis and the quantities per time period on the horizontal axis. (2) Always make the prices per unit increase by equal amounts as you move up the grid lines of the vertical axis, and make the quantities per time period increase by equal amounts as you move from left to right on the grid lines of the horizontal axis. Following these rules, we see that demand curves—visual images of the price effect—always slope downward to the right.

3. One reason demand curves are not identical is that the strength of the price effect is often different for different goods. One primary reason for this difference is that substitutes are available. When there are more substitutes for a good, the price effect is stronger. When there are fewer substitutes, the price effect will be weaker. The *price elasticity of demand* is defined as a measure of the price effect. It compares the percentage change in quantity purchased with the percentage change in price. When the price effect is strong, demand is elastic. When the price effect is weak, demand is inelastic.

4. There are two other reasons for the price effect. First, we place different values on the various uses of goods and services; as the price of a good increases, we exclude the uses we value less than the higher price. Second, as price goes up or down, the buying power of our money incomes changes.

5. The effect of price on the amount purchased, given the demand for the product, must be carefully distinguished from

a change in demand. Changes in the amount purchased of any good or service that are caused by price changes are examples of the price effect. A change in demand for any good or service is a change in the entire list or schedule of amounts that we will purchase at all possible prices. A change in demand can be caused by changes in incomes, changes in tastes or preferences, changes in expectations, and changes in the prices of substitutes. If our demand for a product decreases, the amount we will purchase at each possible price is less than it was before. This decrease in demand is shown graphically by the demand curve's shifting down to the left. An increase in demand is shown graphically by the demand curve's shifting up to the right.

6. We show a change in demand by shifting the demand curve to the right or left, but we show the price effect by moving up or down an existing demand curve. Because price changes often occur at the same time that the determinants of demand change, the price effect is often camouflaged.

Review Questions

1. What is meant by the term *market demand?*

2. What is the difference between a *demand schedule* and a *demand curve?*

3. When you are graphing demand, what is measured on the horizontal axis? What is measured on the vertical axis?

4. Draw a demand curve. Does it always slope downward to the right? Explain.

5. Explain how the price effect of one good might be strong while that of another might be weak.

6. What is meant by the term *price elasticity of demand?*

7. What is the difference between the *price effect* and a *change in demand?* Illustrate this difference graphically.

8. Draw a curve showing an increase in demand. Now draw one showing decrease in demand. Describe verbally or in writing the difference between the two.

1. When graphing demand, what rules should you follow? Explain.

2. What factors might cause you to increase your purchases of compact disks at the same time that their price increases? Would your behavior disprove the price effect? Why or why not?

3. Some economists have advocated a higher tax on beer and other alcoholic beverages as one of the most effective means of reducing drunk driving among teen-agers. Use a graph of demand to analyze whether or not such a proposal could work. Do you favor the proposal? Why or why not?

Activities

1. Survey your parents to determine how many chocolate chip cookies (5″ diameter) they would be willing to buy at $1.00 per cookie, $.50 per cookie, and $.25 per cookie. The cookies will be made by students at school. Chart this information on a demand schedule. Then use the information on the demand schedule to construct a graph of demand.

2. Convince your parents that a scientific survey has revealed that the above cookies taste much better than do the ones they can buy in the store and that the money you earn will go to charity. Now, given this new information, how many chocolate chip cookies would they be willing to buy at each of the above prices? Chart this information on a demand schedule, and then use the information to construct a graph of demand.

3. Poll other members of your class to find out if there were any differences in demand between situation 1 and situation 2. Then write a short paragraph explaining the reason for any differences in demand that might or might not have occurred.

4. Write a short paragraph evaluating the following statement: In order to show that less of a good will be demanded

at higher prices than at lower prices, you must draw a demand curve that slopes downward to the right.

5. Use the following demand schedule to construct a graph of demand:

Price	Dishes of frozen yogurt sold each week
$3.00	1,000
2.50	2,000
2.00	4,000
1.50	7,000
1.00	11,000
.50	16,000

(a) If the price per dish increases from $1.00 to $2.00, does the demand for frozen yogurt decrease?

(b) Suppose the number of dishes sold at each price drops by half. Calculate the new demand schedule, and use this information to draw the new demand curve on the graph you have already constructed. What are some of the factors that could have caused this change?

(c) The changes in part a and part b demonstrate an important point made in this chapter. Explain that point.

Additional Readings

Amos, Orley M., Jr. *Economics: Concepts, Analysis, and Applications.* Belmont, Calif.: Wadsworth, 1987. 52–59.

Byrns, Ralph T., and Stone, Gerald W. *Microeconomics.* 3d ed. Glenview, Ill.: Scott, Foresman, 1987. 43–50.

Heyne, Paul. *The Economic Way of Thinking.* 5th ed. Chicago: Science Research Associates, 1987. 18–35.

Why does the price of eggs affect the quantity of eggs suppliers want to sell?

Supply

■ Student's Goals ■

1. Define the concept of *supply* as it is used in economics.

2. Explain the *price effect* as it applies to supply.

3. List and explain the determinants of supply.

4. Graph a supply curve from a given supply schedule.

5. Use a graph to illustrate an increase and a decrease in supply.

6. Distinguish between the *price effect* and a *change in supply*.

Stripper Wells and Drilling Rigs

A stripper well sips less than ten barrels of oil a day from the earth's crust. However, there are hundreds of thousands of these wells throughout the United States. As a result, stripper wells account for about one out of every seven barrels of oil produced in our nation.

The amount of oil produced by stripper wells is sensitive to price changes. When the price of oil spurted to $30 a barrel in the early 1980s, the number of stripper wells was increased and more oil was produced. When the price sank below $15 in

The amount of oil supplied is sensitive to price. At higher prices, producers have an incentive to incur higher costs in order to provide more oil. But at lower prices, they provide less oil because it doesn't pay to bear the high costs of squeezing more oil out of existing wells and fields. Would you behave the same way if, for example, the price of baby-sitting increased to $50 per hour or decreased to 20 cents per hour?

the mid-1980s, many stripper wells were closed down. Indeed, one study predicted that more than a fifth of all stripper wells would be shut down as a result of the lower price of $15 a barrel.[1]

The amount of oil produced by bigger wells also is sensitive to price changes. The fact that the number of large rigs drilling for oil is increased and decreased with the price of petroleum supports this conclusion. When the price of oil was high in 1981, more than 4,000 rigs were busily probing the ground like thirsty mosquitoes. After the price of petroleum declined, however, the number of rigs drilling for oil was decreased to less than 1,000 by 1986.

These few facts about oil rigs and stripper wells demonstrate an important economic principle called **supply:** producers supply more of a good or service at higher prices and less at lower prices. But if this is true, how can we explain the following fact? Although the prices of personal computers, hand calculators, and some other products have dropped noticeably over the years, companies are willing to supply more, not less, of these items. Doesn't this fact disprove the principle of supply?

The question is a good one and it cannot be answered adequately in a few sentences. First, you need to have a clear understanding of supply.

The Price Effect and Supply

Supply is a list of the various quantities of an item that a producer is willing to sell at different possible prices.

> **Supply:** A list of the various quantities of an item that a producer is willing to sell at different possible prices.

This definition is similar to that given for demand in Chapter 3. There, demand refers to the various quantities that a consumer

[1]See, for example, Allanna Sullivan, "As Oil Prices Decline, Stripper Well Owners Struggle to Hang On," *Wall Street Journal,* May 15, 1986; or Robert B. Horton, "Oil and the World Today," *Vital Speeches* (August 1, 1986): 616–19.

will *buy* at different prices. Here, supply refers to the various quantities that a producer will *sell* at different prices.

Chapter 3 describes the effect that price changes have on the amounts that consumers want to purchase. Lower prices make them buy more, and higher prices make them buy less. There is also a price effect for supply, but it is the opposite of that for demand. Higher prices encourage suppliers to sell more of an item, and lower prices encourage them to sell less.

Price changes have this effect on supply because of the relationship between the amount produced per time period and the item's cost of production. In this case, the cost of production means the *marginal cost* of production—the cost of producing an additional unit of the good or service. (For an explanation of *marginal*, see "Thinking About Choice" in Chapter 1.) As a supplier produces more of an item per time period, its marginal cost of production usually increases. As a result, suppliers must receive higher prices if they are to have an incentive to produce the additional, more costly units.

Consider the fictional story of Rudy and Judy, two teen-agers who start a business that produces peeled, hard-boiled eggs.[2] Every peeled egg is not perfect: some are smashed and others are torn. Eggs that are smashed are sold to a company that makes egg and potato salads; those with small tears are sold to restaurants for salad bars and sandwiches; and perfect eggs are sold to a local pickling company. Rudy and Judy can produce a gross (twelve dozen or 144) of peeled eggs in an hour. If they work one hour per day, they will produce a gross of peeled eggs per day. If they work ten hours per day, they will produce ten gross per day.

Their time isn't free, so the number of peeled eggs they are willing to produce per day depends on the price at which they can sell them. Their time has an opportunity cost because the hours they devote to cooking and peeling eggs must be taken from other uses, such as studying, eating, sleeping, and having fun. If Rudy and Judy are already spending many hours at these other activities, the first few hours they give up for egg production will have relatively low value. But imagine what happens if they are spending twenty hours per day boiling and

[2]For an account of an actual business producing this product, see Yalita Sellers, "Boiled-Egg Peelers Aim for Perfection, and That's No Yolk," *Wall Street Journal*, July 9, 1985.

The number of eggs you would boil and peel depends on many factors, one of which is the price at which you could sell the peeled eggs. Imagine learning that you could sell all the peeled eggs you wanted for $100 per dozen. Would your willingness to boil and peel eggs diminish if you could get only 10 cents for each dozen?

peeling eggs and devoting only four hours to other activities. In that case, the production of an additional gross of eggs per day requires an hour that is very valuable—especially for sleeping.

As Rudy and Judy produce more eggs, the additional hours they devote to production become more and more valuable in their alternative uses. In order to produce more eggs, therefore, they must draw on successively more costly hours. As their marginal cost increases, Rudy and Judy become willing to produce and sell more eggs per day only if they can sell them at a higher price. Other producers' marginal costs rise in the same fashion.[3]

Marginal cost usually goes up as production increases because a supplier must draw on more costly resources and use

---

[3]You might wonder why a larger volume of production does not result in *lower* production costs. Over time, a supplier might be able to alter production techniques or use additional equipment and facilities and thereby reduce costs through the economies of large scale production. But given the producer's current size, larger quantities can be produced only by using higher-valued resources. This means that the marginal cost of production rises as more output is produced.

The Boston Celtics are practicing in order to improve their play and score more points. But scoring more points per game is like squeezing more oil out of an oil field or squeezing more peeled eggs out of one's daily efforts. The marginal costs of points, oil, or peeled eggs all rise as the quantity produced increases. Haven't you encountered a similar event when trying to improve a particular skill, such as guitar playing or tennis playing? At first, a little effort (and a small opportunity cost) produces substantial gains. But as you get better, the improvements become harder (and more costly).

more costly production methods. Take oil production as an example. By using more expensive drilling and pumping methods, a producer can recover more oil from a particular field. Steam, chemicals, or gases can be injected into some wells in order to increase pressure and, thereby, recover more petroleum. Crews can be paid overtime for working more hours. But when a producer employs these costly methods in order to squeeze more oil out of a particular well, the marginal cost rises. Moreover, the cost of obtaining a barrel of oil varies considerably among wells. If the price of oil rises, it pays to use the more costly wells, just as higher egg prices would pay Rudy and Judy to use their more costly hours.

Suppliers' marginal costs can increase as their outputs expand because they must use more costly resources and methods. If a product's price increases, therfore, suppliers produce more because they have an incentive to bear these higher costs. On the other hand, if the price decreases, suppliers produce less because they are discouraged from bearing these higher costs.

The impact that price changes have on the amount supplied is called the **price effect.** Because the price effect applies to all goods and services, it is the universal characteristic of supply. The higher the price, the greater the quantity suppliers are willing to produce and sell. The lower the price, the smaller the quantity they are willing to offer.

> **Price effect:** Higher prices cause producers to supply more of an item, and lower prices cause them to supply less.

The Determinants of Supply

The price received for a good or service has a powerful influence on the amount suppliers produce. But what are the factors that determine the amount of a product that will be produced at each and every possible price?

Technological change is an important determinant of supply. Here, a robot helps to manufacture the chips used in computers. This technology helps to increase the supply of computer chips.

Thinking About the Price Effect

Suppose you have your own business and the price of your product is just equal to your cost of production. If the price of your product suddenly falls, will you produce more or less at the lower price?

Noneconomic Way of Thinking

At the new, lower price you will have to sell more units in order to make up for the lower price you receive for each one. In this way, your profits can be protected.

Economic Way of Thinking

At the lower price there is no way you can make as much money as you did before. All you can do is make the best of a worse situation, and that means producing less. Here's why. Before, you were producing at such a level that the old, higher price was just equal to your marginal cost of production. But now that the price has dropped, those last units cost you more to produce than they give you in revenues. It just doesn't pay to produce those last few units. Consequently, you should reduce your production until your marginal cost falls far enough so that it equals the new, lower price.

Questions

1. What happens to your incentive to produce when the price you can get rises? Why?
2. What limits the amount of additional output you would produce at a higher price?

Assembly-line production in large plants has enabled auto companies to use new technologies to shift the entire supply curve to the right. But if a plant of a given size were to continue increasing its production, the marginal cost of an automobile would increase. It would increase because more valuable resources, such as overtime labor, would be used. See footnote 3 for a brief explanation.

One of these determinants was illustrated when dry weather reduced the supply of peanuts by almost 50 percent. *Events of nature*—weather, floods, earthquakes, and so on—can significantly affect the amounts of a product that will be made available at different prices during a particular time.

A more important determinant of supply, however is the *cost of production*. A higher cost of production decreases the supply of a product, and a lower cost of production increases its supply. Two factors affect the cost of production. One of them is technological change, the introduction of a new production method, such as the computer, that increases productivity. As an illustration, suppose a newly invented, inexpensive egg-peeling machine enables Rudy and Judy to increase their hourly egg production. Because the new machine enables them to produce more peeled eggs in a shorter period of time, they can take less time away from studying, eating, sleeping, and having fun in order to produce more eggs. If the new machine enables them to save enough time to compensate for the machine's expense, the cost of production will drop, and they will be willing to sell more eggs each day.

Another factor affecting the cost of production is the price of resources. If the price of fresh eggs goes down, then the cost

Thinking About Cost and Supply

Sometimes producers must pay higher or lower prices for their raw materials and then keep these materials in stock for manufacturing their products. Put yourself in the shoes of one of these producers. Suppose you stock and use large amounts of silver to produce a special film for cameras. If the price of silver doubles overnight, will you produce more, less, or the same amount of film?

Noneconomic Way of Thinking

If you have already bought the silver, why would the higher price change anything? Your costs will be the same, so why should you alter the amount of film you produce?

Economic Way of Thinking

Your costs do change when the price of silver rises. They rise because the opportunity cost of using silver in the production of film is the price at which it could be resold to others who would buy it in the silver market. If the price of silver rises, this (opportunity) cost also rises. Consequently, you will have more incentive to sell your stock of silver and less incentive to use it for the production of film. You will produce less film at each and every price for the film.

Questions

1. How will the supply behavior of the airlines change if the cost of jet fuel falls? How will the supply curve of travel change in this instance?

2. Ann is a high school senior who often baby-sits on weekends. Will Ann's incentive to baby-sit change if she acquires a steady boyfriend?

of making peeled, hard-boiled eggs also declines. With lower production costs, Rudy and Judy will be willing to produce and sell larger quantities of eggs per day.

In summary, the cost of production is the most important determinant of supply. Moreover, the two major factors affecting the cost of production are changes in technology and changes in resource prices. Accordingly, when technology or resource prices alter production cost, they change the entire list of amounts that a supplier will produce at every possible price. These changes can be shown clearly on a graph of supply. The next section explains how to construct such a graph.

How to Graph Supply

Supply is a list of the various amounts of a good or service that a producer will offer for sale at different prices during a particular time. The list shows that producers offer more at higher prices and less at lower prices. Supply can be shown on the same graph that is used in Chapter 4 to show demand. In that chapter, a graph presents *market demand,* which is the sum of consumers' individual demands. Similarly, market supply is obtained by adding the individual supplies of all sellers in a particular market. **Market supply** is a list of the *total* quantities of a good or service that *all* producers would sell at different possible prices.

> **Market supply:** A list of the *total* quantities of a good or service that *all* producers would sell at different possible prices.

Suppose there are four suppliers in the same hamburger market for which we have constructed the demand curve in Chapter 4. In Table 5–1 the individual supplies of all four producers are added in order to show market supply.

The first and last columns of Table 5–1 show the market supply of hamburgers. When this relationship is shown numerically, as in Table 5–1, it is called a *supply schedule.* In Figure 5–1 the numbers representing market supply (the first and last columns of the table) have been plotted in order to show the *market supply curve.*

Table 5–1   Computing Market Supply

Price	Producer A's Supply per Day		Producer B's Supply per Day		Producer C's Supply per Day		Producer D's Supply per Day		Total
$2.50	200	+	50	+	100	+	150	=	500
2.00	180	+	40	+	90	+	140	=	450
1.50	160	+	30	+	80	+	130	=	400
1.00	130	+	10	+	60	+	100	=	300
.50	100	+	0	+	40	+	60	=	200

This table shows the daily hamburger supplies of four producers. Producer A's supply is the number of hamburgers he or she would be willing to sell each day at different possible prices. At $2.50, Producer A would want to sell 200 hamburgers per day, but at $2.00, she or he would want to sell 180 hamburgers per day. Market supply is the sum of the supplies of all four producers. The total supplies are found by adding the quantities that each producer would be willing to sell at every price. The first column labeled *Price* and the last column labeled *Total* show the *total* quantities of hamburgers that *all* suppliers will sell at different possible prices. Therefore, they give us the market supply for hamburgers per day.

The prices that could be charged per hamburger are put on the graph's vertical axis, and the quantities supplied per day are put on the horizontal axis. Table 5–1 shows that at a price of $.50, producers will supply 200 hamburgers per day. This relationship can be shown on the graph by placing a dot at a location that aligns with $.50 on the vertical axis and 200 hamburgers on the horizontal axis. Plot this dot by going up the vertical axis and locating the grid line marked $.50. Then move to the right along this line until you come to the grid line that comes up from the quantity 200. Here is where you place the first dot. After you have plotted the remaining four points and then connected all the dots with lines, you will have drawn a graph of the daily market supply for hamburgers.

Can Supply Curves Be Shifty?

Some of the same warnings about demand are also true for supply. For example, supply is *not* a single amount; it is a list or schedule of all the amounts that suppliers will offer at various prices during a particular time. If supply changes, the entire schedule changes, so that different quantities are offered at each possible price.

In addition, do not confuse a change in supply with the price effect. The price effect is shown by a single supply curve, such as that in Figure 5–1. If the price increases from $1.50 to $2.50, for example, suppliers increase the number of hamburgers offered for sale each day from 400 to 500. Because it is the price change that causes the number of hamburgers offered for sale to increase by 100, the supply curve does not shift to the right or left. Instead, the price increase brings about a *movement up the existing supply curve*, which is an example of the *price effect*.

A *change in supply* is different because it refers to a *shift of the entire supply curve*. When supply changes, therefore, the schedule of amounts offered for sale *at all possible prices* also changes. The two factors that can alter this schedule and cause the supply curve to shift have been identified earlier in this chapter. They are (1) natural events, and (2) changes in the cost of production, caused by technological changes or changes in the price of resources.

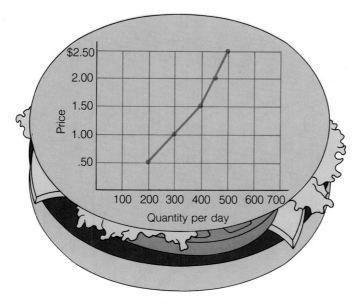

Figure 5–1 The Market Supply of Hamburgers

The money prices that could be charged for a hamburger are shown on the vertical axis of the graph. The quantities supplied at each of these prices are shown on the horizontal axis. The supply curve slopes upward to the right because producers offer more hamburgers for sale at higher prices than they do at lower prices. At $2.50, for example, producers want to sell 500 hamburgers per day. At $.50, however, they want to sell only 200 hamburgers per day.

Table 5—2 A Decrease in the Supply of Hamburgers

Price	Old Supply	New Supply
$2.50	500	300
2.00	450	250
1.50	400	200
1.00	300	100
.50	200	0

This table shows a decrease in supply because the amounts that producers are willing to sell decrease at all possible prices. At $2.50, for example, producers were originally willing to sell 500 hamburgers per day. After the change in supply, however, producers were willing to sell only 300 hamburgers per day.

A Decrease in Supply

Suppose the price of beef increases, making it more costly for producers to make hamburgers. The higher cost of hamburger will alter the entire supply schedule. In this instance, supply

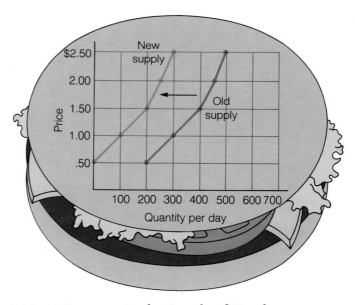

Figure 5—2 A Decrease in the Supply of Hamburgers

Higher beef prices have caused the supply of hamburgers to decrease. This decrease in supply is shown graphically as the supply curve shifts to the left. The leftward shift from *Old supply* to *New supply* shows that at all possible prices producers are now willing to sell fewer hamburgers than they did before. At $1.50, for example, the amount that producers want to sell has dropped from 400 to 200 hamburgers per day.

decreases because producers are offering fewer hamburgers for sale at all possible prices. Table 5–2 shows the decrease in supply.

Figure 5–2 shows this change in supply graphically. Notice that the entire supply curve has shifted to the left, showing that producers are now offering fewer hamburgers at each possible price.

An Increase in Supply

Go back to the original supply shown in Table 5–1 and Figure 5–1. Now assume a newly invented microwave cooker enables producers to cook better-tasting hamburgers at both a faster rate and a lower cost. Businesses can now offer more hamburgers at each price. Table 5–3 shows this increase in supply.

The market supply of hamburgers has increased, because suppliers are offering more at each possible price than they did before. Figure 5–3 shows this increase as a shift of the entire supply curve to the right.

Thinking Correctly About Supply

In the first section of this chapter we presented a question about supply. Is the economic principle of supply disproved by the fact that more computers and hand calculators are produced today at lower prices than were produced in past years at higher

Table 5–3 An Increase in the Supply of Hamburgers

Price	Old Supply	New Supply
$2.50	500	700
2.00	450	650
1.50	400	600
1.00	300	500
.50	200	400

This table shows an increase in supply because the amounts that producers are willing to sell increase at all possible prices. At $2.50, for example, businesses originally wanted to sell 500 hamburgers per day. After the change in supply, however, they wanted to sell 700 hamburgers per day.

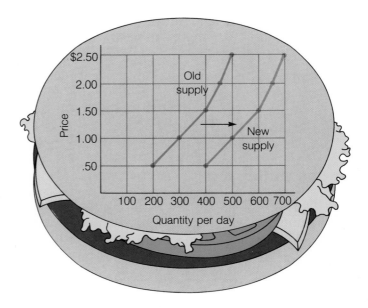

Figure 5-3 An Increase in the Supply of Hamburgers

A lower production cost for hamburgers has caused the supply of hamburgers to rise. This, in turn, has caused the supply curve to shift to the right. The rightward shift from *Old supply* to *New supply* shows that at all possible prices businesses are now willing to sell more hamburgers than they did before. At $1.00, for example, the amount that producers want to sell has increased from 300 to 500 hamburgers per day.

prices? The question can be clearly answered by distinguishing between the price effect and a change in supply. Consider the two supply curves shown in Figure 5–4.

Check the original supply curve, labeled *Old supply*. At the original price of $3,000, 6,000 computers are produced and offered for sale per month. If the price falls to $1,000, the price effect causes the quantity supplied to fall to 3,000 per month.

But suppose that as the price falls technological changes in computer production reduce the production cost and shift the supply curve to *New supply*. This increase in supply means that at the new, lower price of $1,000, 8,000 computers are offered for sale per month. As a result, the price has fallen from $3,000 to $1,000, but the quantity supplied has also increased from 6,000 to 8,000 computers per month. If the price had not decreased to $1,000, the quantity supplied would have risen even more—to 10,000 computers per month. The price effect, caused by a price reduction from $3,000 to $1,000, prevents the quantity supplied from rising as much as it would otherwise

(text continues on page 129)

Now and Then

The Driving Force of Supply

When Berta Benz began a 72-mile drive with her two sons, she probably had no idea of the record she was about to set. On this trip in the 1880s, Berta Benz became the first woman to drive a car. She bravely set out on her trip in a vehicle designed and constructed by her husband, the German inventor Karl Benz. The primitive vehicle was one of the first automobiles to run on petroleum. Its small engine could muster only three horsepower. When going up hills, Berta and her sons had to get out and push. Going down hills must have been frightening, however, for the flimsy brakes were constructed of leather pads that quickly wore out. No doubt, Berta had to stop in more than one village to have a shoemaker nail new pads on the vehicle. At one point, a broken spring prevented one of the engine valves from closing, so Berta creatively employed one of her garters and the automobile clattered on its way.

Although steam coaches had coughed and hissed in London as early as the 1820s and 1830s, their large size, considerable weight, and slow speed made them impractical. Then, in France in 1860, Etienne Lenoir invented the internal combustion engine. But it was Karl Benz who helped to develop the idea further around 1885.

Few people had any idea how drastically and suddenly the world was about to change. For example, the 1888 *German Yearbook of Natural Science* commented that "Benz also had made a petrol car which caused some stir at the Munich Exposition. This employment of the petrol engine will probably be no more promising for the future than the use of the steam engine was for road travel."

That prediction was as wrong as some of today's weather forecasts. Within fifteen years, more than 50,000 cars were being produced per year around the world. In 1900, the United States produced about 4,000 automobiles. This number is tiny compared to today's production figures, but manufacturing methods were much different in those days. At that time, automobiles were prohibitively expensive because they were handmade by people skilled in the wood and iron crafts. Moreover, in order to make additional cars, a supplier would have to pay these skilled artisans even more to get them to work harder and longer.

As a result, the production of more cars during a given period of time would have increased the marginal cost of a car, thereby pushing the supplier up an existing supply curve. Therefore, suppliers would produce more cars only at higher prices. But consumers were unwilling and unable to pay such high prices, so there was little incentive to produce large numbers of new automobiles.

In the United States, however, automobile production was beginning to stir like an awakening giant. The early companies included Studebaker, which had been the world's largest carriage builder; Buick, which had produced bathtubs and plumbing accessories; and Olds, which had produced engines. And then there was Henry Ford.

After building his first car in 1896, Henry Ford and others established the Detroit Automobile Company in 1899. When Ford left the new com-

pany after a couple of years to start his own business, the Detroit Automobile Company became the Cadillac Automobile Company. In 1903, Ford began producing his own automobile, which had an eight-horsepower engine with a top speed of thirty miles per hour. In 1908, the company began producing the famous Model T (see Figure A).

That year also marked the formation of General Motors, which soon purchased many independent companies including Buick, Cadillac, and Olds (Chevrolet was added in 1918). But it was Henry Ford who first used the assembly line in 1913. No longer

Figure A Ford's Model T

More than 15 million Model Ts were produced by Ford between 1908 and 1927. Though simple and inelegant, its price was relatively low.

were motor vehicles individually handcrafted. The age of mass production had begun.

By using the new assembly-line technology, automobile companies were able to produce more automobiles at a lower marginal cost. These so-called economies of scale enabled manufacturers to increase the supply of cars. That is, producers were able to shift their supply curves down to the right, thereby providing more automobiles at a lower price. As Figure B shows, the effects on automobile production were astounding.

Except during the Great Depression of the 1930s and World War II in the 1940s, U.S. auto producers generally continued to shift their supply curves to the right by continually advancing the new technology of mass production. Then came the 1970s. In 1973 and 1979, oil prices suddenly and unexpectedly soared. At the same time, consumers turned a favorable eye toward imported cars. Like a prize fighter caught with his guard down, the U.S. auto industry was stunned by the blow. As the shaded area in Figure B shows, U.S. auto production declined between 1978 and 1983. During those years,

Figure A U.S. Automobile Production, 1900–1986

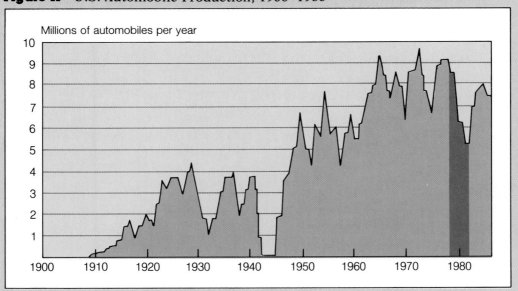

Source: *Historical Statistics of the United States, Colonial Times to 1970; Survey of Current Business*, April 1987, Vol. 67, No. 4, U.S. Department of Commerce, Bureau of Economic Analysis, p. 32.

rebates, special financing plans, and other price reductions pushed auto producers down their supply curves.

The auto companies suffered some hefty losses during these years. But General Motors, the biggest car company with close to half of all car sales in the nation, planned a comeback. Early in 1979 it unveiled a seven-year, $40 billion plan that would utilize the company's economies of scale. By redesigning its factories to incorporate robots and other advanced technology and by making smaller, fuel-stingy, front-wheel-drive cars, GM planned to fight back. But gas prices did not continue to rise as GM's managers had thought they would. Instead, gas prices fell in the mid-80s, and consumers began looking at larger cars, not the smaller ones GM had planned to make. GM's production costs also soared to the highest level in the industry. As a result, in 1986 Ford earned more profits than GM for the first time since the heady days of the old Model T Ford.

The chairman of General Motors claimed the difficulties were the predictable, but temporary, result of the company's shift to a new, more automated production system. Others argued that GM's relatively large size denied the company the flexibility it needed to succeed. While GM was criticized for being too big, Chrysler Corporation was busy getting bigger. It purchased the ailing American Motors Corporation in order to enlarge its production capacity.

Whether its size ought to be bigger, smaller, or unchanged, each auto company must continually seek new technologies to shift its supply curve down to the right. Without the driving force of technological change, an automobile producer will be left far behind by many other companies that eagerly compete in the world marketplace.

References

Beaulieu, Lord Montagu of. "The Early Days of Motoring." *History Today* 36 (October 1986): 43–49.

General Motors: The First 75 Years. By the editors of *Automobile Quarterly Magazine* New York: Crown Publishing Co., 1983.

Hampton, William J. and Norman, James R. "General Motors: What Went Wrong." *Business Week* (March 16, 1987): 102–110.

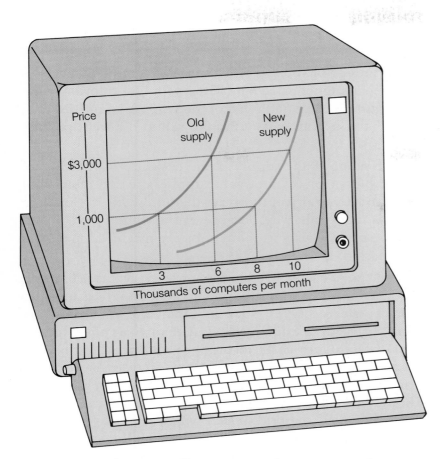

Figure 5—4 The Price Effect versus a Change in Supply

If the price of computers falls from $3,000 to $1,000, the *Old supply* curve shows that the quantity offered for sale will drop from 6,000 to 3,000 per month. But if technological change causes the supply to increase to *New supply,* the number of computers offered for sale will increase from 6,000 to 8,000 per month, *at the same time* that the price falls from $3,000 to $1,000. Because a decrease in price occurs along with an increase in the number of computers supplied, you might incorrectly conclude that the price effect is absent. Although it is not readily apparent, the price effect still exists. If the price had remained at $3,000, production would have increased from 6,000 to 10,000 computers per month. But the lower price of $1,000 caused movement down the *New supply* curve from 10,000 to 8,000 computers per month. As a result, the lower price has prevented computer production from rising as much as it would otherwise have risen, a fact that confirms the price effect.

have risen. The fact that more computers are produced and sold today at lower prices does not disprove the economic principle of supply. Important technological changes in computer production have shifted the supply curve, thereby enabling production to rise and the price to fall.

Chapter Summary

1. The principle of *supply* is this: more of a good or service is supplied at higher prices and less is supplied at lower prices. By definition, supply is a list of the various quantities of an item that a producer is willing to sell at different possible prices.

2. The price effect for supply is the opposite of that for demand: higher prices motivate suppliers to sell more of an item, and lower prices motivate them to sell less. Suppliers tend to react this way because the marginal cost of production usually rises as more units are produced in a given time period.

3. The marginal cost of production increases as more units are produced in a given time period because suppliers must use more costly resources, such as labor and materials, and more costly production methods. Because suppliers have to bear these higher costs to produce additional units, they usually increase their production only in response to higher prices which will compensate them for these higher costs. The influence that price changes have on the amount produced is called the *price effect*, which is a universal characteristic of supply because it applies to all goods and services.

4. Two factors determine how much of any good or service suppliers will produce at all possible prices. These factors are events of nature (such as floods or earthquakes) and changes in the cost of production. The cost of production can be increased or decreased by technological changes (such as a new computer that lowers the cost of production) and by changes in the price of resources (such as a decrease in the cost of materials).

5. *Market supply* is a list of the total quantities of a good or service that all producers will sell at different possible prices. When this list is presented numerically, it is called a *supply schedule*. When a supply schedule is plotted on a graph, the result is called a *supply curve*. The possible money prices of a product are put on the vertical axis, and the possible quantities supplied at each of those prices are put on the horizontal axis.

6. Supply is not a single amount. It is a list or schedule of all the amounts that would be offered for sale at various prices during a given time period. If supply changes, the entire list changes, so that different quantities are offered at each possible price. When a price change causes the amount offered for sale to change, we have an example of the price effect, which is a movement up or down an existing supply curve. When there is a change in supply, the entire supply curve shifts: the schedule of amounts offered for sale at all possible prices is different than it was before. A shift in the supply curve can be caused by natural events or changes in the cost of production.

7. If the price of a product, such as computers, falls at the same time that producers are willing to sell more of the product at this new, lower price, this does not contradict the principle of supply. The price effect still occurs along the new supply curve, but it is not as noticeable because of the positive change in supply, made possible, for example, by technological changes in computer production that lower the production cost.

Review Questions

1. Explain the term *supply* as it is used in economics.
2. What is the universal characteristic of supply?
3. What are the factors that determine the amount of a product suppliers are willing to produce at each possible price?
4. What is meant by the term *market supply?*
5. What is the difference between a *supply schedule* and a *supply curve?*
6. What is the distinction between the *price effect* and a *change in supply?*
7. Draw a supply curve, and explain why it is shaped the way it is.
8. Draw a curve showing an increase in supply. Then, draw a curve showing a decrease in supply. Describe verbally or in writing the difference between the two.

9. For a particular product, explain how the price effect can be overshadowed by an increase in supply.

Review Questions

1. Why do suppliers usually have to receive higher prices to produce additional quantities of a good or service?

2. What is the most important determinant of supply? Why?

3. In the past, video recorders decreased in price at the same time that more of them were produced. Does this fact disprove the principle of supply? Why or why not?

4. Discuss your agreement or disagreement with the following argument: The fact that supply curves slope upward to the right suggests something very scary for the future. It tells us that suppliers can only produce more of what we want by incurring higher and higher production costs. At some point, costs will go so high that suppliers will not be able to provide us with any more of the things we want. It's obvious that economic growth must inevitably come to a grinding halt.

Activities

1. In your own words, explain how the price of a particular item at a particular time influences its supply.

2. Construct a hypothetical supply schedule. Then convert that supply schedule into a supply curve. In two or three sentences, describe the shape of the curve and explain why it is shaped the way it is.

3. Select a product and draw a supply curve for it. Then draw a curve showing a decrease in that supply. Write a short essay describing what might have caused the decrease in supply.

4. Select a product and draw a supply curve for it. Then draw a curve showing an increase in that supply. In a short essay, describe three events that could have caused the increase in supply.

5. The following is a supply schedule for eggs:

Price per Egg	Eggs Produced per Week
10 cents	10,000
9 cents	9,500
8 cents	8,500
7 cents	6,500
6 cents	4,000
5 cents	1,000
4 cents	0

(a) Use this information to graph the supply curve of eggs.

(b) If the price rises from 7 cents to 10 cents per egg, what will happen to the weekly production of eggs? Why?

(c) Why are no eggs at all produced at a price of 4 cents or less?

(d) Suppose a disease among chickens causes the number of eggs offered at each of the prices above to drop by half. Compute the new supply schedule, and plot the new supply curve on the graph you have already constructed.

(e) Now suppose instead that each of the quantities in the table increases by 50 percent. Compute the new supply schedule, and plot the new supply curve on your graph. What might have caused this shift in the supply curve?

(f) Suppose the price of eggs is 10 cents. According to the original supply schedule shown above, how many eggs will be produced per week? Now assume that the price of eggs falls from 10 cents to 9 cents at the same time that each of the quantities supplied increases by 50 percent. What will happen to egg production? Does this outcome deny the price effect? Why or why not?

Additional Readings

Browne, M. Neil, and Haas, Paul F. *Modern Economics: Principles, Goals and Trade-offs.* Englewood Cliffs, N.J.: Prentice-Hall, 1987. 51–57.

Byrns, Ralph T., and Stone, Gerald W. *Microeconomics*. 3d ed. Glenview Ill.: Scott, Foresman, 1987. 50–59.

Schiller, Bradley R., *The Economy Today*. New York: Random House, 1980. 33–37.

Would a shortage of gasoline mean that its price is too low?

Balancing Demand and Supply

Chapter

6

■ Student's Goals ■

1. Explain why the demand curve slopes downward to the right and the supply curve slopes upward to the right.

2. Explain the significance of *equilibrium price*.

3. Graph and determine the equilibrium price when given demand and supply schedules.

4. Identify, both verbally and graphically, situations involving price ceilings and price floors.

5. From given information, draw demand and supply curves, identify the equilibrium price, draw a price ceiling, and identify the resulting shortage.

6. From given information, draw supply and demand curves, identify the equilibrium price, draw a price floor, and identify the resulting surplus.

───────

Surpluses and Shortages

In a cool limestone cave in Independence, Missouri, sacks of powdered milk tower above a forklift operator who is busy as a bee storing honey in a hive. The dried milk is part of the government's stockpile of surplus milk, butter, and cheese that totals more than two billion pounds. That represents more than eight pounds for every person in the United States. Elsewhere in the United States, government silos burst with surplus wheat, corn, and other crops.

In contrast, farmers in some poor nations produce less food than consumers want to purchase. Why does the United States have food *surpluses* while some nations have food *shortages?* In order to answer this question, you must first understand the relationship between demand and supply.

A Price That's Right

Although the last few chapters have explained the meaning of demand and supply, they have not pointed out how the two

In this underground storage facility, a government worker stacks sacks of powdered milk. The milk is part of the government's stockpile of surplus milk, butter, and cheese that totals more than two billion pounds.

concepts are connected. The connection is not obvious because demand and supply represent two entirely different relationships between the prices and quantities of a good or service.

On one hand, market demand tells us that consumers will buy *more* of something if its price is reduced. On the other hand, market supply tells us that producers will sell *less* of something if its price is cut. How can consumers and producers agree on the amounts they want to buy and sell?

We can find the answer by combining the original market demand for hamburgers given in Chapter 4 with the original market supply of hamburgers given in Chapter 5. Table 6–1 summarizes the market demand and supply presented in these two chapters.

As the price changes, the amount of hamburgers consumers want to *buy* and the amount of hamburgers producers want to *sell* move in opposite directions. Figure 6–1 visually presents these two different relationships between price and quantity. The demand curve slopes downward to the right because consumers want to buy more at *lower* prices. The supply curve slopes upward to the right because producers want to sell more at *higher* prices.

Figure 6–1 shows that $1.00 is a special price. It is special, not because it is high or low, but because of what it does. Only at this price does the demand curve cross the supply curve, so $1.00 is the only price that balances the amounts demanded and supplied. Because the price of $1.00 *balances* the amounts demanded and supplied, it is called the **equilibrium price.**

Table 6–1 The Demand and Supply of Hamburgers

Price	Market Demand	Market Supply
$2.50	100	500
2.00	150	450
1.50	200	400
1.00	300	300
.50	500	200

Market demand shows consumers want to buy *more* hamburgers at lower prices than they want to buy at higher prices. Market supply shows the opposite relationship between price and quantity: suppliers want to sell *fewer* hamburgers at lower prices than they want to sell at higher prices.

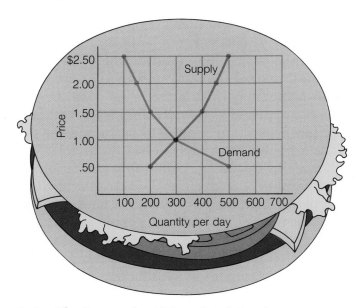

Figure 6–1   The Demand and Supply of Hamburgers

The demand curve slopes downward to the right because consumers want to buy more at *lower* prices. The supply curve slopes upward to the right because producers want to sell more at *higher* prices. Only at a price of $1.00 do the demand and supply curves cross. This fact shows that $1.00 is a special price because it balances the amount consumers want to buy with the amount producers want to sell.

> **Equilibrium price:**   The price that *balances* the amount of a good or service demanded with the amount supplied.

There is no other price that allows buyers to obtain all they want to buy *and* suppliers to sell all they want to sell. At a price of $1.00, consumers want to buy—and businesses want to produce and sell—300 hamburgers per day. At prices below $1.00, buyers will be frustrated because they cannot obtain all they want to buy. Consequently, they will bid the price up. At prices above $1.00, suppliers will be frustrated because they cannot sell all they want to sell. They will then reduce the price. Only at the equilibrium price do buyers and sellers agree on the quantities they want to buy and sell. Because buyers and sellers are both satisfied, the equilibrium price is the only one that persists.

Look what would happen, for instance, if the price of a hamburger is $2.50. Businesses will produce 500 hamburgers, but consumers will be willing to purchase only 100 hamburgers. The result will be a surplus of 400 hamburgers (500 − 100 = 400). A **surplus** is the amount by which the quantity supplied exceeds the quantity demanded at a particular price. A surplus occurs when the actual price of a good or service is *above* the equilibrium price. If suppliers want to sell all 500 hamburgers, they will have to cut their price to $.50.

> **Surplus:** The amount by which the quantity supplied of a good or service exceeds the quantity demanded at a particular price.

At a price of $.50, however, businesses will not continue to produce and sell 500 hamburgers per day. Indeed, at that price they will produce and sell only 200 hamburgers a day. Although 200 hamburgers will be supplied at that price, 500 hamburgers will be demanded. The result will be a shortage of 300 hamburgers (500 − 200 = 300). A **shortage** is the amount by which the quantity demanded exceeds the quantity supplied at a particular price. A shortage occurs when the actual price of a good or service is *below* the equilibrium level.

> **Shortage:** The amount by which the quantity demanded of a good or service exceeds the quantity supplied at a particular price.

When a shortage exists, consumers want to buy more than suppliers want to sell. Competition among buyers then pushes the price up toward its equilibrium level. On the other hand, a surplus exists when suppliers want to sell more than consumers want to buy. As a result, competition among suppliers pushes the price down toward its equilibrium level.

If you ever encounter a surplus or a shortage, you'll know that the price is above or below its equilibrium level. Unless

When American consumers shop at fast-food restaurants, they usually pay equilibrium prices that balance the amounts of food demanded and supplied. This occurs because competition among consumers pushes fast-food prices up to their equilibrium levels, and competition among sellers pushes them down to their equilibrium levels.

something, such as price controls, keeps the price either high or low, competition among buyers will push it up, or competition among sellers will push it down, until the price attains its equilibrium level.

Price Ceilings

Government price controls keep prices above or below their equilibrium levels. For example, a **price ceiling** is a legal limit on how high a price can rise. As a result, the law keeps the price below its equilibrium level. Sellers cannot legally charge a price that is higher than this ceiling, nor can buyers legally pay a price above this legal limit.

> **Price ceiling:** A government limit that keeps a price from rising to its equilibrium level.

Shortages

Many times you read or hear that the supply of a product has been diminished. For example, a frost in Brazil might kill coffee plants, bad weather in Florida might destroy oranges, or the policies of oil-exporting countries might cut the supply of oil. Do these events cause shortages?

Noneconomic Way of Thinking

Brazil produces much of the world's coffee supply. If the supply of coffee falls because of a killer frost in that nation, then we cannot avoid coffee shortages here. Supermarket shelves will be empty of coffee, and people will not be able to purchase all they would like. The same is true for other products, too. If their supplies fall, we will experience shortages.

Economic Way of Thinking

A reduced supply does not create a shortage. Instead, a smaller supply of coffee or some other product causes its equilibrium price to rise. The higher equilibrium price then shrinks the amount we demand to fit the smaller supply. Even with a killer frost in Brazil, we will still find coffee on supermarket shelves. The coffee will sell at a higher price, but the higher price prevents people from wanting to purchase more than is available. A reduced supply does not cause a shortage; it causes a higher equilibrium price.

Questions

1. Suppose a frost drastically reduces the supply of coffee. What will happen if our government keeps the price of coffee at the level it was before the frost?
2. After a frost reduces the supply of coffee, will the price of coffee rise a lot or a little? (*Hint:* Does the answer depend on how much the coffee supply falls and also on the willingness of coffee consumers to switch to substitutes?)

Government officials often establish price ceilings when they feel it is in the best interest of the public to set maximum prices. During wars or emergencies, they sometimes argue that price ceilings are necessary to prevent inflation or to prevent price increases for products believed to be especially important. During normal times, when there are no emergencies, the government sets price ceilings on particular items to allow more citizens to afford them.

Good intentions don't necessarily mean good results, however. Price ceilings can backfire and harm those who are supposed to benefit. Take peanut butter as an example. Suppose the government puts a price ceiling on peanut butter in order to make it more affordable. Figure 6–2 shows what will happen.

Without government control, the price of peanut butter is at its equilibrium level; the amounts demanded and supplied both equal 3,000 jars per day. Look what happens, however, when the government sets a price ceiling. The lower price increases

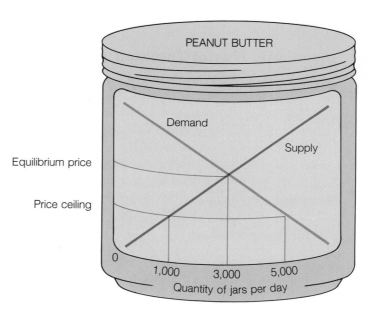

Figure 6–2 The Effects of a Price Ceiling on Peanut Butter

In the absence of a government price control, peanut butter will sell at its equilibrium price. At this price, the amounts demanded and supplied will both equal 3,000 jars per day, so there will be no shortage or surplus. If the government puts a price ceiling on peanut butter, the amount consumers want to buy will increase to 5,000 jars, and the amount suppliers want to sell will decrease to 1,000 jars. The result will be a shortage of peanut butter equal to 4,000 jars per day.

When our government put price ceilings on gasoline in the late 1970s and early 1980s, it prevented prices from balancing the amounts of gas demanded and supplied. Shortages of gasoline resulted, as this picture demonstrates. When gas was available, consumers usually had to wait in long lines. These events quickly disappeared when the government allowed gasoline prices to rise to their equilibrium levels.

the amount consumers want to buy from 3,000 to 5,000 jars per day. It also decreases the amount producers want to sell from 3,000 to 1,000 jars per day. The result is a *shortage* of peanut butter equal to 4,000 jars per day (5,000 − 1,000 = 4,000).

The purpose of the price ceiling might have been to enable consumers to obtain more peanut butter, but the actual result is a shortage of peanut butter because the amount available has been reduced from 3,000 to 1,000 jars per day. Consumers end up with less, not more, peanut butter.

Shortages occurred in the early 1970s when our government put price controls on many products in an effort to keep their prices from rising. Like Mother Hubbard who found her cupboard bare, many shoppers found empty shelves in their supermarkets. In the late 1970s and early 1980s, our government also put a price ceiling on gasoline. The resulting shortage forced angry, frustrated drivers to wait in long lines in an effort to obtain gasoline. When the price ceiling was lifted, the shortage of gasoline disappeared, and drivers no longer had to wait in long lines.

Similar results have occurred in some nations when governments have enacted price ceilings on food in order to make it more affordable for city dwellers. Despite these good intentions, the price ceilings actually created food shortages. As a result, people in those nations ended up with less, not more, to eat.

Price ceilings create shortages because they prevent prices from rising to balance the amounts that people want to buy and sell. When there are shortages, many buyers will eagerly pay more than the ceiling prices to obtain more of those things that are in short supply. No wonder shortages put a lot of pressure on prices to rise. In order to prevent prices from rising above their legal ceilings, the government must enforce the law by imposing penalties on those who violate them. Still, there are often buyers and sellers who are willing to risk these penalties in order to trade with one another at prices that exceed the legal limits. These illegal or *black markets* occur, for example, in cities that enact price (or rent) ceilings on apartments. Because rent ceilings produce apartment shortages, some prospective tenants offer landlords illegal payments in an effort to obtain housing. Black markets would not occur if prices could legally rise to their equilibrium levels, at which there would be no shortages.

Price Floors

A price ceiling is an attempt to prevent a price from *rising* to its equilibrium level. But governments also pass laws to prevent prices from *falling* to their equilibrium levels. This kind of government price control is called a **price floor.**

> **Price floor:** A government limit that keeps a price from falling to its equilibrium level.

Government officials establish price floors to increase the incomes of sellers. For many years, for example, our government has put price floors on various farm products in an attempt to raise the incomes of farmers. Milk is a good illustration.

Figure 6–3 shows that the equilibrium price will balance the amounts demanded and supplied at 6 million cartons of milk per day. But look what happens when a government price floor prevents the price of milk from falling to its equilibrium level.

Because of the price floor, the amount of milk producers want to sell increases from 8 million to 9 million cartons per day. At the same time, the amount of milk consumers want to buy decreases from 8 million to 6 million cartons per day. The result is a *surplus* of milk equal to 3 million cartons per day (9 million − 6 million = 3 million).

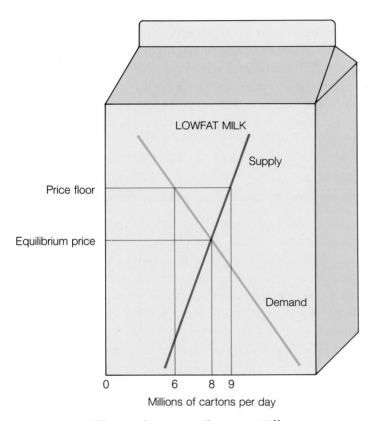

Figure 6–3 The Effects of a Price Floor on Milk

In the absence of a government price control, milk will sell at its equilibrium price. At this price, the amounts demanded and supplied will both equal 8 million cartons per day, so there will be no shortage or surplus. If the government puts a price floor on milk, the amount consumers want to buy will decrease to 6 million cartons, and the amount suppliers want to sell will increase to 9 million cartons. The result will be a surplus of milk equal to 3 million cartons per day.

What happens to the surpluses of milk and other farm products that are created by government price floors? These surpluses end up in the government stockpiles mentioned at the beginning of the chapter. In the example above, the government would purchase and store the 3 million cartons of milk consumers did not want to buy at the higher price set by the government. Instead of keeping the surplus as perishable milk, however, the government would store it as dry milk, butter, and cheese, which can be kept for longer periods of time. In 1985, for example, our government purchased about 64 percent of all nonfat dry milk, 24 percent of all butter, and 20 percent of all cheese produced.[1]

As you can see, a government price floor can mean more income for those who produce and sell the product—and higher prices for consumers who buy the product. A price floor can also mean that taxpayers must pay higher taxes to enable the government to purchase and store the resulting surplus. The incomes of consumers and taxpayers are reduced, therefore, so that the incomes of producers can be increased.

The Goal of Equilibrium

Figures 6–2 and 6–3 show that price floors keep prices *above* their equilibrium levels, and price ceilings keep them *below* their equilibrium levels. This description might seem upside down because it puts the floor on the top and the ceiling on the bottom. In order to avoid confusion, remember that the floor on the top keeps the price from *falling* and the ceiling on the bottom keeps it from *rising*.

In addition to government price controls, there is another reason why prices might not balance the amounts consumers want to buy and the amounts suppliers want to sell. That reason is the continual change in demand and supply.

As an illustration, suppose you are told to drive to a given destination. Before you arrive, however, your destination is changed. If your destination continues to change in this way, you will never get to where you are headed. Similarly, before a particular price ever reaches equilibrium, demand or supply

[1]*Economic Report of the President*, (Washington, D.C.: U.S. Government Printing Office, February 1986), 139.

(*text continues on page 153*)

Cultivating America's Farms

America's farmers endured hard times in the 1980s. Not only did farm exports dip, but also farm prices tumbled. These events represented a big change from the heady days of the 1970s. In those years, farm prices soared and foreigners couldn't seem to get enough of our food. Expecting these happy events to continue, many farmers borrowed heavily in order to purchase more farmland. Then came the 1980s. Farm demand stopped growing, and farm prices fell. Without the growing incomes they had expected, many farmers could not make payments on the farmland loans they had rushed to obtain just a few years back. Like a swarm of hungry locusts, bankruptcy threatened to destroy many farmers.

Our nation's farmers have encountered similar problems in the past. For example, during World War I, a strong foreign demand for U.S. food caused farm prices to spurt. When European agriculture was restored after the war, however, the demand for our farm exports dropped. Prices and incomes fell on our nation's farms, causing a depression in agriculture during the 1920s. Farm prices and incomes were further crushed under the weight of the Great Depression of the 1930s. In an attempt to remedy the problems of our country's farms, the federal government in the 1930s initiated farm policies that remain essentially unchanged to this day.

Evidence of these policies can be seen in the Food Security Act of 1985. Like its predecessors in the 1930s, this act attempts to increase farmers' incomes by keeping farm prices above the equilibrium levels that the market would otherwise determine. Government attempts to accomplish this objective are channeled through the Commodity Credit Corporation (CCC), which was created by the Agricultural Adjustment Act of 1933. Because the CCC sets minimum farm prices that exceed their equilibrium levels, surpluses arise. The CCC, in one way or another, must then purchase and store these surplus products. In the 1930s minimum prices were originally set for wheat, corn, and cotton. Other products, such as rice, peanuts, and tobacco, were soon added to the list. Because milk is one of the products on this list today, the government must purchase and store enormous quantities of powdered milk, cheese, and butter.

Before the Food Security Act of 1985 was passed, President Ronald Reagan wanted to slash milk price supports in order to shrink milk production and curb the large surpluses. The act included a compromise, however, in which the government would tax dairy farmers and then use the revenues to purchase dairy cattle for slaughter. The intent was to reduce milk production by decreasing the number of cows producing milk. The slaughter of additional cattle would increase the supply of red meat, however, so the act also instructed the government to purchase additional quantities of meat to prevent its price from falling.

This compromise illustrates a flaw contained in the farm policies that have been enacted since the 1930s. By setting prices above their equilibrium levels, the government increases production and creates surpluses. Agricultural surpluses began to swell in the 1950s and 1960s. When export demand soared during the 1970s, farm surpluses receded, but the price floors set by our government threatened to undermine our sales of farm goods abroad. As a result, the Agriculture and Consumer Protection Act of 1973 was passed to allow the government to make "deficiency payments" to farmers for particular products. Put simply, under this program, the government does not purchase farmers' surplus production in order to raise the actual selling price of a product. Instead, farmers sell all their output at the lower market price. Buyers pay lower prices under this policy, therefore, but farmers still receive the higher price for their products. The

difference is made by the U.S. Treasury (and U.S. taxpayers).

Whether subsidized through deficiency payments or through price floors, farmers still receive more than the equilibrium price for what they produce. As a result, government subsidy programs increase the production of farm goods. This conclusion holds despite attempts over the years to pay farmers for keeping some land out of production. Although farmers have retired some lands from the production of particular crops, they have idled the least productive lands and then used their remaining acres to produce more of the same crop or of other crops.

The basic flaw of government farm subsidies remains. Because subsidies are tied to the amount produced, farmers end up producing more products in order to obtain more subsidies. Consequently, since the 1930s, government farm programs have ignored or worked against the solution of American agriculture's fundamental problem. That problem is too many resources devoted to farming.

Since the turn of the century, transportation improvements, new lands in the West, new and better farm machinery, and scientific advancements have caused agricultural productivity to increase by leaps and bounds. Because the supply of farm

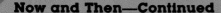

products has grown much more rapidly than has the demand for them, the equilibrium prices of farm products have dropped in comparison to those of nonfarm goods and services. These lower prices are the market's way of directing inefficient resources out of farming and into other areas where they can produce more value for consumers. Fewer farm resources would then produce less food, resulting in higher farm prices that would enable the remaining farmers to earn a living.

Though often distressing, this change has been occurring for decades. In 1985, for instance, farm output per hour of work was more than 16 times what it had been in 1929.

As fewer hours of work produced more farm goods, fewer farmers could produce more food. No wonder only about 2 percent of our population lives on farms today, although 25 percent lived there in 1929 (see Figure A).

Since the 1930s, as we noted above, government farm programs have worked against the market's solution to excessive farm production. They have increased farm production and encouraged resources to remain in farming. In 1987, President Reagan proposed to "decouple" agricultural subsidies from grain production. Under this proposal, grain farmers could receive government subsidies if they stopped farm-

Figure A Farm Population as a Percentage of Total Population, 1929–1985

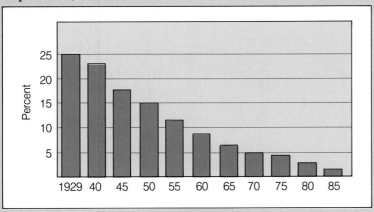

Source: Economic Report of the President. Washington, D.C.: U.S. Government Printing Office, February 1986, p. 362.

ing their lands altogether. This proposal illustrates an attempt to cope with the problem that has haunted farm policies since the 1930s: how to reconcile farm subsidies with the fact that American farmers already produce more food than consumers want to buy at prices that enable farmers to cover their costs of production.

References

Economic Report of the President. Washington, D.C.: U.S. Government Printing Office, February 1986. Chapter 4.

Gray, Ralph, and Peterson, John M. *Economic Development of the United States*. Homewood, Ill.: Richard D. Irwin, 1974. 479–99.

Karr, Albert R. "White House to Propose Grain Growers Be Paid to Quit Farming to Cut Surplus." *Wall Street Journal,* January 5, 1987.

might change and thereby alter the equilibrium level. Figure 6–4 illustrates this event using the demand for and supply of hamburgers presented at the beginning of this chapter.

With the original demand and supply, the original equilibrium price is $1.00 per hamburger because the original demand and supply cross at point **a** on the graph. If the price is above this level, there will be a surplus, and competition among sellers will push the price down. If the price is below this level, there will be a shortage, and competition among buyers will push it up. Suppose that before the price ever settles at this equilibrium level, the price of beef rises and causes the supply of hamburgers to decrease from *Old supply* to *New supply*, as shown on the graph. In that case, the equilibrium price will rise from $1.00 to $1.50 per hamburger because the demand curve and the new supply curve will now cross at point **b** on the graph.

Imagine both the supply and the demand curves dancing around this way, and you can see why equilibrium prices are

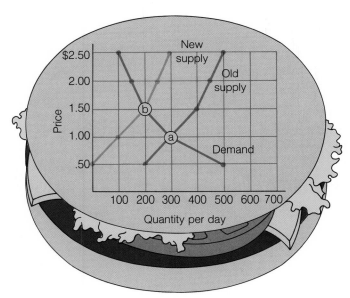

Figure 6–4 A Change in the Equilibrium Price of Hamburgers

The original equilibrium price is $1.00 per hamburger because the original demand and supply curves cross at point *a*. If the price is above this level, competition among sellers will push it down. If the price is below this level, competition among buyers will push it up. Suppose, however, that the supply curve decreases to *New supply* before the original equilibrium price of $1.00 is reached. In that case, the equilibrium price will rise from $1.00 to $1.50 because the demand curve and the new supply curve now cross at point *b*.

The Economic Way of Thinking

Higher Prices

When meat prices rise, are supermarkets to blame?

Noneconomic Way of Thinking

Higher meat prices result from the greed of grocers who exploit us by increasing prices.

Economic Way of Thinking

Higher meat prices often result from an increased demand by consumers. For example, if many of us decide to buy more beef, grocery stores will find their meat inventories declining. As a result, the stores will order more beef, causing the demand for cattle to increase. The higher demand for cattle then will raise the price of cattle, thereby increasing the price that grocery stores must pay for meat. The stores, in turn, raise the prices they charge us. Although it seems as though the stores are the source of the higher meat prices, we are actually the ones who made them rise.

Questions

1. If grocery stores do not increase their meat prices in the face of a higher demand by consumers, what will happen? Why?
2. Explain what will happen to apartment rents in your community if more people want to move there and rent apartments. Should landlords or tenants be blamed for the result? Why?

Although bad weather sometimes reduces the supply of fresh tomatoes, it does not usually produce a shortage. Instead, consumers bid the price of tomatoes up to a higher equilibrium level. By reducing the amount of fresh tomatoes consumers want to buy, the higher price keeps demand in line with the smaller available supply.

continually changing. But as the actual prices we observe chase after their equilibrium levels, they help buyers and sellers adapt to change. In this way, consumers and producers are more likely to agree on the amounts of particular products they want to buy and sell. Surpluses and shortages are then reduced or eliminated.

By balancing demand and supply, equilibrium prices play a vital part in a market economy. Because they direct and coordinate the actions of many independent consumers and producers, prices have been compared to the directions of an enormous puzzle. The next chapter will explain how prices help to put this puzzle together.

Chapter Summary

1. Price changes enable consumers and producers to agree on the amount of any good or service they want to buy and sell. Market demand tells us that consumers want to buy *more* of an item at lower prices than they do at higher prices.

On the other hand, market supply tells us that sellers want to sell *less* of an item at lower prices than they do at higher prices. When we graph demand and supply curves, they intersect at a special price, which is called an *equilibrium price*. An equilibrium price is special because it balances the amount producers want to sell with the amount consumers want to buy.

2. A *surplus* is the amount by which the quantity supplied of a good or service exceeds the quantity demanded at a particular price. A surplus occurs when the price of a good or service is above the equilibrium price.

3. A *shortage* is the amount by which the quantity demanded of a good or service exceeds the quantity supplied at a particular price. A shortage occurs when the price of a good or service is below the equilibrium level.

4. If a shortage exists, consumers want to buy more than suppliers want to sell. Competition among buyers will tend to push the price up toward its equilibrium level. If a surplus exists, suppliers want to sell more than consumers want to buy. Competition among suppliers will tend to push the price down toward its equilibrium level.

5. A *price ceiling* is a government limit that keeps a price from rising to its equilibrium level. A price ceiling creates a shortage because it does not allow the price to rise to its equilibrium level, that point at which the amount suppliers want to sell equals the amount consumers want to buy. Sometimes, individuals risk penalties in order to buy and sell in black markets at prices that exceed the legal limits.

6. A *price floor* is a government limit that keeps a price from falling to its equilibrium level. A price floor creates a surplus because it does not allow the price to fall to its equilibrium level, that point at which producers want to sell equals the amount consumers want to buy. Because government price floors have been set for many farm products, surpluses of these products are common.

7. Because demand and supply are constantly changing, equilibrium prices are always moving up and down. In this way, prices are continually changing in a market economy in order to reduce or eliminate surpluses and shortages.

Review Questions

1. Why does the demand curve slope downward to the right?
2. Why does the supply curve slope upward to the right?
3. Why is the equilibrium price special or significant?
4. What is meant by the term *surplus*, and why does it occur?
5. What is meant by the term *shortage*, and why does it occur?
6. What will tend to happen to price if a shortage exists? Why? If a surplus exists? Why?
7. What are legal *price ceilings*, and why does the government enact them?
8. What are the predictable effects of a price ceiling?
9. What are legal *price floors*, and why does the government enact them?
10. What are the predictable effects of a price floor?
11. What is another reason (in addition to government price controls) that prices might not balance the amounts consumers want to buy and the amounts suppliers want to sell?

Discussion Questions

1. How do demand and supply interact to bring about an equilibrium price?
2. If the government puts a price ceiling on compact disks, what is likely to happen?
3. If the government puts a price floor on compact disks, what is likely to happen?
4. A city government is debating whether or not to remove its rent controls on apartments. Use your knowledge of demand and supply to explain why you support or oppose the city's elimination of rent controls. Explain why you expect each of the following people to agree or disagree with you: (1) a poor person living in a rent-controlled apartment, (2) a person thinking about moving to the city, (3) an owner of a rent-controlled apartment, (4) a contractor who remodels

and repairs apartments, (5) a teen-ager who will soon be looking for an apartment in the city, (6) a real estate developer looking for good investments, and (7) a member of the city council.

Activities

1. Following are an imaginary community's demand and supply schedules for bread:

Price per Loaf	Loaves Demanded per Day	Loaves Supplied per Day
$2.00	1,000	7,000
1.75	2,000	6,000
1.50	3,000	5,000
1.25	4,000	4,000
1.00	5,000	3,000
.75	6,000	2,000
.50	7,000	1,000
.25	8,000	0

(a) Graph the demand and supply curves, and determine the equilibrium price that would exist in the absence of any government interferences. Write a paragraph explaining why the market promotes this equilibrium price.

(b) Suppose the government enacts a price ceiling of $.50 per loaf of bread. Draw the price ceiling on your graph. Write a paragraph explaining why the government might impose such a ceiling and what the probable results will be.

(c) Suppose the government enacts a price floor of $1.75 per loaf of bread. Draw the price floor on your graph. Write a paragraph explaining why the government might impose such a floor and what the probable results will be.

2. Utilizing your knowledge of supply and demand, write an essay responding to the following dilemma: "I believe the prices of one-bedroom apartments near the college are too high. But even though landlords are charging $1,000 an apartment, people are standing in line to rent one."

Additional Readings

Allen, William R. *Midnight Economist: Broadcast Essays*, various issues. San Francisco: Institute for Contemporary Studies.

Alston, Lee. "The U.S. Farm Problem." *Contemporary Economic Issues*, Spring 1985, No. 13. Los Angeles: Pacific Academy for Advanced Studies.

Dooly, Peter C. *Elementary Price Theory*. New York: Appleton-Century-Crofts, 1973. Chapter 1.

Ehrbar, Aloysius. "Facts Vs. the Furor over Farm Policy." *Fortune* (November 11, 1985): 114–20.

"The Energy Crisis Explained." *Wall Street Journal*, May 27, 1977.

Schuettinger, Robert L., and Butler, Eamonn F. *Forty Centuries of Wage and Price Controls*. (Washington, D.C.: The Heritage Foundation), 1979.

Markets and Governments

The price of this computer serves two important functions. What are they?

The Functions of Price and the Role of Profit

Chapter 7

■ Student's Goals ■

1. Explain how market prices ration goods and services among those who want them.

2. Explain how market prices provide an incentive to produce goods and services.

3. Describe at least three methods of rationing goods and services.

4. Analyze any one method of rationing goods and services in terms of how it satisfies and screens out wants.

Food for Thought

If we consume less meat in our country, will hungry people around the world have more to eat?

You might think so if you consider biological food chains. By feeding cattle, we convert grain to meat and move up a food chain to a more complex kind of food. However, not all the grain calories consumed by cattle and other animals are changed into meat calories. Instead, some are always lost in the conversion. As a result, more grain calories are required to obtain a given number of meat calories. When we eat meat, therefore, we indirectly consume more grain than if we had just eaten the grain to get the same number of calories.

So, if we cut our meat consumption, we can still obtain the same number of calories, but from a smaller amount of grain. By consuming less grain, therefore, won't we leave more to eat for hungry people around the world? Many people believe so, but the answer is not so obvious. In order to answer the question, you must first understand the functions of market prices. After explaining these functions, we will return to the question about world hunger.

On Baking and Slicing

Prices have two important functions in a market economy. One of those functions has been discussed in Chapter 5 on supply. That chapter has explained that prices provide an *incentive to produce* goods and services. This task is important for any economy, even if the economy doesn't rely on market prices to carry it out. Unless producers have an incentive to bake the economic pie, there will be nothing available for us to consume. Prices provide this incentive by rewarding producers for their productive efforts. If the price of a good or service rises, the incentive to produce it increases. If the price falls, the incentive to produce it decreases.

The second function of market prices is to *ration* goods and services among those who want them. Once the economic pie is baked, it must be sliced and distributed among the hungry consumers who want to eat it. The **rationing function** is the task of determining how scarce goods and services are divided among those who want them.

Some people believe that if we ate less meat in our country, more grain would be available for hungry people around the world. In light of the functions of price and the role of profit, however, this belief might be wrong.

Rationing function: The task of determining how scarce goods and services are divided among those who want them.

There are many different ways of rationing goods and services among possible users. Because scarcity prevents the satisfaction of all of everyone's wants, some method must be used to determine how people share what is produced—to choose which wants will be filled and the extent to which they will be satisfied.

This choice means that we must somehow *discriminate* among the possible uses and users of a good or service. To discriminate is to identify differences and to use these differences to make a choice. For example, you probably don't think all ice cream flavors are equally as tasty, which means that you discriminate among them when you pick the ones you like best. You do the same thing when you purchase clothes or when you decide what to wear to school on a particular day. You also discriminate among the people at school when you pick your friends or decide whom to date. In one way or another, everyone discriminates because everyone must make choices.

Similarly, in any economy, scarcity necessitates discrimination among the possible consumers of goods and services. No one method of rationing will satisfy everyone. Under one system of rationing you might get more of something; under another system you might get less (or even none at all). Consequently, you probably will like a rationing method that discriminates in your favor, but you will dislike one that discriminates against you. Discrimination cannot be avoided, however, because scarce goods and services must somehow be rationed. Whenever something is scarce, some uses (and users) must be partially or completely screened out.

The methods of rationing goods and services differ from each other in the ways in which they determine whose wants will be screened out and whose will be satisfied. Before looking at how market prices accomplish this task, consider the following nonprice methods of rationing.

Nonprice Rationing

Lottery

Goods and services can be rationed on the basis of chance or luck. Suppose, for example, that 70 students want to enroll in a particular economics class, but there is room for only 40.

These teen-agers discriminated when they decided to wear these clothes. Discrimination means identifying differences and using these differences to make a choice. Because of the variety in clothes usually available in people's closets and always available in stores, people discriminate whenever they choose a particular outfit. What motives do you think made these teen-agers discriminate in favor of these clothes?

Thirty students will have to be screened out. Some form of lottery, such as drawing names out of a hat, can be used to determine who enrolls in the class. Under this system, the lucky can attend the class, and the unlucky will be screened out.

First Come, First Served

A good or service can also be rationed among possible users by allowing those who want it to wait in line until the available supply is gone. The space in the economics class can be rationed in this way by having students line up on registration day and then enrolling the first 40 people in line.

In this system, the first in line are entitled to the good or service and, thus, have their wants satisfied. Those at the rear of the line are not entitled to it, so their wants remain unsatisfied. Parking spaces are a good example of something that is often rationed by the first come, first served method. In addition, the first come, first served method sometimes rations seats at theaters or sporting events. The number of people who want seats (and who are willing to pay the admission price) often exceeds the number of seats available. Would-be buyers then line up, and the scarce seats are sold to those who are first in line.

First come, first served rationing is common in the command economies described briefly in Chapter 2. In Poland, for example, a newspaper reporter once wrote, "On a recent stroll through town, one could see people spilling out of shops into streets everywhere. They were waiting for sugar, butter, eggs, and chocolates. . . There was only one happy scene. Some 50 teen-agers waited patiently for their one scoop of vanilla. Ewa Hirsz, 16, giggled: 'This is worth the wait. But I had to stand all night one day last week for school supplies. That made me angry.' "[1]

Personal Characteristics

Goods and services can also be rationed on the basis of personal characteristics, such as age, beauty, sex, religion, race, intelligence, and personality. Beauty contests award prizes to those who are thought to be most beautiful. Parking spaces at school

[1]Frederick Kerpe, "Poles Survive Collapse of Currency by Using Own System of Barter," *Wall Street Journal*, October 23, 1981.

Finding a parking space sometimes can be a tedious, frustrating experience. The reason is because parking spaces are usually rationed to those who get to them first. First come, first served rationing has allocated all of the parking spaces on this street.

are often set aside for the principal and for teachers, and there have been tragic instances, such as the sinking of the *Titanic* in 1912, when the limited spaces on lifeboats have been rationed to women and children.

Need

Perhaps more appealing to you is the rationing of goods and services on the basis of need. This standard appeals to a lot of people because they think it is fair to take care of people's needs. Surely, they say, it is reasonable that someone who needs a good should have it in preference to someone who does not need it.

The problem with this rationing method is the difficulty of defining *need*. Suppose that gasoline is rationed by need. When you want gasoline, you can't just drive down to the service station and buy some. Instead, you will have to convince the people in charge of dispensing the gas that you really need it. What if you want the gas to get to school or to work? Will the authorities think this use is a need? Will it be considered more or less important than if you want the gas to visit some friends or just drive around and have fun? Will these uses differ in importance from your wanting the gas to drive 50 miles to see a rock concert? What if the purpose of the 50-mile trip is to care for your ailing grandparent?

If you turn back to Chapter 3, you will find a discussion of "Uses of Different Value." That discussion has told you each consumer has many different uses for something like gasoline. Some of those uses are more important to the consumer than are others. When the price of gasoline rises, therefore, we "need" less gas because we willingly exclude the uses we value less than the higher price. On the other hand, we "need" more gas when its price falls. Which of all these possible uses represents our real needs? You can argue that *all* your possible uses are needs, but the same argument will probably be offered by others, too. Because there isn't enough gas to go around to satisfy all of everyone's "needs," the person dispensing the gasoline will have to judge which of all these possible uses represents someone's real needs. Then, the real needs of this individual will have to be compared with the real needs of everyone else.

Rationing by need boils down to having someone decide for you how much gas or other goods and services you really need. Imagine how convincing everyone would try to be when arguing that his or her intended uses represent needs. You can see that rationing by need is difficult, no matter how honest or equitable its administrators try to be. Need is a lot like potter's clay: it takes on different shapes for different people.

Force

Strength is another method of determining who is entitled to the scarce supply of something. Those who are powerful get more of the good or service, and those who are weak get less. A king can toss food from the balcony and allow the hungry multitudes to fight for it. A commander of a prison camp can throw a supply of food or medicine into the prison compound and let the prisoners fight for it.

If you think that force is an unpleasant way to ration things, you're not alone. But it *is* a method, and it *is* often used. Fist-fights over parking spaces, muggings on the street, squabbling over the use of scarce toys, even the Indian Wars from our own nation's history—these and many more events illustrate force as a method of rationing. No wonder those who prize a civilized society prefer some other method of rationing.

Rationing by Market Price

The market prices that evolve naturally from demand and supply are another method of rationing goods and services. With this method, people's wants are satisfied according to their willingness and ability to pay the market price.

The market price is the equilibrium price that has been discussed in Chapter 6. This price balances the amount of a good or service people want to buy with the amount producers want to sell. Although there is no shortage or surplus at that price, the item is still scarce. It is still scarce because we *want more* than is available, even though at the equilibrium price we choose to *buy less* than we would want if there were no price at all.

By choosing to buy less in this way, you deny the satisfaction of those wants that you value less than the equilibrium price. No one tells us which wants are to be satisfied and which are

New computers are usually rationed by the equilibrium price. We want more computers than are available, but the equilibrium price causes us to buy fewer than we would want if there were no price at all. Those of us who are willing and able to pay the price get more computers, and those of us who are less willing and able to pay the price get less.

Competition

Is a market economy more competitive than other types of economies?

Noneconomic Way of Thinking

In a market economy people are always competing: consumers compete with each other to obtain the rights to use the scarce goods produced. Competition can be eliminated if prices are abandoned as a way of rationing scarce goods and if nonprice methods, such as need, are adopted. In fact, cooperation will replace competition if the market economy is scrapped.

Economic Way of Thinking

No matter what rationing method is used, there will never be enough to satisfy all of everyone's wants. People will compete to get what is available, regardless of the rationing method used. If first come, first served is used, people will compete by trying to get in line earliest. If personal characteristics are used, then people will compete by attempting to exhibit those characteristics. If need is used, then people will compete by trying to convince the rationing authority that their needs are the greatest. Competition is not just a feature of a market economy; it is found everywhere. When people compete on the basis of market prices, however, they have an incentive to cooperate with one another in order to produce the incomes that enable them to buy the goods and services they want. As a result, the price rationing of a market economy channels people's competitive activities to cooperative ends.

Questions

1. Anarchy is a "system" in which no laws or rules prevail. Under such a system, what form does competition for goods and other property take?

2. Why does competition imply discrimination against some consumers?

3. What types of people compete most effectively in the price system? In first come, first served? In a system based on personal characteristics?

to be denied. We make these choices for ourselves. Those of us who are more willing and able to pay the price get more of the item, and those of us who are less willing and able to pay the price get less. We satisfy some of our wants and deny others. By balancing the amount we want to buy with the amount available, the equilibrium price rations the scarce supply of a good or service.

Don't conclude, however, that every time a market price performs its rationing function, everyone gets at least a little of the quantity available. Not long ago, for instance, an Impressionist painting by Vincent van Gogh was sold at a New York auction for $9.9 million. There was only one original painting, so the price rose to that astronomical level in order to screen out all but one of the individuals who wanted this painting of a wheat field.

Speaking of wheat fields, if the price of Grade A winter wheat on the Chicago Board of Trade is $5 per bushel, buyers who are willing and able to pay this price can obtain some of it. People who do not believe that wheat is worth this price will be screened out and left unsatisfied. In this case, wheat is not rationed by need, luck, force, or willingness to stand in line. It is rationed by market price.

If the demand for wheat increases (or if the supply decreases), there will be a shortage of wheat at a price of $5 per bushel. As a result, the price of wheat will rise to a new equilibrium level, at which point it will once again ration the available supply of wheat among those who want it.

On the other hand, suppose the demand for wheat decreases (or the supply increases). That will cause a surplus of wheat at a price of $5 per bushel because people will not want to buy all of the available supply at that price. The price of wheat will drop to a new equilibrium level, at which point the available stock of wheat is divided among those who want it.

Scalpers and Rationing

Rationing by market price can be illustrated by the way tickets to music concerts and sporting events are sometimes distributed. People often complain about the evils of scalpers, who buy blocks of tickets to certain events and then sell them above their official prices. The official prices are often below their equilibrium levels, however, so people wait in long lines or sleep overnight in parking lots in order to be first in line when the ticket booth opens.

Scalpers ration their tickets by market price, not by first come, first served. Those willing and able to pay the price can then buy tickets without having to wait in long lines. You may think this rationing method is unfair because those with little money are less likely to obtain tickets. It is true that people who are *not* willing and able to pay the scalper's price will not get tickets, while those who *are* willing and able to pay the price will get tickets. But do you think this rationing method is necessarily worse than one that causes people to wait in long lines or sleep in parking lots?

Suppose that a frail, elderly woman has a strong desire to see a World Series game, a Super Bowl, or a famous singer before she dies. Her health does not permit her to stand in long lines or to sleep overnight in parking lots. She prefers to pay the higher price of the scalper instead of waiting in line. That is, she prefers rationing by price to rationing by first come, first served. Is she less deserving than people who are unwilling to

Scalpers ration tickets by market price, not by first come, first served. Those willing and able to pay the price can then buy tickets without having to wait in long lines. Would you conclude that scalpers are doing some people a favor?

pay the higher market price, but who are willing to sleep in the parking lot or even force their way to the head of the line?

You have to make this value judgment for yourself. Although economics cannot tell you which method of rationing is best, it can tell you what to expect when different rationing methods are used. Every method of rationing has some advantages and disadvantages—and some who gain and some who lose.

No matter what method is used, however, goods and services must still be divided among their possible uses and users. Consequently, some of us will have more of our wants satisfied, and others will have fewer wants satisfied. Some of us might even be completely screened out, so that a particular want is left totally unsatisfied.

Scarcity and Discrimination

There isn't any way to satisfy all of everyone's wants. No matter how hard we try, we can't wish away scarcity. Even hard work and prolonged effort can't chase it away. Whether we like it or not, we have to cope with scarcity, and that means having some method by which we ration goods and services among those who want them.

Whatever rationing method we use, we cannot avoid discrimination. Because of scarcity, we all receive less of a good than we want. Figure 7–1 summarizes how the rationing methods presented in this chapter determine whose wants—for vanilla ice cream and all other goods and services—will be satisfied and whose will be screened out.

In the case of a *lottery*, those with losing tickets are discriminated against. With the *first come, first served* method, those who are unable or unwilling to stand in line or who get to the line too late are the losers. Older people who cannot withstand the strain of standing in long lines and people whose time is very valuable are hurt by this rationing method. When *need* is the method, people who cannot convince the authorities of their needs are discriminated against. When *force* is used as a means of rationing, the meek and the weak are hurt. When *market price* is used to ration the available supply, the ones who are unwilling or unable to pay the price are discriminated against.

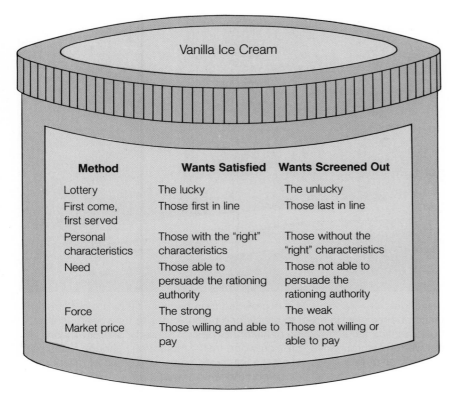

Vanilla Ice Cream

Method	Wants Satisfied	Wants Screened Out
Lottery	The lucky	The unlucky
First come, first served	Those first in line	Those last in line
Personal characteristics	Those with the "right" characteristics	Those without the "right" characteristics
Need	Those able to persuade the rationing authority	Those not able to persuade the rationing authority
Force	The strong	The weak
Market price	Those willing and able to pay	Those not willing or able to pay

Figure 7–1   How Different Rationing Methods Discriminate

Even if the available supply of a good could be equally divided among all consumers, those who value it more than others would be treated unfavorably. During World War II, the government distributed rationing coupons in an effort to apportion equal shares of gasoline and other goods among consumers. Discriminated against were the consumers who valued the gasoline more than did others who received the same quantity.

Regardless of how we cope with scarcity, someone is left out or some wants are left unsatisfied. Discrimination is an unavoidable consequence of our wants' exceeding our abilities to satisfy them. No rationing system can avoid this reality.

There is nothing necessarily wrong with a system that rations a good or service to those who are willing and able to pay for it. Some people favor such a system because those who get the benefit of the good also pay the cost of producing it. Remember, too, that if we believe market prices sometimes deny goods and services to people who ought to receive them, we can take up

Passengers are standing on this crowded train because there are not enough seats for everyone. In order to satisfy one person's desire for a seat, another must sacrifice the satisfaction of his or her desire. Similarly, scarcity means that we travel through life "on a crowded train:" there aren't enough resources to satisfy all of everyone's wants, so we must use some method of rationing available goods and services among those who want them.

a collection or pay the taxes necessary to provide those people with the money needed to buy them.

Profits and the Incentive to Produce

The rationing of *scarce goods and services* among possible consumers cannot be avoided. Nor can the rationing of *scarce resources* among producers be escaped. The distribution of resources among possible productive uses refers to the choices of what and how to produce, which have been explained in Chapter 2.

Just as market prices can ration finished goods and services among uses in consumption, so, too, can they ration resources among various uses in production. Prices perform this function by affecting the profits and losses of businesses. By altering these profits and losses, prices affect the *incentive to produce*.

Most people have some notion of what a profit is, but it is not uncommon to find that different people attach different

Controlling Prices

Do we as consumers benefit if the government reduces particular prices by enacting price ceilings?

Noneconomic Way of Thinking

It is obvious that we benefit if the government decreases the price of what we buy. It should lower the cost of renting apartments and of obtaining other important items. Then, all of us who desire these necessities could afford them.

Economic Way of Thinking

Government price ceilings do not guarantee that we will be able to buy what we want. Indeed, just the opposite can occur. If sellers are restricted to receiving lower prices, they will have less incentive to produce the item. Furthermore, the amount we demand will increase at the government's artificially low price. When a smaller amount is supplied and a larger amount demanded, a shortage occurs. We will then be frustrated by our inability to obtain all we are willing and able to buy at the low price. As a result, we will compete in other, nonprice ways to get what is available. For example, we might spend time in lines, and that waiting involves a cost. For some of us, the cost of waiting in line is greater than the cost we would otherwise incur if the government permitted the price to rise to its equilibrium level. In this case, we incur a higher cost at the same time that producers' reduced incentives make a smaller quantity available. Because we pay more for less, we are actually harmed by the government's price ceilings.

Questions

1. Evaluate the cost of your time spent waiting in line to buy a ticket.
2. Who benefits from price ceilings? Who loses?
3. If you lived in a community that had an apartment shortage, would you suggest rent controls as a solution? What alternative solutions could you suggest?

meanings to this word. **Profit** is the amount by which the earnings of resources exceed their opportunity cost. **A loss** is just the opposite: it is the amount by which the earnings of resources fall short of their opportunity cost.

> **Profit:**   The amount by which the earnings of resources *exceed* their opportunity cost.
>
> **Loss:**   The amount by which the earnings of resources *fall short* of their opportunity cost.

Chapter 1 has defined opportunity cost as the best opportunity given up when a choice is made. If revenues exceed opportunity cost, then revenues exceed what resources could earn in their best alternative employment.

The beef and chicken industries clearly illustrate how profits and losses distribute productive resources among possible uses in our economy. When we consumers shifted our preferences from beef to chicken, the price of beef fell relative to the price of chicken. While profits increased in chicken farming, they fell in cattle raising. Through our dollar votes in the market, there-

As consumers' preferences shifted from beef to chicken, profits increased in chicken farming and decreased in cattle raising. Profits (and losses) perform an important role, therefore, because they enable consumers to direct producers to supply the goods and services consumers want most.

fore, we told producers we wanted more resources producing chickens and fewer resources producing cattle. As losses mounted in cattle production, resources began to move out of this industry because they could earn more in their best alternative employment. As profits rose in chicken ranching, however, resources increasingly moved into that industry because they could earn more there than in their best alternative employment. These changes illustrate how market prices, through their effect on economic profits and losses, ration resources among their many possible uses.

This conclusion takes us back to the question posed at the beginning of this chapter: If we consume less meat in our nation, will hungry people around the world have more to eat?

If we eat less meat, our total demand for food could decrease as we consume more grain directly rather than indirectly through meat. The smaller demand for grain will then cause its price to drop. If we consider only the rationing function of price, we might conclude that others around the world will end up with more food to eat. They could have more to eat because the lower price of grain permits more grain to be rationed to the world's hungry people who can't afford to buy it at the current high price. We eat less; hungry people eat more. It's as simple as that. Or is it?

Doesn't this thinking ignore the incentive to produce? It is true that less meat eating in our nation could depress the price of grain by reducing our total demand for food. But if the price of grain falls, less grain will be grown because the incentive to produce it will decline. Consequently, there is no guarantee that hungry people around the world will end up with more to eat.

This conclusion illustrates that the method a nation uses to ration its goods and services also determines whether or not suppliers have the incentive to produce these goods and services. Suppose the method of rationing chicken in grocery stores is changed from market price to the nonprice method of first come, first served. If that happens, you will see many consumers waiting in lines to obtain chicken. But if consumers no longer *pay* a market price to obtain chicken, then producers will no longer *receive* a market price for raising them. Without the incentive to produce, farmers will stop supplying grocery stores with chickens.

(text continues on page 183)

A Long Drive to the Quarter-Pound Patty

The ground trembled, the air filled with dust, and the dry grass crackled under the weight of a deafening roar. It was not an earthquake, although a city dweller caught in its midst might easily have mistaken it for one. Instead, it was one of the long drives, in which cattle were coaxed and coerced from as far away as Texas, Wyoming, and Montana to busy centers, such as Kansas City and Abilene. There, enormous stockyards waited to be filled, like a vast empty American stomach.

By stretching their fingers into the grassy Great Plains, the railroads helped make the long drives possible. Where the cattle drives ended, the railroads took over. Not only did the railroads ship live steers to the cities of the east, but also the meat-packing companies that sprang up near the stockyards transported fresh meat after the invention of refrigeration in the 1870s.

But the days of the long drive and the cowboy were brief, reaching only from the end of the Civil War to the late 1880s. What the railroad helped create, it also helped destroy. By opening up the Great Plains to farmers and sheepherders, the railroads helped to push cattle off the open ranges. Also important was the invention of barbed wire, which settlers eagerly strung to keep hungry cattle away from crops and grasses.

The barrier of barbed wire blocked the flow of cattle like a dam holding back a rush of water. The long drives quickly dried up, a disappearance aided by cattle diseases and severe winters in the mid-1880s.

Although cattle raising retreated from the open ranges and the long drives, it began to flourish on ranches, where owners could use barbed wire to their advantage. Figure A shows how the number of cattle on U.S. ranches has increased from about 60 million steers in 1888 to a peak of more than 130 million in the 1970s. The incentive to increase the nation's cattle population came from the market prices American consumers willingly paid for beef. Because the market price of beef usually made cattle raising profitable for efficient ranchers, they had the incentive to maintain and add to their herds.

But the market price of beef has done more than offer ranchers an incentive to produce. Over the decades, the market price of beef has also allocated the scarce supply among consumers. Like all other goods and services, beef has been scarce because consumers have always wanted more of it than has been available. Over our nation's history, the market price of beef has balanced the amounts of beef demanded and supplied. True, Americans wanted more

Figure A   Number of Cattle on U.S. Farms, 1888–1986

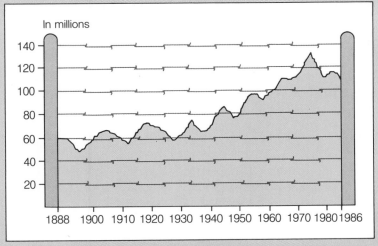

Source: *Historical Statistics of the United States, Colonial Times to 1970*, pp. 520–21; *Statistical Abstract of the United States*, various years.

beef than was available. If there had been no price at all, therefore, they would have wanted to consume more than was supplied. But the equilibrium price has made consumers demand less beef than they actually wanted, thereby keeping consumers' demands in line with available supplies.

In the 1970s, however, the demand for beef weakened as consumers came to prefer relatively more chicken, fish, vegetables, and other foods. Figure B shows how the per capita consumption of beef and veal dropped in the 1970s. Because of the weaker demand, the market price of beef began to fall relative to the mar-

ket prices of other foods, such as broiler chickens. Though consumers still wanted more beef than was available, their changing preferences made it less scarce. Consequently, a lower market price was able to ration existing supplies of beef among consumers. But the lower price of beef also reduced the incentive of ranchers to raise steers. The effects of this diminished incentive can be seen in Figure A, which shows that the number of cattle on U.S. farms dropped after 1975.

From the long drives of the last century to the hamburgers of today, the price of beef has accomplished two vital tasks. Not only has it ra-

Figure B Per Capita Consumption of Beef and Veal, 1930–1985

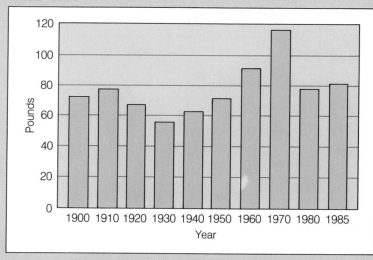

Source: *Historical Statistics of the United States, Colonial Times to 1970*, pp. 329–30; *Statistical Abstract of the United States*, 1986, p. 121; *Statistical Abstract of the United States*, 1987, p. 110.

tioned existing supplies of beef among consumers, but also it has provided the incentive to produce beef. Our nation's history shows that these two tasks of market prices are as complementary as a beef patty and a bun.

References

Bailey, Thomas A., *The American Pageant: A History of the Republic*. Vol. 11. 4th ed. Lexington, Mass.: D. C. Heath, 1971. 609–11.

Morison, Eliot Samuel, and Commager, Henry Steel. *The Growth of the American Republic*. Vol. 2. New York: Oxford University Press, 1950. 90–95.

Faulkner, Harold Underwood. *American Economic History*. 8th ed. New York: Harper & Row, 1960. 351–53.

This example shows that market prices accomplish some important tasks. Although it is not the only method of performing these functions, market prices (1) ration scarce goods and services among consumers, and (2) provide incentives to produce and, in so doing, distribute resources among their many possible uses in production.

Chapter Summary

1. Market prices provide an incentive to produce goods and services, and they ration goods and services among those who want them. Since scarcity means that all of everyone's wants cannot be fully satisfied, some method must be used to determine whose wants will not be satisfied and whose will. Any method chosen will force discrimination among possible uses and users of a good or service. *Discrimination* is the identification and use of differences among people in order to make a choice. Scarcity necessitates discrimination among the possible users of goods and services, and no way of rationing satisfies everyone.

2. Various nonprice methods of rationing exist. Goods and services can be rationed by a lottery; by first come, first served; by need; or by personal characteristics, such as beauty, intelligence, and age. Force is another nonprice rationing method, by which the powerful obtain more of the good and the weak obtain less.

3. Market prices represent another method of rationing goods and services. According to this method, our wants will be satisfied when we are both willing and able to pay the market price for any good or service we desire. The market price is the equilibrium price. Although there is no shortage or surplus at this price, the item is still scarce because we still want of it more than is available. By balancing the amounts people want to buy and sell, the equilibrium price rations the scarce supply of a good or service.

4. Economics cannot tell anyone which method of rationing is best, since that is a value judgment. Any method of rationing produces winners and losers.

5. Different methods of rationing produce different kinds of discrimination. When market price is used as a rationing

device, it discriminates against those who are unwilling or unable to pay the equilibrium price. Discrimination is an inevitable result of our wants' exceeding our abilities to satisfy them. Some people favor a market rationing system because those who get the benefit of the good also pay the cost of producing it. It is possible, through charity and taxation, to provide goods and services to those people who are denied them through market price rationing.

6. Market prices can also be used to ration resources among their different uses of production. By altering the profits and losses of businesses, prices influence the incentive to produce. *Profit* is the amount by which the earnings of resources exceed their opportunity cost. *Loss* is the amount by which the earnings of resources fall short of their opportunity cost.

Review Questions

1. What are the two functions of prices in a market economy?
2. Explain this statement: In any economy, scarcity necessitates discrimination among the possible users of goods and services.
3. Describe three nonprice methods of rationing goods and services among possible users.
4. Discuss the advantages and disadvantages of any *one* of the nonprice methods of rationing goods and services among possible users.
5. Does scarcity exist when market prices ration goods and services? Explain.
6. When a market price performs its rationing function, does everyone get at least a little of the quantity available? Explain.
7. Explain how scalpers ration their tickets.
8. Explain why you agree or disagree with the following statement: Whatever rationing method is used, discrimination cannot be avoided.
9. What are the economic meanings of *profit* and *loss*? How do

profits and losses distribute resources among possible uses in a market economy?

1. Briefly explain how market prices help to get goods and services produced and distributed.
2. Why is the rationing of goods and services necessary in any economic system? Which system of rationing do you prefer? Why?
3. What advantages and disadvantages are associated with rationing by market price? Explain.
4. Evaluate the effects of using price and two specific nonprice methods to ration the scarce spaces at state universities and colleges among all those who would like to attend.
5. Assume you are an economic advisor to a poor nation with many hungry people. The government of that nation is about to reduce the legal prices of food items so citizens can afford to eat more. What advice would you give the government?

Activities

1. Describe a situation in which there has been an interference with the rationing function of price. Then illustrate that situation using graphs and make a case for or against the interference.
2. At the next event at which you expect scalpers, interview at least two of them, and determine the price charged for the ticket and why the scalper expects to get that price. Then interview at least two individuals who have bought a ticket from a scalper and find out the price paid and why the person was willing to pay that price.
3. Write an essay responding to the following statement: scalping should be declared illegal, and the law should be strictly enforced.
4. The following information shows the market demand and market supply for pistachio nuts:

Price per Pound	Market Supply	Mary's Demand +	Joe's Demand +	Jean's Demand =	Market Demand
$5	12	0	1	2	_____
4	10	0	2	3	_____
3	8	1	3	4	_____
2	6	2	4	5	_____
1	4	3	5	6	_____

(a) Compute the weekly market demand for pistachio nuts.

(b) What is the equilibrium price? Explain how this price provides an incentive to produce and also rations the available supply among the three consumers.

(c) Assume a price ceiling of $1 is put on pistachio nuts. Explain how the two functions of price will be affected. How can the three consumers compete for the available supply?

(d) Will the price ceiling of $1 benefit the consumers? Why or why not?

Additional Readings

Bradley, Michael. *Microeconomics*. 2d ed. Glenview, Ill: Scott, Foresman, 1985. 151–54.

Hazlitt, Henry. *Economics in One Lesson*. New York: Arlington House, 1979. 103–109.

Heilbroner, Robert L., and Galbraith, James K. *The Economic Problem*. Revised 8th ed. Englewood Cliffs, N.J.: Prentice-Hall, 1987. 447–51.

Heyne, Paul. *The Economic Way of Thinking*. 5th ed. Chicago: Science Research Associates, 1987. 229–40.

Why is most high school education financed and produced by the government?

The Role of Government

■ Student's Goals ■

1. Define and give examples of *public goods*.

2. Explain how government plays a role in determining what is and is not produced in a market economy.

3. Explain how government plays a role in modifying the way in which a market economy distributes income.

4. Identify and describe at least three of the major types of taxes that citizens pay.

5. Explain why an increase in income will not result in a decrease in take-home pay.

6. Define *external costs,* and describe three ways in which government can intervene if external costs are harmful.

7. Define *monopoly,* and give at least one example of how government attempts to control or regulate monopolies.

Letters to the Authors

Public Goods

After reading and thinking about the last few chapters, I have a much better understanding of how market prices can provide incentives to produce a lot of the goods and services we all demand. But it seems to me that you're ignoring many important things that a market economy would never produce. What about fire and police protection, education, roads, national defense, national parks, and the administration of justice in our courts? Aren't these examples of things that are provided by the government because market prices don't give enough incentive for their production?

David Ramirez
California

Redistribution

Until I read the last few chapters, I never realized how market prices get people to cut back voluntarily on the amounts they use, so that demands and supplies are balanced. This gives people the freedom to choose for themselves the amount of something they are going to buy. No authority has to tell them how much they really "need." As you said in Chapter 2, a market economy has both consumer freedom and consumer sovereignty.

When discussing the circular flow in Chapter 2, however, you also pointed out that in a market economy the ability to buy what one wants in the goods and services markets depends on the amounts and productivities of one's resources. Those who have few resources or who have resources with little productivity will, thus, earn little income and receive few goods and services. In order to give more goods and services to some citizens, doesn't the government tax the incomes of some people and then transfer this money to those who have lower incomes? It seems to me that an important role of government is to redistribute income to assure that poor people can buy goods and services, too. Shouldn't you mention this role?

Sandy Frost
Alaska

Pollution

I read the first seven chapters with a lot of interest and care, but I find it hard to believe we're looking at the same world. You talk about how market prices and profits cause private resource owners to use their property carefully, so that the things consumers want get produced and distributed. In Chapter 2 you even point out that with private ownership, the desire to do what is best for oneself can also work in the interest of everyone else.

But I just read a story about how our desires for lumber and recreation are destroying the few remaining grizzly bears in our nation. That reminds me of what we're doing to the populations of whales and seals, and what we did to the valuable buffalo herds earlier in our nation's history.

Aren't these just a few more examples of how we pollute our environment by ignoring valuable resources, like grizzly bears, air, water, and land? If we left the use of these valuable resources to be determined by prices and profits, wouldn't they all be polluted?

Kathy Wheatley
Kansas

Monopoly

I thought your discussion of equilibrium price was interesting but unrealistic. You say that when a price is below its equilibrium level, competition among buyers will push it up and eliminate the shortage. Okay, I can accept that. But then you say that when the price is above its equilibrium level, competition among sellers will push it down and eliminate the surplus.

But what about monopoly? Aren't you ignoring that? Don't sellers sometimes hold goods and services off the market, so that the price won't come down to the competitive level you describe? I know from my history classes that there have been lots of examples of so-called "robber barons" and other monopolists. Why don't you mention them?

Matthew Todd
New York

Changing What's Produced

These fictional letters show the government plays a very important role in our economic system. Why, then, have the previous chapters generally ignored it? Until now, the economic functions of government have been omitted so that you could concentrate on learning about markets.

National defense is a good example of a public good. Everyone can use it at the same time, and those who do not pay for it cannot be prevented from using it. Because many who enjoy national defense would not willingly pay for it, private businesses do not have an incentive to provide adequate national defense. As a result, the government taxes citizens and compels them to pay for this important service.

Although our economic system is largely a market economy, it is still a mixture of both markets and government. No wonder many refer to it as a *mixed economy*. In a mixed economy, one important function of government is to alter the kinds of goods and services produced. Government has to do this because a market economy does not guarantee sufficient production of certain kinds of goods and services consumers want. Instead, government provides these goods and services, which are called public goods.

A **public good** (or **public service**) has the following characteristics: (1) everyone can use it at the same time, and (2) those who do not pay for it cannot be prevented from using it. The classic example of a public good is national defense. If national defense is provided for one citizen, all other citizens can benefit from it at the same time. A public good is certainly different from a milk shake and other ordinary goods. Your drinking a milk shake necessarily prevents others from also consuming it. But your benefiting from national defense does not prevent others from benefiting from it, too.

> **Public good:** A good or service that has the following two characteristics: (1) everyone can consume it at the same time, and (2) those who do not pay for it cannot be prevented from consuming it.

Imagine what would happen if a private business, rather than our federal government, tried to produce and profitably sell a public good like national defense. Once in place, our defense system protects everyone—even those who do not pay for it. Consequently, sellers of national defense and other public goods in a market economy would seldom profit because people could use them, even though they do not pay for them. Lacking an incentive to make such payments, therefore, consumers do not spend enough money on these goods to make it worthwhile for private businesses to produce them.

As a result, markets do not produce enough public goods, even though people prefer to have them. Through its power of taxation, the government can purchase these goods and ensure that those who consume them will pay for them. It is not easy to know, however, when the government ought to provide something or how much it ought to make available of those items it does supply. The reason is because many things the government supplies are *not* public goods: not only can prices be charged for many of these goods and services, but also non-payers can be prevented from using them. As a result, markets can sometimes offer private businesses enough incentive to produce some of these things. For example, private businesses now profitably produce and sell some fire and police protection, some parks, and some education.

Many things that citizens ask the government to purchase are not pure public goods. How, then, do you distinguish between requests to have the government provide important items that markets will not otherwise provide and requests to have the government force taxpayers to subsidize the consumption of others?

Our government's role in providing goods and services has grown over the years. At the turn of the century, it purchased approximately 5 percent of the total goods and services produced in our nation. By the 1950s, that number had reached about 20 percent.

Figure 8–1 shows that between 1950 and 1986, the total of federal, state, and local government purchases of goods and services has remained about 20 percent of our nation's total production.

Figure 8–1 also shows that the stable proportion of 20 percent hides a changing mixture of expenditures between the federal government and state and local governments. While the relative size of federal purchases of goods and services has tended to fall during this time, the relative size of state and local purchases has tended to rise. That's why the line indicating state and local government expenditures rises, and the line indicating federal government expenditures falls.

You can see that the government is an important source of dollar votes in the goods and services markets of our economy. These votes encourage the production of certain things government representatives believe should be produced. But just

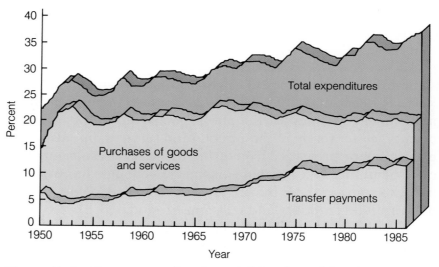

Figure 8–1 Government Purchases of Goods and Services as a Percentage of National Production, 1950–1986

Total government purchases of goods and services consist of purchases by state and local governments and purchases by the federal government. The graph above shows that local government purchases of goods and services (the top line) have remained about 20 percent of national production between 1950 and 1986. During this period, purchases by state and local governments have risen as a percentage of national production. Consequently, the line marked *State and local governments* rises from left to right. Federal government purchases of goods and services have fallen as a percentage of national production, so the bottom line slopes downward from left to right.

Source: Economic Report of the President, 1987.

State and local expenditures are responsible for the existence of this high school. The services provided by the school are part of our nation's total production. What changes do you think would occur in education if we depended less on government and more on the "invisible hand" of the market for the provision of education?

as the government encourages the production of particular goods and services, so, too, does it discourage the production of others that citizens and their government representatives believe are undesirable.

For example, in the absence of government intervention it might be more profitable for landowners to grow illegal drugs than to grow food. In the warm, humid jungles of South America, *campesinos* (peasants) have been doing just that. Because of the strong market demand for cocaine, many *campesinos* have stopped growing oranges and bananas and started growing the coca leaves used to produce cocaine.[1] In order to curb the production of cocaine, various governments have tried to reduce the profitability of producing coca leaves. This profitability can be reduced if consumers in the United States and elsewhere can be influenced to purchase less cocaine or if the government can somehow raise the cost of producing coca leaves. By making the good unlawful, for example, our government discourages consumers from demanding it. Moreover, by im-

[1]For an interesting discussion of this event, see "Can South America's Addict Economies Ever Break Free?" *Business Week* (September 22, 1986): 40–44.

posing a cost of fines or imprisonment on producers, the government increases the cost of producing the good. Still, attempts to outlaw certain products sometimes backfire. When enforcing laws against a certain product eliminates some producers of that good, its production might become so profitable for the remaining illegal producers that they will take very high risks to continue supplying it.

Whether the government is attempting to decrease or increase the production of particular goods and services, it still tries to work through markets by influencing demand and supply. Consequently, the government tries to alter the results of the market economy by modifying the profitability and consequences of various types of production.

Redistributing Income

Another role of government is to redistribute income. As the letter from Sandy Frost has pointed out, a market economy distributes income unequally. Those who have more resources or who have resources with greater productivity earn more income and are able to purchase more goods and services. The fact that individuals obtain unequal shares of a market economy's total production often violates our feelings about fairness.

Because some minimum standard of living is an accepted goal in our society, the government often supplements the incomes of certain individuals. This modification is generally accomplished by taxing the incomes of some citizens and then transferring that income to others. However, most of these *transfer payments* go to individuals who are not poor. Examples of such transfers are Social Security payments, unemployment compensation, and farm subsidies. These transfer payments are not included in government purchases of goods and services because they are redistributions of income, not expenditures made to obtain a product or service. Consequently, total government expenditures contain both transfer payments and purchases of goods and services. Indeed, these two kinds of government expenditures now account for more than 90 percent of all government spending.

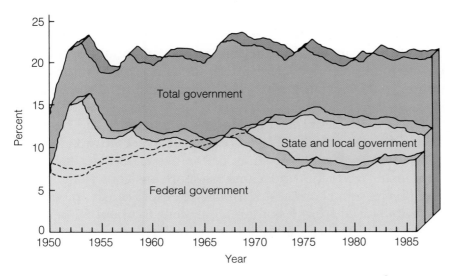

Figure 8–2 Government Expenditures as a Percentage of National Production, 1950–1986

Total government expenditures include both transfer payments and purchases of goods and services. The top line shows that total government expenditures have grown from about 22 percent of national production in 1950 to about 35 percent in 1986. The increase is the result of growing transfer payments, which are shown by the rising line at the bottom of the graph. The middle line, which is neither rising nor falling, shows that government purchases of goods and services have remained fairly constant at about 20 percent of national production.

Source: Economic Report of the President, 1987.

Figure 8–2 shows how spending by federal, state, and local governments has changed during the period from 1950 to 1986. The top line of Figure 8–2 shows that total government expenditures as a percentage of national production have grown from less than 25 percent in the early 1950s to about 35 percent in the mid-1980s. The increase is the result of an increase in transfer payments, not in the purchases of goods and services. You can see this by comparing the middle and bottom lines on the graph. The middle line shows government purchases of goods and services as a percentage of national production. This line is relatively flat, meaning that government purchases of goods and services have not been rising as a percentage of national production. The bottom line has risen, however, showing that government transfer payments as a percentage of national production have been going up.

Figure 8–2 reveals an important fact about government spending: total government expenditures (the top line) have been rising relative to national production primarily because transfer payments (the bottom line) have also been rising relative to our nation's production. Since the amount of transfer payments reflects government's role as a redistributor of income, you can see that this role has grown during the last few decades.

The growth of transfer payments is generally the result of changes in the pattern of *federal* expenditures. Figure 8–3 shows that since 1960 a bigger share of the federal budget has gone to transfer payments and a smaller share has gone to the goods and services that comprise national defense. Transfer payments have increased from less than 25 percent to about 37 percent. At the same time, expenditures for national defense have dropped from almost 50 percent to about 27 percent.

The Taxes You Pay

If federal, state, and local governments are going to make transfer payments and are going to purchase goods and services,

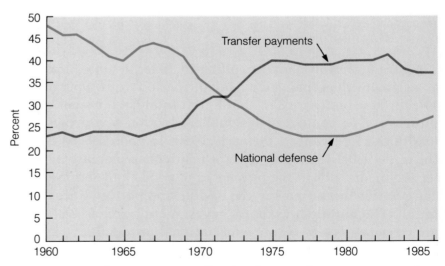

Figure 8–3 The Percentage of Federal Expenditures Accounted for by Transfer Payments and by National Defense, 1960–1986

Between 1960 and 1986, transfer payments as a share of the federal budget have grown from under 25 percent to about 37 percent. At the same time, expenditures for national defense have declined from almost 50 percent of the federal budget in 1960 to about 27 percent in 1986.
Source: Economic Report of the President, 1987.

they must get money by taxing citizens. No wonder Benjamin Franklin once wrote that "in this world nothing is certain but death and taxes."

Figure 8–4 shows the major kinds of taxes we pay. Personal taxes, such as federal and state income taxes, are the most common taxes we pay. The federal personal income tax requires us to pay a larger percentage of our incomes as tax as our incomes rise. Therefore, it takes a larger percentage of a richer person's income and a smaller percentage of a poorer person's income. This type of tax is called a *progressive tax*. In contrast, a tax that takes a larger percentage of a poorer per-

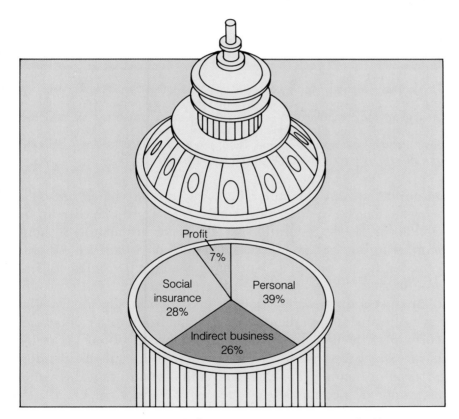

Figure 8–4 Major Types of Taxes as a Percentage of All Tax Revenues, 1985

Federal, state, and local governments receive money through four major types of taxes. Personal taxes include federal and state income taxes and local property taxes. Indirect business taxes, which include sales and excise taxes, are not levied directly on the profits of a business. Social insurance taxes include tax for Social Security. Taxes on corporate profits are also a source of government revenue.
Source: Economic Report of the President, 1986.

Filling out your federal income tax return can be a difficult task. No wonder there are so many lawyers and accountants who make a living doing just that. But although the computation of your tax can be difficult, the principle behind it is quite simple. You subtract various deductions and exemptions from your income to obtain your taxable income. Then, you look up your taxable income in a tax table to determine the total income tax you owe.

son's income and a smaller percentage of a richer person's income is a *regressive tax*. Sales tax is an example of a regressive tax. Poorer people generally spend a larger proportion of their incomes to buy goods and services than do wealthier people. Consequently, a poorer person pays a larger *percentage* of income in sales tax, even though the sales tax charged on each dollar of spending is the same for everyone. In contrast, a tax that takes an equal percentage of income from both richer and poorer persons is a *proportional tax*. A proportional tax is illustrated by proposals for a flat-rate federal income tax. Under this type of income tax, each individual would pay the same percentage of income as tax.

Some people believe that if they earn extra money, their take-home pay will drop because they will move into a higher income tax bracket: that is, they will have to pay a higher percentage in taxes. It's true that more income can put you into a higher tax bracket, but your total take-home pay will still rise, not fall. This is because the higher tax rate applies only to the income that falls in the higher bracket. The tax law of 1986 reduced the number of tax brackets from fourteen to two;

these are 15 percent and 28 percent. For an individual taxpayer, the lower bracket applies to taxable income up to $17,850.[2] (For a married couple filing a joint return, the lower bracket applies to taxable income up to $29,750.) An individual with a taxable income of $1,000 falls into the lower bracket and will pay an income tax of $150 (15% × $1,000).

That individual will also pay as tax 15 percent of each extra dollar of taxable income he or she earns up to $17,850. Because the tax rate applies to the additional (marginal) income received, it is called the *marginal tax rate*. If an individual has a taxable income of exactly $17,850, he or she will pay a total tax of $2,677.50 (15% × $17,850).

Now suppose that individual's taxable income rises from $17,850 to $20,000. In that case, he or she still pays a tax of only $2,677.50 on the first $17,850 of income. The higher 28-percent rate applies only to the *additional* income of $2,150 ($20,000 − $17,850). As a result, here is what the person's total tax payment would be:

$$
\begin{array}{rl}
15\% \times \$17,850 = & \$2,677.50 \\
28\% \times \$\ 2,150 = & \$\ \ \ 602.00 \\
\hline
\text{Total tax} \quad\quad = & \$3,279.50
\end{array}
$$

There is no tax bracket for which the tax on *added income* is greater than 100 percent. Therefore, even if you earn more income and move into the higher tax bracket, you will still take home most of the additional money.

Still, when it comes time to file your income tax return in April, it's not always easy to know exactly how much your tax is for the year. Filling out your income tax forms can be complicated, which is why there are so many accountants and lawyers who earn their livings doing just that. Although the actual computation of your federal income tax can be difficult, the principle behind it is quite simple. You start by calculating your income. Next, you subtract certain deductions and exemptions in order to arrive at your taxable income. Then you look up the amount of your taxable income in a tax table to determine how much tax you owe.

In addition to federal and state income taxes, indirect business taxes provide government with much revenue. These busi-

[2]Taxable income is calculated by subtracting allowed deductions and personal exemptions from total income.

ness taxes, such as sales and excise taxes, are called indirect taxes because they are not levied *directly* on the profits of a business. Excise taxes are a kind of sales tax, but they are levied only on certain kinds of products, such as gasoline, alcoholic beverages, and cigarettes. Because indirect business taxes are included in the prices of goods and services, you pay for them as a consumer.

Taxes for social insurance have become an important source of revenue for the federal government. As a worker, for example, you pay Social Security tax, which usually shows up on your paycheck as a deduction for FICA (Federal Insurance Contributions Act). This tax enables the federal government to make Social Security transfer payments to retired citizens.

Taxes on corporate profits represent another tax source that is important to the federal government. The slice of the tax pie contributed by these taxes has dwindled over the years, falling from about 16 percent of federal, state, and local government receipts in 1960 to 8 percent in 1986. A major reason for this decline is the fact that corporate profits have declined relative to the size of the economy.[3] Many people believe that corporations, not individuals, pay the profits tax, but this is not the case. Corporations collect the profits tax for the government, but consumers, stockholders, and employees of those companies actually bear the burden of the tax in the form of higher prices, lower stock earnings, and reduced wages.

Pollution and External Costs

The various taxes you pay help federal, state, and local governments to finance their transfer payments and their purchases of goods and services. But these expenditures and taxes are not the only ways in which government alters the economy. Government also intervenes in the economy because our decisions about what to buy and sell do not always account for

[3]For example, in 1960 corporate profits represented more than 12 percent of national income, but by 1985 they had dropped to about 9 percent. A reduction of three or four percentage points might not seem like much. However, national income is such a large number that even a small reduction in the percentage of national income represented by corporate profits makes a big difference in the total amount of profits that can be taxed.

all the costs they create. Kathy Wheatley's letter about grizzly bears, whales, seals, and buffalo makes this point.

Why have these and other valuable resources often been neglected or destroyed, while others, such as beef and dairy cattle, have been well cared for? Why do we abuse and pollute some resources at the same time that we carefully use and preserve others?

The answer has to do with property rights, which have been discussed in Chapter 2. Consider what happened to the buffalo during the last century. Because buffalo were not privately owned, no one had the legal right to control their use. Instead, they were common property that belonged to whomever killed them first. The cost of shooting a buffalo would not, therefore, be borne by a hunter. Compare this case with that of a private cattle owner who would bear the costs if his or her herd were destroyed.

Because buffalo were not privately owned, the rights to kill or use them were not exchanged in the market. There were no market prices for buffalo that would provide the necessary information and incentives to prevent their wasteful use. The

Litter is a good illustration of the pollution that occurs because individuals do not have to pay for the right to use resources as a dump. Without private property, resources are not assigned a caretaker with an incentive to assure their careful use. As a result, so-called common property resources are often abused and polluted.

lack of market prices made the scarce, valuable herds of buffalo seem like they were free and limitless. The predictable result was what ecologists call "the tragedy of the commons."

Beef and dairy cattle were not affected by this tragedy because they were privately owned. In order to obtain cattle, therefore, one had to purchase them in the market. The costs of carelessly destroying cattle would have been borne by their owners because they would have been unable to sell them in the market. Unlike buffalo, beef and dairy cattle had market prices that provided the information and incentives necessary to conserve them for their most valuable purposes.

An absence of private property rights causes people to abuse valuable resources and to pollute excessively. Air and water are seldom privately owned, for example, so there are no market prices to tell us the costs we inflict on others when we use these resources. These costs are called *external costs* because they remain outside the consideration of those who are making decisions about resources. External costs have been briefly described in Chapter 1 in terms of the barking dogs that continually disturbed the writer who worked at home.

When people behave in ways that are harmful to the general community, external costs are large. Government can then intervene in three ways: (1) it can pass laws to regulate the behavior; (2) it can tax the behavior in order to control it; and (3) whenever possible, it can create private property rights for the abused resources, so that market prices will control the behavior. The threatened extinction of animals, factory pollution, noisy all-night parties, highway litter, theft, speeding— all these are behaviors that cause other people to bear involuntarily the costs of someone else's decisions. These are examples in which the absence of markets and market prices for certain resources leads to wasteful behavior, behavior that the government then attempts to correct.

Monopoly

The role of government in dealing with external costs and pollution is to expand and improve, not overrule, the market economy. The government tries to assure that people behave according to the rules of the game by making sure that they are

Litter

Why do people often throw trash on highways and in other public places?

Noneconomic Way of Thinking

People throw trash on highways and in other public places for the same reason they pollute the atmosphere with exhaust fumes: they are irresponsible people who lack a social consciousness.

Economic Way of Thinking

It would be nice if people voluntarily considered all the costs they inflict on other people, but this wish doesn't mean that irresponsibility is the cause of litter and pollution. The same people who discard their trash on the highway usually don't act that way in their own homes. Irresponsibility, therefore, is not the reason for the destruction and abuse of valuable public resources. Rather, the reason is that people do not directly bear the costs of abusing public resources, such as highways, parks, and the air. People abuse valuable resources because they are not penalized for such behavior.

Questions

1. Are public rest rooms generally better maintained than are those in private homes? Explain.
2. Are privately owned lakes likely to be more or less polluted than those open to the public? Why?
3. How can government minimize the abuse of public resources?
4. If people's property rights to resources were clearly spelled out, would those resources be abused and polluted?

responsible for the costs they produce. Government has another role in which it tries to enforce the rules of the game in a market economy. This role has been identified by the letter from Matthew Todd.

Matthew points out that sometimes a product is supplied by a single seller or a small group of sellers, so that market competition is restricted and the price is kept artificially high. The resulting **monopoly** is a concern of government if new producers are somehow prevented from entering the market. In that case, *barriers to entry* into the market prevent the threat of new competitors from driving prices down to a competitive level.

> **Monopoly:**   A market in which there is only one seller.

Sometimes monopoly results naturally from the production of a good or service. These instances of *natural monopoly* usually occur in businesses having large, fixed costs of production. A single seller is able to obtain the lowest production cost per unit by spreading the huge fixed costs over larger quantities of output. By being the only producer in the market, a supplier can thereby produce each unit at a lower cost. For example, instead of having two or more local telephone companies— each with its own system of wires—it is cheaper to have only one. In these instances of natural monopoly, the government creates regulatory commissions in an attempt to assure the lower prices that would otherwise result from greater competition. However, some people doubt the incentive of these commissions to serve the interests of consumers. Indeed, they often view government regulation as a means of protecting producers from the competition that would benefit consumers.

Natural monopoly is the exception, not the rule. In most cases the stated role of government is to prevent monopolies and to promote a competitive economy. The laws designed to accomplish these objectives are called *antitrust laws* (because early monopolies were often called trusts). The first antitrust law passed in the United States was the Sherman Act of 1890, which prohibited price fixing and monopolization. Other major antitrust acts are the Clayton Act and the Federal Trade Commission Act, both passed in 1914. The Clayton Act and the Federal Trade Commission Act outlawed certain business prac-

SIMPLICITY

INTRODUCING
MCI PRISM PLUS.

For simplicity, service and savings, it's the greatest innovation in long distance since WATS.

New MCI PRISM PLUS combines the simplicity of ordinary long distance with sophisticated features and savings superior to AT&T WATS. Or *anything* else AT&T has to offer your business.

If you use more than an hour and a half of long distance a day, PRISM PLUS can give you universal interstate coverage at savings of 10 to 35% vs. AT&T. And with PRISM PLUS there's no time-consuming installation or special lines required.* No difficult, costly analysis. You get complete, detailed billing for efficient, effective management. And you can count on PRISM PLUS to grow with your business as fast and as far as you go.

The simplicity--and strength--of PRISM PLUS is another example of MCI's commitment to superior communications solutions. MCI* has invested over $5 billion to bring you the most flexible, sophisticated service available. MCI's coast-to-coast fiber optic network and other state-of-the-art facilities can guarantee the clearest, cleanest connections and the most reliable, cost-efficient service.

Let PRISM PLUS revolutionize your business' capabilities. Call MCI today.

For more information,
call 1-800-888-0800.

MCI
COMMUNICATIONS
FOR THE NEXT 100 YEARS.

For many years, AT & T was thought to be a natural monopoly. But technological change helped to alter this thought. For example, as satellites, fiber optics, and microwaves drastically changed the nature of long distance telephone calls, new companies began competing with AT & T. MCI is one of the new competitors that has used new technology to reduce costs for consumers.

tices that were thought to restrain competition and create monopolies. The Federal Trade Commission Act also created the Federal Trade Commission (FTC) to investigate methods of competition, to issue complaints against businesses that are restraining competition, and to conduct hearings. The purpose of antitrust legislation, therefore, is to promote a competitive economy, in which buyers have access to a wide variety of products at reasonable prices.

What's Ahead

The letters at the beginning of this chapter have identified some important roles of government. Not only does government alter the kinds of goods and services produced in a market economy, but also it redistributes income in order to modify the way goods and services are distributed among citizens. In addition, when there are significant external costs, government tries to reduce the pollution and abuse of valuable resources. So, too, does government attempt to control and restrict monopoly.

(text continues on page 213)

The Economic Way of Thinking

Copyrights

In the United States, records and films are copyrighted by the government. This makes it illegal to duplicate and tape them without permission. Should consumers be deprived of the right to copy or to buy pirated copies of records and films?

Noneconomic Way of Thinking

It is wasteful to stop people from duplicating videos and other recordings. Once the film or recording is made, why limit the number of people who can enjoy it? It doesn't cost the producing company anything extra, and it doesn't hurt the consumers who buy the originals.

Economic Way of Thinking

The government's prohibition of pirating makes sense for both producers and consumers. While it might seem wasteful to limit the use of a product or service that has already been produced, you have to consider what pirating does to the incentive to produce those items in the first place. If a producer anticipates weak sales for a recording because listeners are apt to purchase less expensive copies, he or she might decide not to make the recording. Then everyone loses. By providing important incentives to produce recorded material, copyright laws help producers and consumers.

Questions

1. In the United States, patent laws prevent other businesses from producing identical products. Why does the government limit competition in this way? Do consumers benefit?

2. Do you believe that composers would create song lyrics if they were not going to be paid for their commercial use?

3. How is photocopying a copyrighted book comparable to tape recording a copyrighted music album?

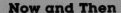
Phone Rates and Government Regulation

Telephones used to be like the Model T Ford: you could get one in any color as long as it was black. Now they come in all sizes and shapes, and make all kinds of sounds. And even though most of us push buttons instead of turning dials, we still listen for dial tones.

Despite the changes, most of us remain concerned about the cost of making a call. Telephone rates are different from other prices, however, because they have been closely regulated by the government. That was not the case during the early years of the telephone industry, which began with Alexander Graham Bell.

As a young man, Bell already had considerable knowledge about sound and hearing. He obtained this knowledge from his father and grandfather, who had done much research in the subject and who had taught the deaf and dumb. Because of Bell's knowledge and interest, he received financial backing to develop a "harmonic telegraph" that would send different pitches of sound over a wire. But Bell was more interested in transmitting voices.

He knew he was onto something in 1875 when his assistant, Thomas A. Watson, plucked a piece of clock wire and Bell heard the sound on a telegraph line in another room. Propelled by their dream, the two worked hard for 40 weeks. Then, on March 10, 1876, Bell transmitted his voice to Watson in a distant room. "Mr. Watson, come here, I want you," he said and, in so doing, transmitted the first words ever spoken on a telephone.

Alexander Bell had the idea patented in 1876. Then Bell, Watson, and their financial supporters formed the Bell Telephone Association. By successfully suing the Western Union Company for violating Bell's patent, the company forced Western Union out of the telephone business. As a result, Bell obtained Western Union's 56,000 phone subscribers and its Western Electric Manufacturing Company, which produced telephone equipment.

The cost of financing the company's growth was immense because of the amount of copper used in telephone lines. A line between New York and Chicago required about 400 tons of copper. The American Telephone Corporation had obtained its charter in Massachusetts, and that state had severely limited the ability of the company to sell new stocks to raise funds for new telephone lines and other capital goods. Consequently, in 1885 the Bell company created a subsidiary under a New York charter that did not cramp the company's ability to raise funds. That subsidiary, American Telephone and Telegraph Company, quickly became the parent company that everyone knows today as AT & T.

When Bell's patent on the telephone expired in 1893, competition intensified as many new telephone companies were created. Between 1893 and 1907, the number of telephones in the nation increased from under 300,000 to more than 6 million. Almost half of all these telephones were provided by companies other than AT & T. Because of the increased competition, the profitability of the Bell company declined. The company responded to this situation by purchasing many competing telephone companies and by refusing to let competing companies use Bell's long-distance lines. More important, however, was the company's new policy of advocating government regulation of the telephone industry.

According to the Bell company, telephone service was a natural monopoly. The company argued that it was in consumers' interests to have telephone service concentrated in one large company that could then be regulated by the government. Others saw the argument as an effort to avoid the market competition that was reducing the company's profitability. The issue was decided in 1910 when the Mann-Elkins Act empowered the government to regulate the telephone industry. Since then, the telephone industry has been closely regulated by the government.

Aided by this regulation, AT & T prospered. Figure A shows how the number of telephones with the Bell System increased relative to the number of those with other companies between 1900 and 1920. Indeed, through its complex of companies, AT & T eventually obtained a virtual monopoly on the telecommunications market. This complex, known as the Bell System, consisted of Bell Telephone Laboratories, (which conducts research), Western Electric Company (which produces telephone equipment), and twenty-three Bell Operating companies.

Despite its regulation, AT & T has been prosecuted for violating the Sherman Antitrust Act. For example, in 1974 the government filed a suit charging AT & T with using its monopoly of local telephone exchanges to restrict competition in the long-distance and telephone equipment markets. But rapid technological change led to an interesting and abrupt end to this suit.

Microwave radio, satellites, and fiber optics are some of the technological developments that allowed competition to develop. These changes enabled new companies, such as MCI and Sprint, to offer consumers alternative long-distance ser-

Figure A Number of Telephones, 1900–1920

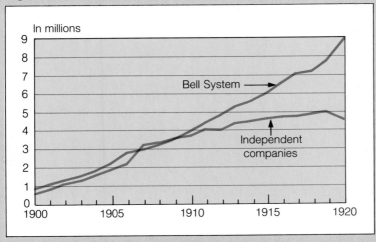

Source: Historical Statistics of the United States, 1820–1970.

vices. And they provided the services at a lower cost than did AT & T. One important reason for this lower cost was the fact that government regulators had set AT & T's long-distance rates above the cost of providing this service. They had done this in order to subsidize local callers by setting their rates below cost. But if AT & T was going to compete with these emerging companies in the long-distance market, it could no longer support this hidden subsidy. Moreover, the company wanted the government's permission to enter the rapidly growing computer-related markets from which it had been legally excluded. As a result, in 1982

AT & T agreed to break up the Bell System. The company retained Western Electric and Bell Laboratories, but it lost its local operating companies. In return, AT & T was allowed to enter computer-related markets. Although we have not yet experienced the full effects of this change, there is little doubt that market competition has replaced some government regulation in the telephone industry.

In the years immediately following the breakup of AT & T, local telephone rates have risen, and long-distance rates have declined. If greater market competition produces a leaner, more efficient industry, the

Now and Then—Continued

total cost of providing our nation's telephone services will decline.

References

Groner, Alex, and the editors of AMERICAN HERITAGE and BUSINESS WEEK. *The American Heritage History of American Business & Industry*. New York: American Heritage Publishing Co., 1972. 180–82 and 334–35.

Ratner, Sidney, Soltow, James H., and Sylla, Richard. *The Evolution of the American Economy*. New York: Basic Books, Inc., 1979. 339–41.

Vedder, Richard. *The American Economy in Historical Perspective*. Belmont, Calif.: Wadsworth, 1976. 414.

In each of these roles, government's stated purpose is to promote, improve, and strengthen a competitive market economy. It is obvious that no market economy is perfect. And government, too, has its imperfections. Not only might it be impossible for government officials to know our preferences on particular issues, but also they might not even have an incentive to satisfy these preferences. Instead, they might cater to special interests that seek government subsidies for which we citizens must pay.

Despite the imperfections of both the market economy and the government, each has its important roles to play in producing and distributing goods and services. Indeed, government must enforce private property rights in a market economy because that enforcement guarantees us the ability to exchange our property in markets. If you didn't own the rights to your labor services, for example, you couldn't sell them in order to obtain the money you want to purchase goods and services. Thus, another important role of government is to assure us the ability to exchange our property rights in labor markets as well as in markets for goods and services. (The circular flow map in Chapter 2 describes these two types of markets and the ways in which they relate to one another.)

In the remaining chapters of this book, you will continue to see the various economic roles of government. In the next two chapters we will examine labor markets in order to show how wage rates are determined and why some people are unemployed.

Chapter Summary

1. Since a market economy does not produce enough of certain goods and services, called *public goods*, these goods are provided by government. Public goods have two distinct characteristics: (1) everyone can consume the good or service at the same time, and (2) those not paying for it cannot be prevented from consuming it. Because we can use these goods without paying for them, there is often not enough profit to interest private businesses in producing them in sufficient quantity. Government's role in the provision of goods and services has grown over the years; now, federal,

state, and local purchases of goods and services are about 20 percent of our total national production.

2. The government encourages and discourages the production of various goods and services. It also redistributes income by taxing the incomes of some citizens and transferring that income to others. These transfers are called *transfer payments*. They are not included in government purchases of goods and services because they are redistributions of income, not expenditures to obtain a product or service. Total government expenditures, which consist of both transfer payments and purchases of goods and services, have grown during the past thirty years. This is largely because transfer payments have increased, which means government's role as a redistributor of income has grown.

3. There are four major types of taxes collected by the different levels of government. *Personal taxes*, such as federal and state income taxes, are *progressive taxes* because they take a bigger percentage from those with higher incomes and a smaller percentage from those with lower incomes. A *regressive tax*, such as a sales tax, takes a bigger percentage from those with lower incomes and a smaller percentage from those with higher incomes. A *proportional tax* takes an equal proportion of income from everyone, no matter what her or his income. The second major type of tax is the *indirect business tax*, such as sales taxes. These business taxes are referred to as indirect because they are not levied directly on the profits of a business. *Social insurance taxes*, such as Social Security taxes, are the third major type of tax, and *corporation taxes on profits* are the fourth.

4. An absence of private property rights causes people to abuse valuable resources and to pollute the environment. *External costs* are costs inflicted on others who bear them involuntarily. Government can employ various means to control external costs, thereby helping the general community to avoid the wasteful behavior that causes them.

5. *Natural monopolies* occur in businesses having large, fixed costs of production. A single seller is able to obtain the lowest production costs per unit by spreading the huge fixed costs over larger quantities of output. One stated role of government is to prevent monopolies and to promote competition. Various antitrust laws, such as the Sherman, Clay-

ton, and Federal Trade Commission Acts, help government meet these objectives.

6. The government and the private market economy both have important roles in the production and distribution of goods and services. For example, government's enforcement of private property rights is necessary for a market economy in which people exchange that property in markets.

Review Questions

1. What are the two characteristics of a *public good?*

2. How does government attempt to increase or decrease the production of particular goods and services?

3. What are *transfer payments,* and why do we have them?

4. How do transfer payments illustrate government's role as a redistributor of income?

5. Explain the differences among a *progressive tax,* a *regressive tax,* and a *proportional tax.*

6. Explain why the following statement is false: "If I earn extra money this year, my take-home pay might drop because I will move into a higher income tax bracket."

7. What are *indirect business taxes, Social Security taxes,* and *taxes on corporate profits?*

8. What are *external costs?* When external costs are large, what are three ways in which government can intervene?

9. What is meant by the term *monopoly?* What is a *natural monopoly?* What is the role of antitrust laws in preventing or controlling monopolies?

Discussion Questions

1. Explain how *public goods* differ from *ordinary goods,* and use examples to show their differences. Why don't private businesses usually produce public goods?

2. Explain how government can influence the kinds of goods and services that are produced in a market economy. Use examples from our economy.

3. Is this statement correct: Although government purchases of goods and services have not increased as a percentage of national production, total government expenditures have increased as a proportion of national production. If so, why? If not, why not?

4. Why have some of our nation's valuable resources been destroyed while others have not been? Explain briefly, and give examples. How can government help to stop this destruction?

5. Government expenditures have grown relative to the size of our economy. What reasons do you think might account for this growth? Do you think this growth helps or hurts our nation? Why?

Activities

1. Write a letter in response to any one of the "Letters to the Authors" at the beginning of Chapter 8.

2. Draw a circular flow chart that illustrates the way in which the what, how, and for whom decisions are made in a market economy. Then write a short paragraph describing how government might use its authority to modify these decisions.

3. Write an essay in response to the following statement: The role of government should be to prevent monopolies and to promote a competitive economy.

4. Defend or attack the following statement: "If my spouse goes to work, we might actually end up with less money because it will place us in a higher income tax bracket."

5. The following table presents our nation's total production and the four major sources of *federal* tax revenues for various years. Calculate the percentage of national production that each revenue source represents for each of these years. Then construct a graph (similar to Figures 8–1 and 8–2) that shows how these revenue sources have changed over the years.

Year	National Production	Personal Income Taxes	Social Security Taxes	Corporate Income Taxes	Indirect Business Taxes
1970	$1,015.5[a]	$ 92.6	$ 52.9	$30.6	$19.2
1975	1,598.4	125.9	101.6	43.6	23.8
1980	2,732.0	257.9	186.8	70.3	38.8
1985	3,998.1	345.6	311.5	73.6	56.1

[a]All figures are in billions of dollars.
Source: Economic Report of the President, 1987, pp. 244, 337.

Additional Readings

Boskin, Michael J., and Wildavsky, Aaron, eds. *The Federal Budget: Economics and Politics.* San Francisco: Institute for Contemporary Studies, 1982.

Goodman, John C., and Dolan, Edwin G., *Economics of Public Policy: The Micro View.* 3d ed. St. Paul: West, 1985. 207–17.

Hailstones, Thomas J., and Mastrianna, Frank V. *Contemporary Economic Problems and Issues.* Cincinnati: South-Western, 1985. 288–304.

Miller, Roger Leroy, and Shannon, Russell. *The Economics of Macro Issues.* 5th ed. St. Paul: West, 1986. Chapter 1.

Markets for Resources

Unit

IV

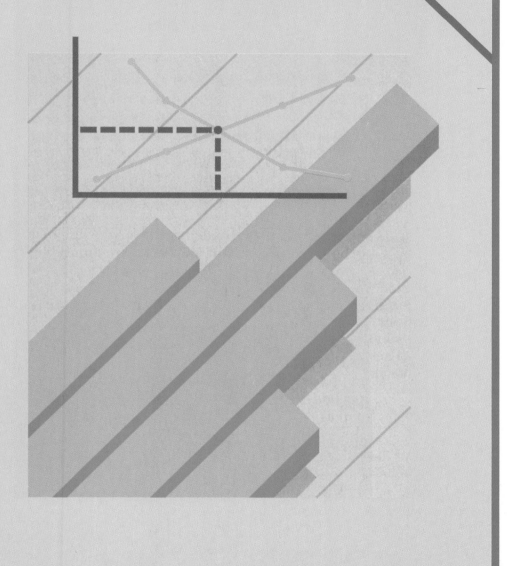

How can the tools and machines with which you work affect the value of your labor?

Labor Demand

■ Student's Goals ■

1. Explain how to compute the value of an hour's worth of work.

2. Explain how the marginal productivity of labor relates to the decision of how many workers to hire.

3. Explain the importance of the law of diminishing returns in making hiring decisions.

4. Explain how the law of downward sloping demand applies to the demand for labor.

The Age in the Minimum Wage

Would a higher minimum wage help teen-age workers? Many people strongly believe it would benefit teen-agers because employers would have to pay them higher wages. If you agree, consider these words written many years ago by the American humorist Finley Peter Dunne: "It ain't the things you know that land you in trouble but the things you know that ain't so."

Many anticipated benefits of a higher minimum wage turn out to be "things we know that ain't so." If Congress increases the minimum wage in the belief that teen-agers will benefit, many teen-agers will have trouble finding jobs.

This conclusion will be explained later in the chapter, after a presentation of labor demand. Usually, when people think of demand, they think of markets for goods and services, such as food, haircuts, and automobiles. In these markets, *individuals* are the consumers who demand the goods and services that businesses produce.

However, the labor market is a market for resources, not for finished goods and services. In resource markets, *businesses* are the demanders or consumers. It might seem odd to think of businesses as consumers, but they purchase land, buildings, equipment, machinery, raw materials, fuel, electricity, and many other resources. When they hire the services of workers, they are also demanding labor resources.

In resource markets, described in Chapter 2, property owners supply labor, land, equipment, and all other productive resources. Those who supply labor services are individuals, just like you, who own the rights to their labor time. You might not think of yourself as participating in a market when you go to work, but you are selling your labor services to an employer in the resource market.

The Value of Labor

In the resource market, employers demand labor services because of their benefits, just as consumers demand goods and services because of their advantages. To a business, however,

Would a higher minimum wage benefit teen-age workers? If the answer seems to be an obvious yes, then consider the warning of the American humorist Peter Finley Dunn: "It ain't the things you know that land you in trouble but the things you know that ain't so."

the benefits of one's work depend on how much that work can produce.

As an example, consider Paula, a high school student who earns money by washing cars at customers' homes. Using a bucket and sponge, Paula can wash an average of one car per hour. When she washes cars downtown, consumers are willing to pay $4 per car. When she washes cars in the suburbs, however, customers pay only $2 for each car washed. It's easy to see that the value of Paula's labor depends on the value consumers place on it. In the suburbs, an hour of Paula's time spent washing cars is worth $2 to consumers, while downtown an hour of her time is worth $4.

Now, suppose Paula thinks her productivity might increase if, instead of a bucket and sponge, she uses a water-powered scrubber that attaches to a hose. After giving the new technique a try, Paula discovers that she can wash two cars per hour with the scrubber. Table 9–1 compares the value of her labor downtown and in the suburbs using the two techniques.

When Paula works in the suburbs and uses the bucket-sponge method, an hour of her time is worth $2 to her business. But if Paula uses the power-scrubber technique, her productivity

The value of one's labor depends on its productivity and on the price consumers will pay for that productivity.

doubles and causes the value of her labor to rise to $4 per hour. Notice what happens, however, when Paula decides to use the power scrubber and also to work downtown. Not only does her productivity double (from washing one to two cars per hour), but also the value of a washed car to consumers doubles (from $2 to $4). By using the power-scrubber technique and by working downtown, Paula can increase her pay to $8 per hour. As you can see, the value of an hour's work is computed by multiplying the physical productivity of labor times the price consumers will pay for it.

$$\boxed{\text{Value of an hour's labor}} = \boxed{\begin{array}{c}\text{Productivity of labor}\\\text{per hour (number of}\\\text{units produced per hour)}\end{array}} \times \boxed{\begin{array}{c}\text{Price consumers will}\\\text{pay for one unit}\end{array}}$$

Table 9–1 Value of Paula's Labor per Hour

Method	Suburbs	Downtown
Bucket-sponge method	1 car × $2/car = $2/hr	1 car × $4/car = $4/hr
Power-scrubber method	2 cars × $2/car = $4/hr	2 cars × $4/car = $8/hr

The worker at this 3M Medical Surgical Division Plant is using a redesigned production line to produce medical supplies. The new production line has increased the value of the worker's services by making the worker more productive.

A Rule for Cleaning Cars

The productivity of labor is very important in determining how much labor a business should hire. Consider Dudley's Discount Detailing Shop, for example. Dudley used every cent he had and borrowed from his family and friends to open a shop that will provide discount automobile detailing services. Armed with waxes, hoses, sponges, electric buffers, toothbrushes, vinyl cleaners, and a building with a few detailing bays, Dudley plans to chase every speck of dirt and grime from his customers' cars. Dudley is sure that speedy service and an unusually low price will enable the shop to sell all the detailing services it can produce each day.

Dudley knows that he cannot do all of the work himself, so he has begun looking for helpers. "How many workers should I hire?" wonders Dudley. Although he has never made a business decision like this before, Dudley knows there is no simple answer. It seems obvious that if he hires a couple of workers, their productivity will be high enough to justify paying them

How many mechanics should this auto repair shop hire? With only one employee, the shop would be unable to do all the work demanded by customers. But with too many employees, the shop would become as crowded as a can of sardines. The shop's manager must decide on a number of employees somewhere between these two extremes. How can the manager make that decision?

the going wage. Dudley also knows that if he keeps hiring more and more people, his shop will eventually look like a can of sardines. In that case, his shop will become so crowded that if he hires one more helper, the productivity of that additional helper will be so low it will not pay to hire him or her.

Although Dudley wants to hire *some* workers, he also knows that he doesn't want *too many*. Instead, he has to choose a number somewhere between the two extremes of no workers at all and a shop crammed full of helpers. How will he decide what to do?

Here Comes the Law

This rule will help Dudley make his decision:

Rule: If the *value* of an additional worker is greater than the *wage* that must be paid, then hire another worker.

But this rule is not easy to follow because it is difficult to know the value of another worker's labor. Because Dudley does not know the exact amount of this value, he will have to use his judgment and try to make the right decision. Indeed, the survival and success of his business depend on his ability to choose the correct number of employees for his shop. If he has too few workers, he will sacrifice much valuable business, but if he has too many workers, wage costs will gobble up the shop's money. Table 9–2 presents some of the information that Dudley could use to make the right decision.

If Dudley hires more workers, the total number of clean cars produced each day increases. The second column shows that nothing is produced when no one works at all. With the addition of one worker (Dudley), a total of five clean cars is produced each day. Two workers clean a total of nine cars a day, three workers clean twelve cars a day, and so forth. More workers enable Dudley's team of labor and nonlabor resources to increase its total daily production. The third column is peculiar, though. It shows how many *additional* clean cars the team can produce each day as each additional worker is hired. Even though *total* production rises, the *additional* number of cars cleaned each day falls.

The declining numbers in column 3 illustrate *thinking at the margin*, which has been explained in Chapter 1. This term applies to Dudley's shop because it is the additional or **marginal**

Table 9–2 Production Statistics for Dudley's Discount Detailing Shop

Employees Working Each Day		Total Cars Cleaned Each Day		Additional cars Cleaned Each Day
0	-------	0		
1	-------	5	-------	5
2	-------	9	-------	4
3	-------	12	-------	3
4	-------	14	-------	2
5	-------	15	-------	1

As Dudley hires more people to work in his shop, the total number of cars cleaned in a day increases, as shown in the second column. But even though an additional worker increases daily production, the *additional* number of cars cleaned each day falls, as shown in the third column.

At this Apple Computer factory, an employee assembles a Macintosh computer. The marginal productivity of labor is the additional quantity of Macintosh computers that can be produced during a given time by hiring one more worker.

productivity of workers that must be weighed when deciding how many workers to hire.

> **Marginal productivity of labor:** The additional production obtained by hiring one more unit of labor.

Dudley's statistics are probably not typical of most producers. At first, the number of additional cars cleaned could increase as more labor makes it easier for workers to specialize. For example, a larger number of employees might permit Dudley to divide their work into related tasks, such as washing, scrubbing, applying polish, and buffing. Workers could then concentrate on a particular task, and this specialization could increase the marginal productivity of labor as the first few workers are hired.

But eventually the marginal productivity of workers will fall, as more workers are employed.[1] Hiring the second worker adds

[1]If enough new workers are employed, the marginal productivity of labor will eventually become *negative*. In that case, an extra worker will decrease total production.

four clean cars to the total that could be produced with one worker, and hiring the third worker adds only three cars to the total that can be cleaned with two workers. Similarly, in any business the marginal productivity of labor eventually falls. Why is this so, and what meaning does it have for the number of workers hired?

The marginal productivity of labor diminishes for Dudley because he has a limited quantity of equipment. As more workers are hired, there aren't enough electric buffers and tools to go around for everyone. With the addition of more and more workers who compete for these available resources, the necessity of sharing increases. Workers then begin to spend more time in idleness, waiting for an opportunity to use the shop's limited resources.

Sharing space also becomes a problem as more workers get in each other's way. Dudley would certainly never be foolish enough to hire 1,000 workers for his small shop, but imagine what would happen if he did. Production would probably come to a complete halt because no one would have enough room to move. It might even take most of the day to figure out a way to fit the last few workers into the shop.

Why doesn't Dudley buy more tools and obtain more space in order to avoid this crowding? Even if Dudley is willing and able to make the additional investment, his management skills remain limited. By hiring more workers, Dudley will eventually crowd his ability to manage the business, in the same way that more workers crowd an existing amount of tools and space.

The crowding of a business's limited resources causes the marginal productivity of labor to fall. No producer, big or small, can avoid this crowding if it continually adds more and more workers to its limited resources. The decrease in marginal productivity caused by crowding is known as the **law of diminishing returns.**

> **Law of diminishing returns:** As more workers share the limited resources of a business, the marginal productivity of labor eventually diminishes.

This law tells us that if a producer that has a fixed quantity of one or more of its resources increases the amounts of labor used, eventually the additions to total production will fall. Even if the producer increases these nonlabor resources, the marginal productivity of labor will fall if the number of workers increases faster than the resources. In that case, the increasing *ratio* of labor to other resources will still produce the crowding that diminishes the marginal productivity of labor.

The Details of Hiring Labor

Like most other businesses, Dudley can only estimate the value of labor to his shop. Earlier in this chapter we explained that you determine the value of labor by multiplying its productivity times the price consumers will pay for this productivity. If Dudley could somehow obtain the useful information shown in Table 9–3, he could accurately calculate the value of labor at his shop. For example, the marginal productivity of the first worker is five cars cleaned per day. If customers pay an average of $20 for each detailing job, then the value of a day's work from the first detailer is $100 (5 × $20).

Because of the law of diminishing returns, however, the productivity of additional workers declines as more are hired. As the marginal productivity of labor declines, the value of work

(text continues on page 235)

Table 9–3 The Diminishing Value of Labor at Dudley's Discount Detailing Shop

Employees Working Each Day	Marginal Productivity		Price Paid by Consumer		Worth of Marginal Product
1	5	×	$20	=	$100
2	4	×	20	=	80
3	3	×	20	=	60
4	2	×	20	=	40
5	1	×	20	=	20

Because of the law of diminishing returns, the marginal productivity of labor decreases as Dudley hires more workers. The second column shows this decline. You calculate the value of hiring an additional worker by multiplying the marginal productivity by the $20 customers will pay for each detailing job. Because marginal productivity fails as Dudley hires more workers, the value of an additional worker diminishes, as is shown in the last column on the right.

Skateboards, Karl Marx, and the Laws of Motion

The *Los Angeles Times* describes him as "an-oh-so-hip, tightly muscled, 5-foot-6 blend of exceptional athlete, teen cult figure, savvy businessman and out-to-party 19-year-old." He is Christian Hosoi, ranked by the National Skateboard Association as one of the top skateboarders in the nation.

Christian tried out his first skateboard while he as a second grader in Hawaii. Made by his father from surfboard fiberglass, the skateboard was a far cry from its primitive ancestors that date back to the 1920s. In those days, skateboards were nothing more than roller skates mounted on wooden packing crates. Not until the 1960s were clay wheels used on stiff wooden boards. Using fiberglass and laminated wood made the boards lighter, and adding urethane wheels increased speed and mobility. Then, in the 1970s, a better wheel assembly opened up the new world of vertical skating, in which one performs on U-shaped ramps and curved walls.

When Christian's family moved to California, he practiced often at a skatepark in Marina Del Rey, where, he stated, "I was just a grommet hanging out. A little skate rat." With all the practice and athletic ability, Christian soon became an expert in the laws of skateboard motion.

In the last century, the laws of motion were of considerable interest to another individual. In that instance, the laws of motion pertained to the development of a market economy, and the individual was Karl Marx. Marx was born in Germany and received his doctorate in philosophy there. After turbulent years as a journalist in Germany and France, he came in 1850 to England, where he and his family would live for the next twenty years. Despite the income provided by Marx's friend and colleague, Friedrich Engels, the family endured poverty while Marx worked tirelessly in the London Museum on his never-finished three-volume work, *Capital*.

Capital was Marx's attempt to explain what he believed were the "laws of motion" of a private-property market economy, which Marx called a *capitalist economy*. By the laws of motion, Marx meant the hidden historical forces that were moving market economies to an inevitable destination. Skilled skateboarders are often unaware of the laws of physics that explain their performance. Similarly, Marx believed that the participants in a market economy are unaware of the historical forces that shape their behavior.

Central to Marx's laws of motion of a market economy was his assertion that the entire value of a product is produced by labor. Because capital goods are private property, however, their owners, whom Marx called *capitalists,* are able to "exploit" workers by withholding some of the value created by their labor. It is not that capitalists are bad or that they consciously cheat their workers. In order to survive the rigors of competition, a business is forced to pay workers less than the full value they create. And if workers are to find employment, they have to accept wages below the value they produce. According to Marx, therefore, profits are surplus value created by workers but kept by those who own the tools, machines, factories, and other capital goods that workers require for their labor.

Marx predicted that as an economy industrializes and more capital goods are accumulated, the yoke of exploitation will tighten around workers' necks. Profits will increase as a fraction of the nation's total income, and the share going to wages will fall. Although a smaller slice of a rapidly growing pie could still mean more income for labor, Marx believed that average pay rates will also decline. Moreover, because capitalists will increasingly substitute capital for labor, employment will diminish. As workers obtain a shrinking share of the nation's income, as paychecks de-

cline, and as employment diminishes, the growing misery of workers will inevitably bring the overthrow of any economy based on private property and markets.

Marx offered no argument or evidence to support his assertion that the value of a good is produced entirely by workers. Indeed, you could assert the opposite—that all value is created by capitalists. Today, economists agree that each of the four major resources—land, labor, capital, and management—contributes to the value of a product. Profit is not a surplus squeezed from workers. Instead, it represents earnings received by owners of capital when they innovate, organize, take risks, and successfully anticipate what consumers value.

A market economy encourages individuals to complete these important tasks successfully, because it is a system of losses as well as profits. Profits reward risk takers for correctly identifying and efficiently satisfying consumer preferences. In contrast, losses punish those who do not efficiently satisfy the demands of consumers.

Take the production of skateboards as an example. Because there was no guarantee that consumers would buy their products, private owners of capital risked their wealth by purchasing the machines, tools, and buildings necessary to produce skateboards. Profits have rewarded only those who have satisfied consumers by introducing new types of wheels, developing new kinds of boards, and keeping costs low. By assuming risks, by innovating, and by weeding out inefficiency, private owners of capital have helped create a product that consumers value. As a result, both workers and owners of capital (and other resources) have contributed to the value of skateboards.

Wages measure the contribution of workers, and profits measure the contribution of capital owners. Marx predicted that labor's share of the nation's income will drop as the market economy develops. Figure A shows, however, that over our nation's history, labor's share of total national income has remained fairly

Figure A Labor's Share of National Income, 1840–1980

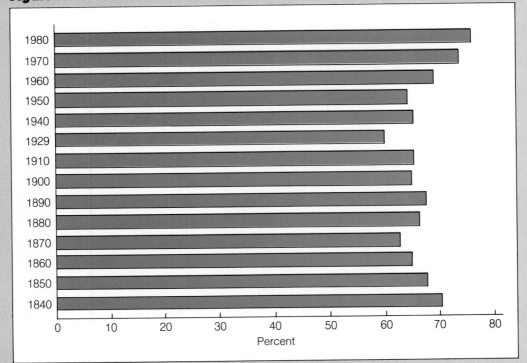

Source: Richard K. Vedder, *The American Economy in Historical Perspective*, p. 303; *Economic Report of the President*, 1987, p. 270.

constant at between two-thirds and three-fourths. Indeed, if any change is noted, labor's share has gone up, not down.

References

Ballo, Paula. "A Skate Rat Grows Up." *Los Angeles Times Magazine*, March 1, 1987. 16–19.

Rose, Jonathan. "Communism's Promises, Communism's Problems." *Scholastic Update* 119, no. 2 (September 22, 1986): 10–13.

Sowell, Thomas. *Marxism: Philosophy and Economics*. New York: Quill, 1985.

Vedder, Richard K. *The American Economy in Historical Perspective*. Belmont, CA.: Wadsworth, 1976.

from an additional employee also falls. Table 9–3 shows how the law of diminishing returns reduces this value.[2]

The number of workers Dudley will want to hire depends on the wage he has to pay. Suppose the going wage for a day's work is $40. In that case, it pays Dudley to hire the first worker because this would add $100 to receipts but only $40 to costs. Don't make the mistake of thinking that the $100 is produced entirely by the first worker. It is produced by a team consisting of this worker and all the other resources of the shop. As a result, the difference between the income of $100 and the wage of $40 is not all profit. Instead, Dudley must use this $60 ($100 − $40) to help pay for the shop's equipment, supplies, building, and other resources. But as long as the hiring of another employee enables the shop to bring in more money than what must be paid out as a wage, the shop gains by employing that additional worker.

Remember that the worth of another worker's time declines as more people are hired. Table 9–3 shows that although the worth of the first worker's time is $100 per day, the value of the second worker's time is only $80. But even though a second worker's time is worth less, the shop still benefits if Dudley hires this additional person. That's because the second employee's work still enables Dudley to add more to the shop's receipts ($80) than the wage ($40) he must pay.

Now look at the worth of a third worker. Would Dudley want to hire this person? The correct answer is Yes. Although a third day of work adds even less value to the business ($60), only $40 is added to wage costs. As long as the worth of another employee's work is greater than the going wage, it pays Dudley to hire that person.

What is the maximum number of workers Dudley will want to hire? The worth of a fourth person's work falls to $40—an amount exactly equal to the daily wage that must be paid. As far as Dudley is concerned, it makes no difference if a fourth worker is hired.

But four is certainly the *maximum* number of workers Dudley will want to have working in his shop each day. If a fifth worker is hired, for example, the additional work will be worth only $20—an amount less than the $40 wage that must be paid.

[2]For simplicity, this calculation ignores the value of materials and other nonlabor resources used up by the worker when producing the additional detailing services.

Dudley will certainly not want to hire more than four workers because by doing so he would add more to his costs than to his revenues.

When the going wage is $40 per day, therefore, Dudley should hire a maximum of four people. But what happens if the going wage rises from $40 to $60 per day? In this case, a fourth worker should not be employed because the work of this person is worth only $40, an amount less than the $60 that must be paid. If the daily wage rate increases from $40 to $60, therefore, Dudley will hire three instead of four workers.

Drawing Conclusions

Businesses wish they could easily obtain information like that shown for Dudley's shop, but they seldom know the exact value of labor. Instead, successful businesses often rely on experience, trial and error, and luck to make the kind of hiring decision described at Dudley's business.

But our purpose in describing these calculations is not to explain how to run a business. Instead, our objective is to explain the demand for labor, which is an important part of our economic system.

Dudley's demand for labor has been presented in Table 9–3. If you think of the fourth column of the table as the daily wage rate, you can then look at the first column to see the maximum number of workers Dudley will hire at that wage. If the daily wage if $40, for instance, Dudley will hire a maximum of four workers. At a daily wage of $20, the maximum number of workers hired will be five. But at a daily wage of $80, only two will be hired.

Table 9–4 has reversed the order of these columns, so you can first look at the wage paid and then determine the number of people that should be hired at that wage. The table thus lists the various quantities of labor Dudley's business would buy each day at different possible wage rates. This description probably sounds a lot like the definition of the demand for a good or service given in Chapter 3. It *should* sound the same because Table 9–4 shows us the shop's **demand for labor.**

Table 9—4 Demand for Workers at Dudley's Detailing Shop

Daily Wage	Maximum Number of Workers Employed
$100	1
80	2
60	3
40	4
20	5

At a daily wage rate of $100, Dudley will hire a maximum of only one worker. If the daily wage is $80, however, he will hire two workers. Because the table lists the maximum number of workers Dudley will hire at different wage rates, it represents the demand for labor at Dudley's Detailing Shop.

> **Demand for labor:** A list of the various quantities of labor that would be bought at different possible wage rates during a particular time.

Chapter 4 has explained how to graph consumers' demands for goods and services. The same rules also apply to graphing the demand for labor. In Figure 9–1 the number of workers (the quantity of labor) is measured along the horizontal axis, and the wage rate (the price of labor) is measured along the vertical axis. By checking Table 9–4, you can see that only one worker will be hired if the going wage is $100 per day. You can plot this point on the graph by moving to the right along the horizontal axis to a quantity of 1, and then by moving up the grid line at that quantity to a wage rate of $100 per day. Here is where you place the first point of the graph. You then plot the shop's demand for labor by placing the remaining points on the graph and connecting them with straight lines.

Figure 9–1 shows that more workers will be hired at lower wage rates, while at higher wage rates fewer will be hired. This relationship exists because the value of an employee's work depends on the number of people employed. When more people are employed, the value added by hiring another worker is less than when fewer are employed. This occurs because of the law of diminishing returns. At a wage rate of $80 per day, for example, Dudley's shop will hire two workers per day. The value

The Number of Jobs

At various times union workers have agreed to cuts in their wages. Don't unions hurt themselves when they make these agreements?

Noneconomic Way of Thinking

It makes no sense for union workers to agree to a wage cut. The lower wage means only that union workers get paid less for doing the same amount of work.

Economic Way of Thinking

The lower wage might not reduce the total income of all union workers because the lower wage will cause employers to hire more labor. The lower wage will be offset by the increase in jobs, so that workers' overall income might be unaffected. It might even rise.

This conclusion follows logically from the economic principle of demand, which tells us that more labor is hired at lower wage rates. By agreeing to a wage cut, a union might help its members if enough new jobs become available for the union's workers.

Questions

1. If union workers bargain for a pay increase, what happens to the number of workers employed?
2. Why does a lower wage cause employers to demand more workers?
3. How does the level of the union wage affect the incentive of firms to automate by using machines in place of labor?

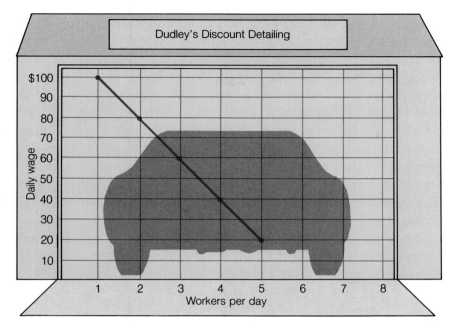

Figure 9–1 The Demand for Labor at Dudley's Detailing Shop

The graph shows the demand for labor at Dudley's Detailing Shop. Dudley will hire more workers at lower wage rates than he will at higher rates. At $80 per day, for example, he will hire no more than two workers. But at $20 per day, he will hire a maximum of five workers. Dudley will hire three more workers when the wage falls to $20 because the lower wage compensates for the lower value of work added by a third, fourth, and fifth worker. Why do diminishing returns cause the value of an additional person's work to decrease as more people are hired?

added by a third worker falls below the $80 wage, so it does not pay Dudley to hire this extra person. But if the daily wage falls to $20, the lower wage compensates for the lower value of a third person's work. As a result, Dudley will hire a third worker. In fact, at the lower wage it pays Dudley to hire a fourth and a fifth worker, too.

Now, consider the opposite case in which the original wage is $20 per day. At this wage Dudley will hire five workers per day. But if the wage rises to $80, it will no longer pay Dudley to employ all five of these people. The work of the third, fourth, and fifth employee would be worth less than the $80 Dudley would pay each of them. If the daily wage rate increases from $20 to $80, therefore, the shop will reduce the number of workers employed from five to two.

The demand for labor at Dudley's shop illustrates the answer to the minimum wage question posed at the beginning of this chapter. A higher minimum wage can eliminate some jobs for teen-agers because it can reduce the quantity of teen-age labor demanded by employers. Suppose, for example, that the going wage Dudley must pay is only $20 per day. For an eight-hour day, therefore, employees receive $2.50 per hour ($20 ÷ 8). At this wage, Dudley wants to hire five workers per day. Notice what happens, however, if the government sets the minimum wage at, say, $4 per hour. For eight hours of work per day, Dudley has to pay no less than $32 ($4 × 8). But at this minimum wage rate, it no longer pays Dudley to hire a fifth worker. The value of that person's labor is less than the minimum wage, so Dudley hires four, instead of five, workers.

When the minimum wage rate is set above the going wage, businesses purchase less labor. It's true that the minimum wage forces employers to pay at least this legal wage. Those workers who obtain or keep jobs paying the minimum wage certainly gain. On the other hand, the law, in effect, tells those whose labor is worth less than the minimum wage that they will not be employed at all. That's because businesses refuse to hire workers whose labor is worth less than the minimum wage. Those most affected are usually teen-agers, who have not yet

Would this person benefit from an increase in the minimum wage? If he keeps his job, he will surely gain. But a higher minimum wage reduces the amount of labor that businesses want to hire. If his productivity is worth less than the higher minimum wage, he will lose his job.

If wage rates rise without a corresponding increase in productivity, businesses will want to substitute capital goods for labor when producing their products. For example, higher wage rates will encourage auto producers to use more robots and less labor when producing automobiles.

obtained many of the skills that make their labor more valuable than the minimum wage.

Timely Substitutes for Labor

The demand for labor slopes downward to the right because the value of labor declines as more people are employed. The value of labor declines in this way because, according to the law of diminishing returns, the marginal productivity of labor is reduced, as more workers crowd the limited resources of a business. But there is another reason that becomes important over time: other resources can be substituted for labor.[3]

[3]A third reason has been ignored. As a business hires more workers, it has to reduce its price in order to sell the additional goods or services produced by the additional workers. The reduced price then pushes down the value added by an additional employee. As a result, the business will hire additional workers only at lower wage rates.

More labor and less equipment could be used in the construction of new roads. One of the factors determining the relative amount of labor used is the wage rate that an employer must pay. When a higher wage is not the result of increased labor productivity, the higher wage encourages businesses to substitute capital for labor.

Just as you can substitute peanut butter and jelly for tuna fish when buying a sandwich, so, too, can a business substitute machines for labor when producing a good or service. And just as your willingness to substitute one item for another depends on the prices you pay for these items, so, also, does the willingness of a business to substitute one type of productive resource for another depend on the prices of these resources.

For example, suppose the wage goes up at Dudley's shop. Dudley will then seek ways to substitute other, less expensive resources for labor. He will not make these substitutions immediately. But over time Dudley will be more likely to purchase machines and other equipment that reduce the number of workers demanded. The longer the time Dudley has to adapt to the higher wage cost, the more likely it is that he will find ways to automate his team of resources. On the other hand, if the price of labor falls relative to the prices of these other productive resources, then Dudley will substitute labor for other resources.

Compare the relative quantities of labor and equipment used by road crews in Mexico and the United States. In Mexico the price of labor is much less than the price of equipment, but

Automation

Automation is a particular type of technological change in which robots and other automatic machines are substituted for labor. Many people believe that automation reduces employment. Is this belief correct?

Noneconomic Way of Thinking

Automated machines, such as robots, have a lot of advantages over workers. They don't get tired, don't take coffee breaks, aren't paid wages, don't take vacations, and don't ask for fringe benefits. Because of the enormous changes in electronics in recent years, machines that were replacing human muscle are now replacing the human brain. That is why automation is spreading from factories to banks, grocery stores, and other service industries. This change might be beneficial for businesses using automation, but it eliminates jobs and causes unemployment.

Economic Way of Thinking

Automation is a continuation and extension of the technological change that has been occurring for centuries. Although this change has eliminated certain jobs, it has increased, not decreased, total employment. Employment has been increased because technological change makes production more efficient and less expensive. Lower production costs drive down prices, and those lower prices stimulate sales and employment.

Take the automation of a car wash. Because automation reduces costs and increases sales, the car wash hires more cashiers, supervisors, and people to vacuum. Although fewer people are used to wash each car, more workers might be employed because more cars are washed at the lower price. Generally, automation has increased, not decreased, total employment.

Questions

1. Are workers in the U.S. automobile and steel industries more or less likely to keep their jobs if for some reason their work productivity rises?

2. Think of a situation in which automation could actually reduce employment. (*Hint:* What if automation reduces costs and, therefore, prices, but buyers don't buy much more than they did before?)

this is not true in the United States. That's one reason why Mexico uses proportionately more labor in its roadwork than does the United States.

You should now understand why any business buys more labor at lower wage rates and less labor at higher wage rates. But how is the going wage determined in the first place? And what makes it increase or decrease? Why are some people unemployed? The next chapter will answer these questions.

Chapter Summary

1. Businesses consume labor and other resources in order to make the finished goods and services we buy. When you sell your labor services to a business, you are selling a service you own in a market for resources.

2. You determine the value of labor by multiplying the physical productivity of labor by the price consumers are willing to pay for that productivity. Therefore, the value of labor increases when its physical productivity increases or when consumers are willing to pay a higher price for what the labor produces.

3. A business will want to hire an additional employee if that worker enables the business to bring in more money than it must pay out. A business will not continue to hire additional labor if the next additional worker's wage is higher than the revenue provided by that worker's marginal productivity.

4. The marginal productivity of labor diminishes because additional workers must increasingly share the equipment and space that the employer provides for them. Because the resources of any business are limited, the marginal productivity of labor will eventually drop. This predictable drop in marginal productivity caused by crowding is the *law of diminishing returns*.

5. An employer will hire an additional employee if that worker brings in more money than what must be paid out as a wage. As the employer hires more workers, the value of each extra worker's time falls. Consequently, the employer will not continue to hire additional labor at the point that an

additional worker's wage is higher than the value of that worker's productivity.

6. The demand for labor shows that as the wage rate increases, the maximum number of workers hired decreases. Because of the demand for labor, a minimum wage law can decrease the number of teen-agers hired by employers. Those teen-agers who keep their jobs and receive the higher minimum wage will gain; those teen-agers who lose their jobs or who are not even hired because their labor is worth less than the minimum wage will lose.

Review Questions

1. When you go to work, are you participating in a market? Explain.
2. How can you figure out the value of an hour of your labor?
3. What is meant by the term *marginal productivity of labor?*
4. Why is it important to a business to know something about the marginal productivity of labor when it is deciding how many workers to hire?
5. What is the *law of diminishing returns?*
6. How does the law of diminishing returns affect the number of workers a business will hire?
7. What is meant by the term *demand for labor?*
8. Does the demand for labor have any characteristic in common with the demand for a good or service? Explain.
9. Give two reasons why the demand for labor slopes downward to the right.

Discussion Questions

1. What factors can change the value of a person's labor?
2. Why does the marginal productivity of labor usually fall as more workers are hired? Can you think of any situation in

which hiring an additional worker will increase marginal productivity? Explain briefly.

3. In industry A, one unit of labor costs much more than does one unit of machinery, but in industry B the costs of each are equal. Would you expect both industries to employ labor and machinery in the same proportions? Why or why not?

4. If the going wage is $3.50 to sweep floors, what will be the effect of establishing a minimum wage of $4.00 per hour? Explain briefly.

5. Discuss your agreement or disagreement with the following argument: Although we may have jobs at particular businesses, our final boss is really the consumer. Our employer is only an intermediary who partially buffers us from finicky buyers. It is really the consumer who determines our wage.

Activities

1. Write a short essay defending or attacking the following statement: The success or failure of someone's business might depend on that person's ability to hire the correct number of employees.

2. Write a one-paragraph response to the following statement: If one can hire a worker whose productivity is worth $50 per day, it is foolish to hire another worker instead whose productivity is worth less than $50 per day.

3. Analyze the following statement, and use a graph to illustrate your analysis: If Congress increases the minimum wage, there might be many unhappy teen-agers.

4. Use the following information to compute the marginal productivity of ditch diggers. If consumers will pay $1 per ditch that is dug, what is the value of each of the marginal productivities you computed? Use these results to graph the demand for ditch diggers. If the hourly wage is $2, what will be the maximum number of ditch diggers hired? What if the hourly wage is $4? Explain why the numbers of workers hired differ at the two wage rates.

Number of Workers	Total Ditches Dug per Hour	Marginal Productivity of Labor
0	0	
1	5	_____
2	9	_____
3	12	_____
4	14	_____
5	15	_____

Additional Readings

Browne, Lynn E. "Conflicting Views of Technological Progress and the Labor Market." *New England Economic Review* (July/August 1984): 5–16.

Eggert, Jim. *Investigating Microeconomics*. Los Altos, Calif.: William Kauffman, 1979. 41–49.

Goodman, John C., and Dolan, Edwin G. *Economics of Public Policy: The Micro View*. St. Paul: West, 1985. Chapter 14.

Hazlitt, Henry. *Economics in One Lesson*. New York: Arlington House, 1979. Chapters 7 and 19.

Schiller, Bradley R. *The Economy Today*. New York: Random House, 1980. 520–30.

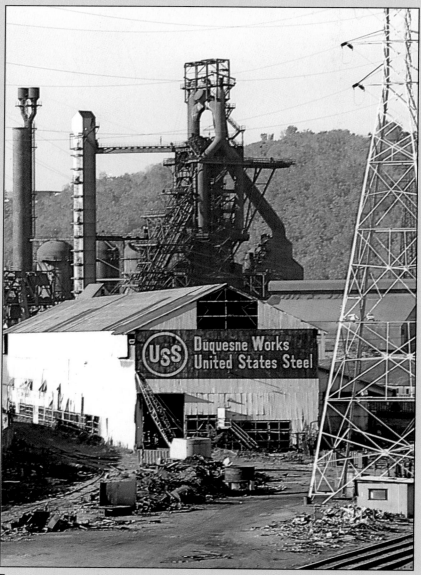

Does most unemployment arise when businesses lay off their workers?

Labor Markets and Unemployment

∎ Student's Goals ∎

1. Define the term *going wage*, and explain why the equilibrium wage could also be the going wage.

2. Describe the goals of labor unions, and explain the ways by which they achieve these goals.

3. Explain the meaning of the *unemployment rate*, and describe at least three ways by which individuals become unemployed.

4. Compare and contrast the following types of unemployment: *seasonal unemployment, frictional unemployment, structural unemployment,* and *weak-demand unemployment.*

5. Explain the meaning of *full employment.*

Heavy Metal

"I'm not going to give them any more concessions," growled a steelworker in an aging factory in Cleveland. "No way. They can shut that plant down for all I care."[1]

This steelworker was referring to the company's proposal to cut wages. The company had made this proposal while the steel industry was being battered by one of the steepest downturns of this century. A weak worldwide demand for steel, coupled with enormous growth in other nations' steel-making capacities, had diminished the demand for American steel and intensified competition in world markets. These changes were felt in the labor market for steelworkers, where declining employment cut membership in the steelworkers' union by more than 50 percent in five years. In addition, some wage reductions had occurred in the early 1980s, but average hourly labor costs in the steel industry remained well above $20 per hour.

[1]J. Ernest Beazley and Mark Russell, "Steel Union is Balking at Further Givebacks, Terming Them Futile," *Wall Street Journal*, July 29, 1986.

In the 1980s, this and many other steel plants were idled when the American steel industry declined. As steel production slumped, however, unemployment increased among steelworkers. Although news stories often emphasized this loss of jobs, most unemployment does not usually result from the loss of jobs.

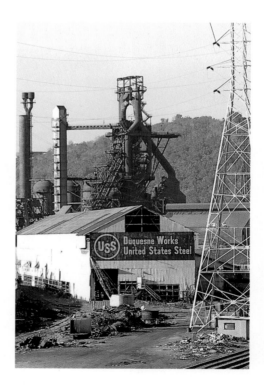

Because the work is hot, dangerous, and dirty, most nations pay steelworkers higher wages than they pay other manufacturing workers. In 1970, the wages of U.S. steelworkers were about 25 percent above those of other U.S. manufacturing workers, a premium common in other nations. After soaring to more than 60 percent in 1980, the premium fell to about 50 percent in 1985.

Although people dispute the causes of the steel industry's problems, there is no doubt it shows how job loss creates unemployment. This chapter explains, however, that most unemployment does not normally result from the loss of jobs. The chapter also examines labor markets and unions, and it does this by beginning with a circular flow map.

Checking the Map

Figure 10–1 reproduces the circular flow map of Chapter 2, but we have added circles at the top and bottom of the map.

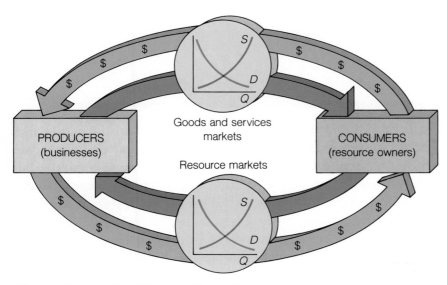

Figure 10–1   The Circular Flow Map

This circular flow map is similar to the one in Chapter 2, but this one includes circles at the top and bottom of the flow. The demand and supply curves in the top circle represent the many markets in which consumers demand and businesses supply goods and services. The demand and supply curves in the bottom circle represent the many markets in which businesses demand and consumers supply resources.

Because most of us are buyers, we are more familiar with the markets for goods and services shown at the top of the map. As consumers in these markets, we *demand* food, clothes, gasoline, auto repair services, and many other things that businesses *supply*. The circle at the top, labeled *Goods and services markets*, shows demand and supply curves. The demand curve represents our demand for a particular good or service, and the supply curve represents the supply of that good or service produced by businesses. The bottom circle represents resource markets in which businesses, not individuals, are the demanders. In these markets, businesses purchase resources in order to make the products they supply in the goods and services markets at the top. In resource markets, businesses purchase resources, such as raw materials, buildings, machines, fuel, and labor services. Markets for labor services are especially important because most of the income that we earn (and then spend in the top markets for goods and services) comes from our participation in labor markets. When we go to work, therefore, we are selling our labor services in the bottom market in order to obtain money to buy goods and services in the top market.

The Going Wage

Until the last chapter, we have concentrated on the goods and services markets shown at the top of the circular flow map. We did this by explaining the demand and supply of a particular item, such as hamburgers or milk. In this chapter we will look at the demand and supply of labor in the resource markets shown at the bottom of the map. In doing so, we will explain how wage rates are determined in labor markets.

Wage rates are prices of labor services. At lower wage rates businesses purchase more labor, and at higher wage rates they purchase less. This relationship is the demand for labor, which was the subject of the last chapter. On the other hand, the supply of labor tells us that workers offer less labor at lower wage rates and more labor at higher wage rates. As a result, demand and supply in labor markets are very much like demand and supply in goods and services markets.

It's no secret why people are willing to supply more hours of labor at higher wage rates and fewer hours at lower wage rates. Take a specific labor market, such as that for workers in fast-food restaurants in a particular city. If these restaurants, sometimes called speed eateries, suddenly want more hours of labor each day, they can persuade some current employees to work more hours. Also, they can draw others not now working at these restaurants away from other jobs, such as baby-sitting, bagging groceries, and clerking at retail stores. They might also persuade others who are not working at all to join the labor force and begin working at the restaurants.

Time is not free, so in order to supply additional hours to the restaurants, these people must sacrifice alternative jobs or nonmarket activities, such as going to school, doing chores around the house, watching television, playing sports, and doing homework. This means, as Chapter 1 has pointed out, that people bear an *opportunity cost* when they supply their labor time to employers.

At first, it will probably take only a small increase in the wage rate for restaurants to persuade people to bear the opportunity cost of supplying a little more labor. That's because

If fast-food restaurants in a particular community want to hire more labor, they will have to pay higher wage rates in order to attract the additional help. Higher wage rates are necessary to compensate workers for the higher opportunity costs of their time.

there are some alternative uses of time with relatively low values, and it won't take big wage increases to compensate people for bearing these small costs. But if a continually increasing number of hours is to be diverted to working at speed eateries each day, then the cost of supplying additional hours will rise. It will rise because people will have to give up progressively better and higher-paying alternative jobs as well as progressively more important nonmarket uses of time.

No wonder businesses must pay higher wages if together they demand more hours of labor in a given job market. The opportunity cost of additional hours increases as more hours are supplied, so employers must pay more per hour to persuade people to sell this additional, more costly labor. Thus, people will supply more labor at higher wages and less labor at lower wages.

Table 10–1 shows a hypothetical daily supply of labor for fast-food restaurants in Eaton City, USA. It also shows the labor demand of all fast-food restaurants in this area. Together, these numbers show the labor market for fast-food workers in Eaton City. As you can see, higher wages increase the total hours of labor workers want to sell, and they decrease the total hours of labor businesses want to buy.

Figure 10–2 presents these numbers visually to show the demand and supply of labor more clearly. Just as there is an

Table 10–1   The Demand and Supply of Labor
at Fast-Food Restaurants (Eaton City, USA)

Hourly Wage Rate	Total Hours Supplied Each Day	Total Hours Demanded Each Day
$1.00	1,000	10,000
2.00	3,000	8,000
3.00	5,000	5,000
4.00	6,000	3,000
5.00	6,500	1,500
6.00	7,000	1,000

This table lists the various amounts of labor that will be supplied at different possible wage rates by citizens in Eaton City, USA. The second column shows that at lower wage rates, citizens will want to work fewer hours than they will at higher wage rates. The table also lists the various amounts of labor that will be purchased by all fast-food restaurants in Eaton City. The third column shows that at lower wage rates, the restaurants will want to purchase more hours of labor than they will at higher wage rates.

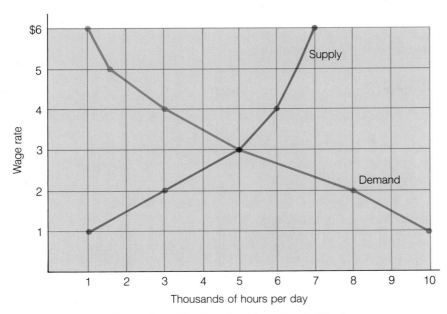

Figure 10–2 The Labor Market for Fast-Food Workers
(Eaton City, USA)

The demand and supply of labor listed in Table 10–1 have been plotted on the graph above. Because people in Eaton City want to work more hours at higher wage rates than they do at lower wage rates, the supply curve of labor slopes upward to the right. On the other hand, the demand curve for labor slopes downward to the right because restaurants want to purchase more labor at lower wage rates than they do at higher wage rates. The graph clearly shows that the equilibrium wage rate is $3 per hour. Only at $3 per hour are the demand and the supply of labor balanced.

equilibrium price that balances the demand and the supply of a product in goods and services markets, so, too, is there an equilibrium wage that equates the demand and the supply of labor in resource markets. Figure 10–2 shows that this equilibrium wage is $3 per hour because that is where the demand and supply curves cross.

If the wage rate is less than $3 per hour, there will be a shortage of labor. At an hourly wage of $1, for instance, businesses will demand 10,000 hours of labor per day, but workers will be willing to supply only 1,000 hours. The difference between 10,000 and 1,000 is 9,000 hours per day, and that is the labor shortage that will occur if the wage rate is only $1 per hour. Because of this shortage, fast-food restaurants will compete for employees, and this will push the wage rate up until it equals its equilibrium level of $3, at which point the shortage is eliminated.

(text continues on page 263)

Labor Shortages

Because of lower birth rates in the 1970s, fewer teen-agers are entering the labor market. Does this fact mean there will be a shortage of teen-age workers?

Noneconomic Way of Thinking

Because there will be fewer teen-agers to take jobs in restaurants, gas stations, and other places, businesses will certainly confront shortages of this type of labor for years to come. Many jobs will simply go begging.

Economic Way of Thinking

The smaller supply of teen-age labor will not mean a labor shortage. That's because the going wage will rise as employers compete more intensely for fewer workers. The going wage will rise until the smaller amount of workers demanded at the higher wage just matches the smaller amount supplied. Given the higher cost of labor, employers will not fill certain, less important jobs. The wage rate can always adjust in this way to prevent a labor market shortage.

Questions

1. If a maximum wage on teen-age labor is imposed by the government, will the labor shortage still persist?
2. What effect will the shrinking supply of younger workers have on firms' incentives to automate production processes? Why?
3. At the same time that a shortage of young workers is projected, a surplus of older workers is also projected. Explain how the larger number of older workers will affect wage rates.
4. Why is it unlikely that any labor shortage will persist over time?

Wages, Workers, and the Standard of Living

In the early morning darkness a weary worker lumbers off to spend another day in a nearby stuffy factory. Surrounding the factory are the slumlike hovels of "wage slaves" who have been trapped in the dreary, unhealthy environment. Many workers at the factory are women and children who somehow survive the sweaty, boring work for twelve or thirteen hours a day, six days a week. In return for meager wages, workers are sometimes brutally whipped, physically stunted, and emotionally battered. There is no relief, no hope—only a dreadful succession of days that are endured like the sound of constantly dripping water.

The picture is grim, indeed, but does it accurately describe the existence of a typical American factory worker of the last century? In the early days of our nation's history, factory workers toiled about thirteen hours a day. By today's standards their pay and working conditions were miserable.

But the development of our economy began to make significant changes. By the time of the Civil War, the average workday had fallen to around ten or eleven hours. During the same period, the earnings of workers also increased. Other changes occurred in the last century as factories began producing goods, such as cotton. The ability to pur-

chase cotton goods freed many women from spinning fibers and weaving cloth at home. Sewing machines and other appliances also increased the productivity of labor. Instead of being forced to work in dreary, unhealthy factories, some women *chose* to work outside the home because they and their families benefited from the employment.

Following the Civil War, wages increased greatly, and the workweek continued to drop, falling from about sixty-six hours in 1860 to about fifty-one hours in 1920. Children were still employed, but after 1870 they represented only about 5 percent of the labor force. Historian Stanley Lebergott thinks it unlikely that any other nation had ever had so few of its children in the labor force. According to Lebergott, "The proportion was . . . so small not because of legislative intervention but because parents' attitudes and income kept them from sending their children to work."

The massive stream of immigrants during our history bears witness to the relatively favorable and improving conditions of American labor. These conditions improved over time because of the efficiency of the American economy. Under the tug and pull of profits and losses, resource owners directed their land, labor, capital, and management skills to

Figure A Annual Earnings Adjusted for Inflation, 1860–1920

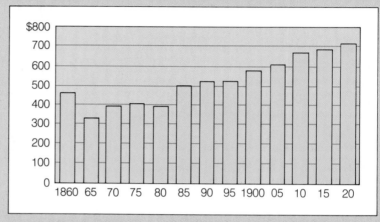

Source: Adapted from Richard K. Vedder, *The American Economy in Historical Perspective*, p. 305.

their most productive uses. Not only did investors and producers make *more* capital goods available, but also technological changes meant *better* capital goods for America's workers.

As workers' productivity increased, businesses bid more intensely for their services, causing wage rates to rise and conditions to improve. As an illustration, Figure A presents the estimated annual earnings, adjusted for inflation, of nonfarm employees between 1860 and 1920. (The next chapter will explain how statistics are adjusted for inflation. Here, the incomes are all measured in terms of the price level of 1914.) The driving force behind the rising living standard of American workers was the increasing productivity of their labor. With the notable exception of the Great Depression of the 1930s, hourly wages adjusted for inflation generally increased after 1920.

Recent statistics suggest a different story. After being adjusted for inflation, both hourly and weekly earnings were lower in 1986 than they were at their peaks in 1972. A similar trend is evident in yearly earnings: annual wages and salaries per employed person in our economy were slightly less in 1986 than they were in 1972.

Before you jump to the conclusion that workers' wages have been falling, consider the fact that each of the above measures ignores the fringe benefits that have become an impor-

Figure B Labor Compensation, Adjusted for Inflation, 1950–1986

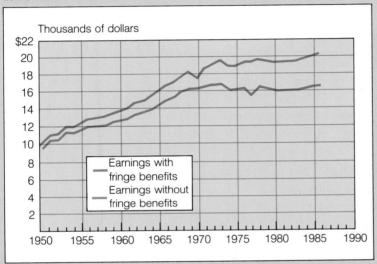

Source: Calculated from *Economic Report of the President,* 1987.

tant part of workers' pay in recent years. In 1950, health insurance, retirement benefits, and other employer-provided supplements accounted for only about 5 percent of total labor compensation. By 1986, this had jumped to 17 percent.

Figure B shows inflation-adjusted earnings per employed worker in our economy between 1950 and 1986. The top line includes fringe benefits, and the bottom line excludes them. When these benefits are recognized as part of workers' pay, earnings per employed worker were higher than ever in 1986.

Despite this fact, the smaller slope of the top line shows that total earnings per employed worker have not been rising as fast as they had been before the early 1970s. One factor holding back the growth of wages has been the relatively slow growth of labor productivity. Table A indicates how the rise of labor income over a period of years depends on the increase in labor productivity.

Over the course of our nation's history, substantial advances in the productivity of labor have brought enormous increases in wages. As technology has advanced and as

Table A Growth of Labor Productivity and Labor Compensation

	Average Yearly Growth	
	Labor Productivity	Labor Compensation (adjusted for inflation)
1950–1972	2.6%	3.1%
1972–1982	0.5	0.1
1982–1986	1.8	1.0

Source: Calculated from *Economic Report to the President*, 1987.

businesses have added to their stock of equipment and facilities, an hour of work has become more productive. By competing against one another to obtain greater quantities of this labor made more valuable by capital, businesses have bid up the wages they pay. In this way the average living standard of America's workers has advanced.

References

Economic Report of the President. Washington, D.C.: U.S. Government Printing Office, January 1987.

Lebergott, Stanley. *The Americans: An Economic Record.* New York: W.W. Norton, 1984.

Vedder, Richard K. *The American Economy in Historical Perspective.* Belmont, Calif.: Wadsworth, 1976.

On the other hand, if the wage rate is $6 per hour, there will be a surplus of labor. In this case, businesses will demand only 1,000 hours of labor per day but workers will want to sell 7,000 hours. The labor surplus will then be 6,000 hours per day (7,000 − 1,000), which means that some people will be unemployed. Because of this labor surplus, workers will compete to sell their labor services and this will depress the wage until it falls to the equilibrium level of $3, at which point the surplus is eliminated.

The wage rate will eventually settle at its equilibrium level, at which point the amounts of labor demanded and supplied are equal. The equilibrium wage can also be the **going wage,** which is the prevailing wage rate in a particular labor market. If an employer wants to hire workers, she or he cannot offer less than the going wage; otherwise, people will not want to work at that business. Moreover, if people want to sell their labor services, they, too, must accept the going wage; anyone asking for a higher wage will not find employment.

Going wage: The prevailing wage rate in a particular labor market.

Labor Unions and the Going Wage

Sometimes efforts are made to raise the going wage. A higher wage rate has certainly been one of the objectives of labor unions, such as the United Steelworkers.

Many people think labor unions came into existence in this century, but highly skilled workers in particular crafts (carpentry or welding, for example) began organizing into local *craft unions* even before the Civil War.[2]

Craft unions were soon replaced by a national federation of labor called the *Knights of Labor*. The Knights of Labor was a secret organization formed in 1869 by a group of workers headed by *Uriah Smith Stevens*. This organization more closely resem-

[2]The factual material in this short summary of the history of the labor movement depends heavily on Lila S. Truett and Dale B. Truett's description in *Economics* (St. Paul: West, 1982), 568–71.

bled modern labor unions because it allowed craft workers as well as workers grouped by entire industries to become members. But the Knights of Labor suffered from bad organization, unsuccessful strikes, and its support of radical and unpopular political changes. For these reasons, membership rapidly dropped from the 700,000 peak it reached in the early 1880s.

That decline in membership was hastened by the rise of another labor organization in the 1880s. That organization, called the *American Federation of Labor (AFL)*, was formally founded in 1886. Under the leadership of *Samuel Gompers*, who was president of the AFL for all but one year between 1886 and 1924, membership rapidly increased.

The success of the AFL was due largely to Gomper's skillful and intelligent leadership. He realized that unionism would be highly successful in the United States if it accepted and worked within our market economic system. If unions promoted other kinds of economic systems, such as socialism in which productive resources are owned by the government, they would risk offending the American public. They would then be doomed to low membership and to weak economic and political power.

Samuel Gompers thus committed the AFL to the aims of higher pay and improved working conditions, rather than to policies aimed at changing the nation's economic system. He thought that the public would like unions if unions made it clear they supported our system of private property and markets. He also insisted on the principle of only one union for each craft, thereby avoiding the organizational problems caused by two unions trying to represent the same group of craft workers.

While the AFL grew to approximately 5 million workers by the 1920s, it still followed the practice of having a separate union for each craft. But since there were many crafts in a particular industry, this practice prevented the AFL from organizing entire industries, such as steel or autos. When membership in the AFL began to drop during the depression in the 1930s, the formation of industrywide or industrial unions began to look more attractive.

As a result, the *Congress of Industrial Organizations (CIO)* was formed in 1935. Now, the unions represented both craft and industrial workers. With many millions of workers organized in the mass-production industries, such as the steel, auto, aluminum, meat packing, and rubber industries, union member-

Samuel Gompers was president of the American Federation of Labor (AFL) for all but one year between 1886 and 1924. Under his skillful leadership, the union worked within our market economy in an effort to increase the pay and improve the working conditions of the union's members.

ship roughly tripled between the early 1930s and 1941, when it totaled about 9 million workers. It increased to about 14 million just before World War II and continued to increase through the 1950s.

In 1955 the AFL and the CIO merged to become the *AFL–CIO*. Despite this merger, union membership as a percentage of all civilian workers has declined in recent decades. In 1960 about 26 percent of all civilian workers were union members, but that dropped to just over 21 percent by 1980 and to under 18 percent by 1985.

Many people think this drop has resulted from the shrinking of our labor force in manufacturing industries, such as steel, in which unions have been very strong. As the productivity of manufacturing workers has increased over the decades, the production of more goods has become possible with the same number of workers. Also, our growing labor force has resulted in increased employment in service industries, so manufacturing workers have become a smaller fraction of our total employment. While unions have been losing members in manufacturing, however, they have been gaining members in the service industries in our economy. Most importantly, gains have occurred in government employment, such as teaching.

Although unions have lost many members in manufacturing industries, they have gained other members among government employees. These teachers are striking in an attempt to raise their pay. If unions succeed in raising teachers' pay, would anything happen to the total number of teachers employed?

Labor unions are still very active and powerful, and they still have as their main goal an increase in economic benefits for their members. That means they try to obtain higher money wages, more fringe benefits (such as medical and dental care), shorter hours, and better working conditions. When added together, these money and nonmoney benefits can be thought of as the total wage received by union members. As a result, unions still have as their major goal an increase in the going wage received by their members.

Labor Unions and Labor Markets

Labor unions use various methods to increase the going wages of their members. Three of these methods are discussed below.

Decreasing the Supply of Labor

Unions know they can raise the wages of their members by restricting the supply of labor. The smaller labor supply intensifies competition among businesses and causes them to bid up wages. One way to reduce the supply of labor is to make sure employers hire only union workers. Unions can then severely restrict the number of people who can join their organizations. They can do this by requiring many months or even years of training for those who want to join, and they can also have very high initiation fees. In order to reduce the supply of non-union labor, unions might pressure Congress to pass retirement laws, child labor laws, or immigration laws.

All of these devices, if successful, restrict the supply of labor (shift the labor supply curve up and to the left) and make the going wages of union members higher than they would other-wise be. But workers who are excluded from union jobs often end up seeking employment elsewhere, causing the labor supply to increase there. As a result, wage rates in these jobs are reduced.

Collective Bargaining

Another method of raising the going wage of union members is *collective bargaining. Collective bargaining* is the process in which a union, as a representative of all its workers, deals with an employer in order to increase wage rates. In effect, the union

During the strike against USX Corporation in 1986, these workers illustrated collective bargaining in action. They opposed the company's efforts to reduce wages and benefits by more than $3 per hour. How would such a cut in wages and benefits affect the employment of steelworkers?

threatens the employer with a strike if the employer does not pay a higher wage to union members. In 1986, for example, the United Steelworkers went on strike against USX Corporation in an effort to prevent wage and benefit cuts of more than $3 per hour.

If successful, this method does not reduce the supply of labor; it merely forces the going wage above the equilibrium level. The higher wage then reduces the amount of labor the employer wants to hire, meaning that some people who are willing to work at the lower equilibrium wage will not get a chance to do so. In addition, the higher wage increases the amount of labor that workers want to sell. Unemployment results because the union creates a surplus of labor by keeping the going wage above the equilibrium level.

Increasing the Demand for Labor

Unions also try to increase the wage rates of their members by increasing the demand for their labor. Chapter 9 has pointed out that an employer's demand for labor depends on the price that consumers are willing to pay for that productivity.

If a union can convince consumers to pay more for union-made products, then it will increase the demand for labor. The demand curve for union labor will shift up and to the right, causing the equilibrium wage to rise. When a union advertises its products on television, it hopes to persuade us to pay more for them. Unions can also try to reduce our demand for nonunion-made products. They might do this by attempting to restrict the entry of foreign-made goods. For example, unions often want import quotas and tariffs in order to decrease the availability of foreign goods. When fewer foreign-made goods are available, the demand for particular goods made by union workers in our country will increase.

The Minimum Wage

Unions (and many citizens) favor minimum wage laws that prevent employers from paying wages below a certain level. The first federal minimum wage law, called the Davis-Bacon Act, was passed in 1931 during the Great Depression. This law covered workers on federal construction projects. Another law, called the *Fair Labor Standards Act*, was passed in 1938. It covered millions of ordinary workers and set the minimum wage at 25 cents per hour. Since that time, the minimum wage has risen substantially, and the proportion of our nation's workers covered by that minimum has risen greatly.

The minimum wage law will not affect employment in those job markets in which going wage rates are much higher than this legal floor. However, in job markets in which the going wage is below this legal floor, the minimum wage reduces employment, as described in the last chapter.

For example, Figure 10–3 shows an equilibrium wage of $3 per hour for fast-food workers in Eaton City. At this wage rate, 5,000 hours of labor are hired each day. If the law then establishes a minimum wage of $4 per hour, the amount of labor hired will fall to 3,000 hours, a decline of 2,000 hours per day. In addition, more workers will seek employment at the higher wage rate, thereby raising the amount of labor supplied from 5,000 to 6,000 per day. As a result, the minimum wage of $4 per hour causes a surplus of labor equal to 3,000 hours (6,000 − 3,000) per day.

A minimum wage law is more likely to affect the employment of unskilled workers. Being unskilled, these workers have low

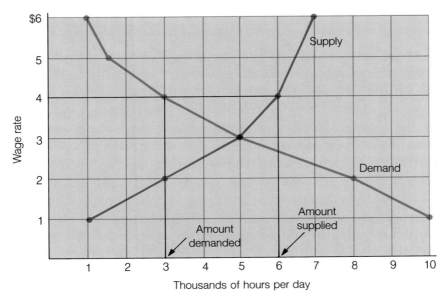

Figure 10–3 The Effects of a Minimum Wage on the Labor Market for Fast-Food Workers (Eaton City, USA)

labor productivity, and this low productivity means low wage rates. When the minimum wage law raises the legal wage above its equilibrium level, therefore, it excludes from employment all those workers whose labor cannot produce at least that much per hour. If fast-food workers must be paid $4 per hour, then those workers whose productivity does not equal $4 per hour will not be hired.

But the effects of a minimum wage are not like the rush of an avalanche that quickly crushes job opportunities. They are more like the steady growth of a jungle's canopy that gradually chokes out the light of employment shining on the unskilled workers below. Jobs that employers would have offered at the lower wage fail to materialize at the higher wage mandated by the government. Fast-food restaurants and other businesses shorten their hours, cut their work crews, and rely more on customer self-service. Businesses gradually redesign production processes to use less unskilled labor and more machines, and other businesses move abroad. Moreover, as unskilled workers lose their ability to pay for on-the-job training through lower wages, they lose an important means of building the skills they need to get better jobs and higher wages.

Unemployment

The minimum wage law has often been cited as contributing to the unemployment of unskilled workers, especially teen-agers. It does this by preventing job seekers whose productivity is less than the minimum wage from selling their labor services in the job market. But the minimum wage is not the reason for most of the unemployment we find in our nation.

In 1986, there were more than 8 million unemployed Americans. According to the government's definition of unemployment, this figure means that 8 million people who were looking for work had not found employment. Each month the government computes the nation's **unemployment rate,** which is reported by television, radio, and newspapers. In order to compute this rate, the government must know two things: (1) the number of people unemployed, and (2) the size of our nation's *civilian labor force,* which consists of all persons at least 16 years of age who are not in the military and who are either working or looking for work. In 1986, the civilian labor force totaled a little less than 118 million people. By dividing the 8 million unemployed people by the labor force of 118 million people, you arrive at an unemployment rate of almost 7 percent.

Unemployment rate: The proportion of the nation's civilian labor force that is not working but is looking for employment. The unemployment rate is calculated as follows:

$$\text{Unemployment rate} = \frac{\text{Number unemployed}}{\text{Number in civilian labor force}}$$

Ways of Becoming Unemployed

It is commonly believed that all unemployment is due to workers' losing their jobs. Job loss, however, is only one of four ways by which people become unemployed.

Many people are unemployed because they have quit their jobs and are now looking for other employment. In 1986, for example, about 12 percent of the 8 million unemployed people became unemployed by *leaving their jobs*. The reasons for leaving a job can certainly vary from person to person. Some quit because they are bored with their jobs; some find the work too hard; others do not like the hours; and some think the pay is too low.

Whatever their reasons for quitting, these people then begin to search for better jobs. This takes some shopping, however, because they must find information about alternative jobs. Searching for the job that best suits you is no different than searching for the best stereo, restaurant, automobile, or college—finding all these things takes time. All those who have quit their jobs and are now busy gathering this costly information are counted as unemployed.

Another way that people become unemployed is by *entering the labor force for the first time*. In 1986 about 13 percent of all the unemployed were people who had entered the labor force for the first time and had begun searching for jobs. Once again,

The Economic Way of Thinking

Unemployment

Is unemployment always undesirable, wasteful, and involuntary?

Noneconomic Way of Thinking

Unemployment occurs because people have been thrown out of their jobs by employers who no longer need them. All workers who don't have jobs are unemployed against their will because there aren't enough jobs available. Unemployment is bad for these people, and it wastes their time because they could otherwise be producing things that people value.

Economic Way of Thinking

Only a fraction of unemployed people have become unemployed by losing their jobs. Many voluntarily quit their jobs in order to look for better ones. Others enter or reenter the labor force and begin searching for acceptable jobs. During this search, these people are classified as unemployed, even though they have become unemployed voluntarily. The time and money devoted to finding a job that matches their skills and preferences are an investment they willingly make. That's because job search can benefit the unemployed by enabling them to find better jobs. Job search produces valuable information, therefore, in the same way that intelligent shopping for a car produces valuable information. Enough jobs are usually available, but people must spend time searching for them. While they search, they are counted as unemployed.

Questions

1. When you graduate from high school or college, will you be likely to take the first job offered to you? Why or why not? If you refuse this job, will you then be voluntarily unemployed?

2. How can an unemployed steelworker benefit from a period of job search? What is the cost of the search to this worker?

3. Suppose the government outlaws unemployment; that is, it becomes illegal to be without a job. Do you think people will end up doing the jobs they do and like best? Explain.

Shopping for a new car is similar to shopping for a new job. Both are necessary to provide information for making a decision. Most of us do not take the first job that comes along, just as most of us do not buy the first car we see. Instead, we usually spend time searching for the right car or the right job.

information about jobs is costly, so they must spend time shopping for the best one. During this time, these new entrants are counted as unemployed.

Entering the labor force for the first time is an especially important concept when explaining unemployment among teenagers. In 1986 about 13 percent of total unemployment could be accounted for by new entrants into the labor force; however, more than 40 percent of teen-age unemployment during that year was due to their entering the labor force and beginning to shop for work.

Still another group of unemployed people is the millions who are *reentering the labor force*. Many people, especially new mothers raising children, have dropped out of the labor force for extended periods of time. Others, such as teen-agers, are likely to leave the labor force after working for awhile and then, after a brief time, return to look for work. When these people choose to reenter the labor force and begin to shop around for employment, they, too, are counted as unemployed. In 1986 about 26 percent of all unemployment was attributed to people reentering the labor force. For teen-agers, reentry into the labor force accounted for more than 30 percent of their unemployment. When added together, therefore, reentrants and new entrants into the labor force totaled almost three-quarters of all teen-agers unemployed in 1986.

The last, and usually the most important, explanation for unemployment is the *losing of a job*. When people lose their jobs and begin searching for another one, they are counted as unemployed along with those newly entering or reentering the labor force and those who have quit their jobs. In 1986 close to half of all unemployment was explained by the loss of jobs.

We have now listed all four ways people become unemployed. Unemployment does not occur just because people are laid off or fired, although these are important reasons for unemployment. Many people choose to become unemployed by quitting their jobs or by entering or reentering the labor force. In addition, once people become unemployed, they usually don't jump at the first job that comes along. Instead, they spend time searching for the right one. But most people who become unemployed don't remain unemployed for long periods of time. In 1986, more than 40 percent of the unemployed spent less than five weeks looking for employment; and more than 70 percent spent less than fifteen weeks searching for a job.

When you hear that a certain number of workers is unemployed during a given year, therefore, don't make the common mistake of thinking the same people were unemployed all year. Instead, think of most of the unemployed as shoppers in a supermarket. During a given day, there is a certain number of shoppers in the store. But their faces are constantly changing as shoppers enter and leave the store. So it is with most (but not all) unemployment. Many people become unemployed during the year, spend a short time shopping around in the labor market, and then leave unemployment. Most do not remain without work for very long.

Kinds of Unemployment

Many people don't know that some unemployment occurs naturally in a market economy. During some parts of the year, various occupations require more workers. The post office hires more workers to help sort and deliver the increased quantity of mail during the busy Christmas season. Department stores also hire more workers to take care of more shoppers who are buying Christmas gifts. The harvesting and food processing industries also add more workers at certain times of the year. And favorite vacation spots demand additional workers for the increased volume of visitors during their busy seasons.

When these busy times pass, some workers will be laid off, only to be hired again when the next busy season arrives. When they are laid off, these workers suffer **seasonal unemployment,** which is the temporary unemployment caused by the normal, seasonal decline in the demand for particular goods and services.

> **Seasonal unemployment:** Temporary unemployment caused by the normal, seasonal decline in the demand for particular goods and services.

Because seasonal unemployment is predictable, it can be easily removed from unemployment statistics. The result is *seasonally adjusted unemployment,* which is the topic for the rest of this chapter.

After the harvest season, this worker could become unemployed. Seasonal unemployment is the temporary unemployment caused by the normal, seasonal decline in the demand for or supply of particular goods and services.

Even when seasonally adjusted, unemployment occurs naturally because people choose to quit their jobs and to enter and reenter the labor force. In addition, constantly changing consumer demands will cause some industries to expand and others to contract. As a result, while new employment opens up for some workers, others will lose their jobs and become unemployed. But whether people lose or quit their jobs or enter or reenter the labor force, they usually spend a short time searching for employment.

This type of brief unemployment occurs normally in an economy in which people move freely into and out of the labor force or move freely from job to job. It also occurs normally in an economy in which consumers determine the kinds and quantities of goods and services produced. Because this unemployment is due to the natural friction of a constantly moving and changing economy, it is called **frictional unemployment.**

> **Frictional unemployment:** Unemployment that occurs normally as people move from one job to another or as they move into and out of the labor force.

Structural unemployment is different from frictional unemployment. A person is structurally unemployed when his or her job skills do not match the requirements of available jobs. For example, teaching jobs might become available, but that doesn't mean that many of the unemployed will have the desired teaching skills for those jobs. In addition, employment in a particular industry, such as steel, might decline, but those losing their jobs in this industry might not have the skills required for new jobs opening up in other industries. Indeed, a considerable period of retraining might be required to give these structurally unemployed people the new skills they need to get different jobs.

Thus, structural unemployment occurs when the skills of unemployed workers don't match the skills demanded for the available jobs. But structural unemployment also occurs when the geographic location of unemployed workers doesn't match that of the jobs available. As a result, time might be required for workers to move from one part of the country to another, just as it can be required to obtain new job skills.

> **Structural unemployment:** Unemployment that results from a mismatch of (1) workers' skills and the skills required for available jobs or (2) the geographic location of workers and that of the jobs available.

Structural and frictional unemployment do not arise because there are not enough jobs for all those who want to work. Think of jobs as holes in a board and workers as the pegs. There are enough holes for all the pegs, but all the pegs are not in them. That's because pegs are always moving from hole to hole, because some pegs might not fit into particular holes, and because some pegs might be at a particular place on the board where there are not many holes.

Weak-demand unemployment is very different, however. In this case, there are not enough holes for all the pegs. Weak-demand unemployment occurs because of a general decrease in the demand for labor in our economy. This lower demand results from less total spending on the goods and services that labor produces. You already know that the demand for labor depends on the demand for the goods and services that labor produces. When consumers demand fewer goods and services, businesses will hire less labor. The result is more unemployment.

> **Weak-demand unemployment:** Unemployment that results from a drop in the total demand for a nation's goods and services.

A good example of this kind of unemployment occurred during the early 1980s. At that time, our economy was growing weaker, and people were buying fewer goods and services than they had before. As you might expect, unemployment increased rapidly, rising from 5.8 percent in 1979 to 9.5 percent in 1982. Beginning in 1983, however, our economy began to grow stronger as people increased their purchases of goods and services. As a result, unemployment then declined, falling to about 6 percent by 1987.

In contrast to weak-demand unemployment, structural and frictional unemployment occur naturally as workers move from job to job, as workers enter or reenter the labor force, as con-

During the Great Depression of the 1930s, unemployment soared because of a weak demand for goods and services. At this New York City soup kitchen in 1931, many unemployed people filled their empty stomachs.

sumers shift their demands from one item to another, and as technological change alters the characteristics of jobs. As a result, **full employment** does not mean an absence of all unemployment. Instead, full employment represents the unemployment that remains when there is no weak-demand unemployment.

> **Full employment:** The unemployment that remains when there is no weak-demand unemployment.

In the 1980s, for example, some economists estimated the sum of frictional and structural unemployment, sometimes called *natural unemployment*, to be about 6 percent of the labor force. Therefore, an unemployment rate of 6 percent would mean an absence of weak-demand unemployment. Accordingly, 6 percent was an estimate of full employment for our economy at that time. Such estimates are important because full employment has been a principal objective of the government's economic policies. These policies will be explained in the next few chapters.

Chapter Summary

1. Consumers are the buyers in goods and services markets, and businesses are the buyers in resource markets. Labor services are an important resource because the incomes people earn from selling them are used to buy goods and services.

2. Wage rates are prices for labor services. Businesses purchase more labor when the price (wage) is lower and less labor when the price (wage) is higher.

3. People supply more labor at higher wage rates because the benefits of those wages persuade them to bear the opportunity cost of giving up other jobs or of sacrificing their leisure. The opportunity cost increases as people give up increasingly valuable options. Accordingly, wages must increase to compensate them for the sacrifice of those options.

4. A lower-than-equilibrium wage causes a shortage of labor, and a higher-than-equilibrium wage causes a surplus of labor. The equilibrium wage is usually the *going wage*, which is defined as the prevailing wage in a job market.

5. Highly skilled workers organized into craft unions before the Civil War, and they were replaced in 1869 by a national organization called the *Knights of Labor*. This organization was followed by the *American Federation of Labor (AFL)*, founded in 1886 and first headed by Samuel Gompers.

6. The *Congress of Industrial Organizations (CIO)* was founded in 1935 as a group of unions that organized industrial workers. In 1955, the AFL and the CIO merged, forming the *AFL-CIO*.

7. Labor unions try to increase the going wage by decreasing the supply of labor, bargaining collectively, and increasing the demand for labor. *Collective bargaining* is an attempt to force the going wage above its equilibrium level. Minimum wage laws also try to force the going wage above its equilibrium level. By so doing, collective bargaining and minimum wage laws create a surplus of labor, which means unemployment.

8. The civilian labor force is defined as all persons at least 16 years of age who are not in the military and who are either working or looking for work. The unemployment rate is calculated by dividing the number of unemployed people by the number of people in the civilian labor force. There are four ways of becoming unemployed: losing a job, entering the labor force for the first time, reentering the labor force, and leaving a job. Most people who become unemployed do not stay that way for long.

9. There are four kinds of unemployment: seasonal, frictional, structural, and weak-demand. Full employment does not mean an unemployment rate of zero. Instead, it means the unemployment left over when there is no weak-demand unemployment.

Review Questions

1. What is meant by the term *going wage?* What would probably happen to anyone asking for a wage higher than the going wage?

2. What is the main goal of labor unions? Discuss three ways by which labor unions achieve this goal.

3. Why are minimum wage laws more likely to affect the employment of unskilled workers?

4. How is the nation's unemployment rate calculated?

5. What are four common ways by which individuals become unemployed?

6. Explain this statement: Some unemployment occurs naturally in a market economy.

7. What is the difference between *frictional unemployment* and *structural unemployment?*

8. What is *weak-demand unemployment,* and why does it occur?

9. What is meant by the term *full employment?* Does full employment imply an absence of all unemployment? Explain.

Discussion Questions

1. If a business wants to obtain more hours of labor, what must it do? Explain.

2. If the equilibrium wage for grocery clerks is $5 per hour, what will happen if stores pay less than this amount? What will happen if the wage rises to $7 instead of its equilibrium level of $5? Why?

3. Write a short paragraph in response to the following statement: Most people become unemployed because they have lost their jobs.

4. Do you agree with this suggestion: The government ought to assure employment for every person who wants to work? Why or why not?

Activities

1. Interview at least three members of labor unions to find out (1) what they believe the goals of labor unions are, (2) how labor unions go about achieving these goals, (3) if they believe labor unions are successful in achieving these goals, and (4) why labor unions are successful or unsuccessful in achieving these goals. Write a brief paper that presents the results of your interviews, and compare your answers with those of your classmates.

2. The average earnings of full-time female workers equal about 65 percent of the average earnings of full-time male workers. Research this topic, and then use the economic principles discussed in this chapter to explain whether you think the disparity is due to sex discrimination or to differences in the labor markets of men and women.

3. The following table presents information about a fictional labor market for teachers:

Average Annual Wage	Number of Teachers Demanded	Number of Teachers Supplied
$40,000	1,000	7,000
35,000	2,000	6,000
30,000	3,000	5,000
25,000	4,000	4,000
20,000	5,000	3,000
15,000	7,000	1,000

(a) Plot the demand for and supply of teachers on a piece of graph paper.

(b) What is the equilibrium wage rate?

(c) What will happen if the wage rate is $40,000 per year? What will happen if the wage rate is $15,000 per year?

(d) Suppose the community suddenly puts more value on education, so that 2,000 more teachers are demanded at each wage rate. Show this change on the graph. What will happen to the equilibrium wage? Why will the wage rate change?

(e) Suppose that stricter licensing of teachers by the state causes the amount of teachers supplied to drop by 2,000 at each wage rate. Show this change on the graph. Compared to the initial equilibrium in part b, what will happen to the equilibrium wage? Why will this change occur?

Additional Readings

Drucker, Peter F. "Why America's Got So Many Jobs." In *Introductory Macroeconomics, 1985–86: Readings on Contemporary Issues*, edited by Peter D. McClelland. Ithaca, N.Y.: Cornell University Press, 1985. 30–31.

O'Neil, June. "Comparable Worth." *Contemporary Economic Issues 3*, no. 111 (Fall 1984).

Sharp, Ansel M., and Leftwich, Richard H. *The Economics of Social Issues.* 7th ed. Plano, Texas: Business Publications, 1986. 301–10.

Shaw, Jane S. "The Case for Paying Teen-Agers a Lower Minimum Wage." In *Annual Editions: Macroeconomics 85/86*, edited by John Pisciotta. Guilford, Conn.: Dushkin, 1985. 9.

Tuerck, David G. "Fair Pay for Women." *Vital Speeches of the Day. LII*, no. 17 (June 15, 1986): 520–23.

Economic Growth and Stability

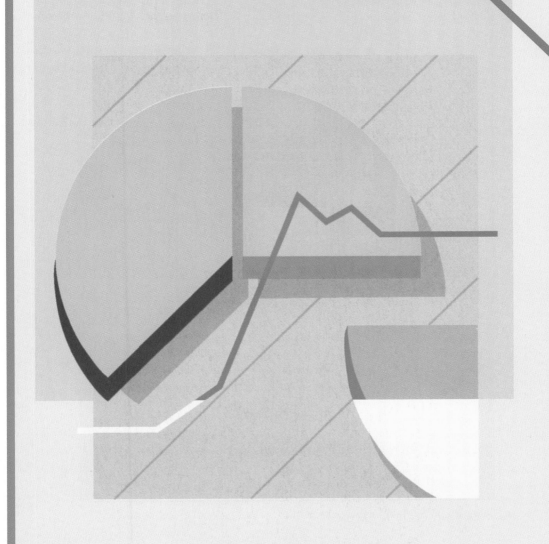

What would happen to your standard of living if no one lent or borrowed money?

Aggregate Demand and Aggregate Supply

Chapter

11

■ Student's Goals ■

1. Define *aggregate demand* and *aggregate supply*.

2. Draw aggregate demand and aggregate income on a circular flow of money diagram.

3. Distinguish between the economist's use of the term *investment* and its everyday usage.

4. Explain why aggregate demand and aggregate supply are balanced only when the outflow of saving is exactly equal to the inflow of investment.

5. Define *gross national product* and *real gross national product*, and distinguish between them.

6. Explain why channeling saving into investment is crucial to the growth of our economy.

To Borrow or Not to Borrow. . .

"Neither a borrower nor a lender be," advised William Shakespeare in the first act of *Hamlet*. Shakespeare was certainly one of the world's most gifted writers. But was he a good economist? Would we be better off if we took his advice and stopped all lending and borrowing?

Doing so would surely eliminate bankruptcies, such as those experienced by many of the farmers you read about in Chapter six. Bankruptcy occurs when individuals cannot pay off their debts. Without any borrowing, there would be no debts, so bankruptcy would be impossible. Shakespeare also wrote that borrowing dulls our desire to save. If we could obtain funds by borrowing them from someone else, he thought, we would be less likely to save the money ourselves. But if individuals did not lend the money they saved, what would they do with it? Would they bury it in their backyards or hide it somewhere in their homes?

Lending and borrowing perform important tasks in a market economy. Our ability to find a job, the wages we earn, and the prices we pay all depend on how well these tasks are performed. The importance of lending and borrowing can be understood by relating them to the economy's aggregate demand and aggregate supply.

Sum Things

Aggregate means that individual items have been combined to form a total or sum. When McDonald's adds up its sales of hamburgers, French fries, milk shakes, and other items, for example, it is calculating its *aggregate* sales. When the market demands for wheat, gasoline, chocolate, movies, eggplant, doctors, dentists, mechanics, and all other goods and services in the economy are somehow added together, the sum is called aggregate demand. **Aggregate demand** is the total of all demands for goods and services in our economy. Similarly, **aggregate supply** is the total of all supplies of goods and services in our economy.

Although Shakespeare advised against being either a borrower or a lender, both activities are vital to our economic well-being. Without borrowers there could be no lenders. If people did not lend the money they saved, how could they put their savings to use?

Aggregate demand: The total of all demands for goods and services in our economy.

Aggregate supply: The total of all supplies of goods and services in our economy.

Aggregate demand and aggregate supply are illustrated by the circular flow map in Figure 11–1. Compared with earlier diagrams of the circular flow, this picture has been simplified by eliminating the large dark arrows showing the clockwise flow or real resources. The circles showing the markets for goods and services and for resources have also been eliminated.

The top loop in Figure 11–1 shows consumers' aggregate demand for goods and services. When consumers make these purchases, they cause dollars to flow through the top loop from right to left. Businesses then use this money to purchase the resources they demand to produce more output. When they purchase these resources, businesses cause dollars to flow through the bottom loop from left to right. The flow of money in the bottom loop represents the combined incomes of resource own-

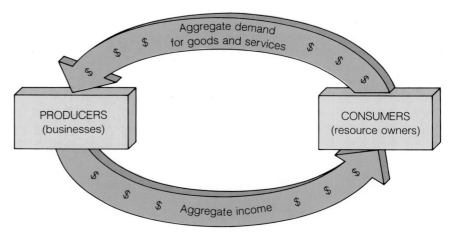

Figure 11—1 The Circular Flow of Money

The top loop shows consumers' aggregate demand for goods and services. By purchasing goods and services, consumers cause dollars to flow through the top loop from right to left. Businesses then use this money to buy the resources they require to produce additional goods and services. When purchasing these resources, businesses cause dollars to flow through the bottom loop from the left to right. The money flow in the bottom loop represents aggregate income because it is the total income of resource owners. When the flows of both loops are combined, they produce a circular flow of money.

ers, so it is called *aggregate income*. Together, the top loop of aggregate demand and the bottom loop of aggregate income produce a circular flow of money.

The Chicken and the Egg

As an example of the circular flow of money, take the imaginary economy of Trigo. To simplify our discussion, assume bread is the only thing Trigo's citizens produce. Suppose consumers spend $500 on a particular day to purchase bread. Consumer expenditures are the same as business revenues, so this action causes $500 to flow from consumers to producers through the upper loop. When businesses use their revenues to buy resources, their outlays generate income for those who own the resources. Even the profits—the money businesses have left after paying for their resources—represent income for those who own the businesses. By producing and selling $500 worth of bread, therefore, the businesses of Trigo also generate $500 of income.

As this bakery uses its revenues to produce more bread, it purchases resources and thereby generates income for those who own the resources.

Consumers then turn this $500 of aggregate income into another $500 of aggregate demand tomorrow. Because of this renewed demand on the following day, businesses again produce bread (aggregate supply) worth $500. As businesses produce this bread, they again generate an income of $500, enabling consumers to demand still another $500 worth of bread on the third day. This example shows how production is connected to income, how income is connected to spending, and how spending is connected back to production. By continuing this circular motion, Trigo's economy generates $500 worth of demand, production, and income each day.

The circular flow map highlights the relationship among aggregate demand, aggregate supply, and aggregate income. As Figure 11–2 shows, aggregate demand leads to aggregate supply, and aggregate supply leads to aggregate income. Aggregate income then leads back to aggregate demand, and the process begins again.

Asking which slice comes first is like asking whether the chicken or the egg came first. Chickens are necessary to have eggs, but eggs are necessary to have chickens. Similarly, any one of the three slices in the diagram is necessary to have the other two. As a result, we won't get anywhere by asking which slice comes first. Just remember that in the circular flow of money, aggre-

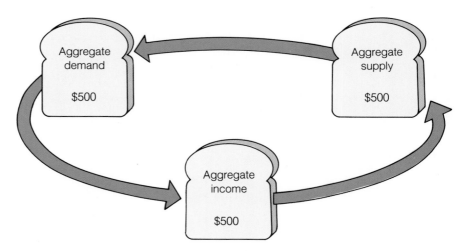

Figure 11–2 Aggregate Demand, Supply and Income in the Economy of Trigo

Aggregate demand, aggregate supply, and aggregate income all depend on one another. The total amount that businesses supply (aggregate supply) depends on the total demand of consumers (aggregate demand). Similarly, the total income of resource owners (aggregate income) depends on how much businesses produce or supply. Total income then determines the total demand of consumers. Because each of these three quantities depends on the other two, asking which one is the starting point is like asking whether the chicken or the egg came first.

In the circular flow of money, aggregate demand, aggregate supply, and aggregate income all depend on one another. When consumers spend their incomes to purchase this bread, they provide revenues for the bakery's continued production. When producing bread, the bakery generates income that resource owners use to demand bread and other goods and services.

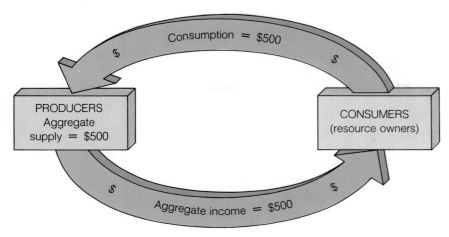

Figure 11–3   The Circular Flow of Trigo's Economy

The top loop shows that aggregate demand arises when consumers spend $500 to purchase bread. The box on the left shows businesses producing an aggregate supply of $500 worth of bread. When producing the bread, businesses generate an aggregate income of $500 in the bottom loop. If consumers spend all of their $500 of income on bread each day, businesses will continue to sell and produce $500 worth of bread, thereby continuing to create for resource owners $500 of daily income. As a result, $500 of money will move completely around the circle each day.

gate demand, aggregate supply, and aggregate income all depend on one another.

Figure 11–3 summarizes this interdependence. Aggregate demand consists of $500 of *consumption* expenditures, shown by the top loop on the map. Aggregate supply is shown by the $500 of *production* taking place inside the producers' box on the left. Aggregate income is shown by the flow of $500 through the bottom loop on the map.

If consumers in Trigo spend all of their $500 of income on bread every day, businesses will continue to sell and produce that much bread and, by so doing, will continue to generate $500 of income each day. Aggregate demand and aggregate supply will then be equal to $500 per day. Accordingly, each day $500 of money makes a complete loop around the circular flow map of Trigo.

Outflows and Inflows

What happens if consumers save some of their income? For example, suppose that consumers decide one day to save $50

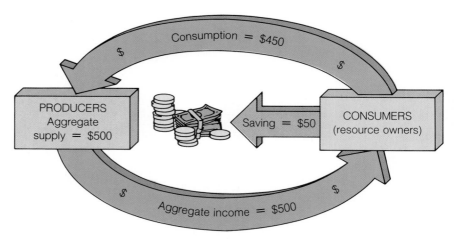

Figure 11–4 Trigo's Circular Flow with an Outflow of Saving

The arrow marked *Saving* on the right shows that consumers are saving $50 of their income by stashing it away in their homes. This outflow of saving causes consumption (aggregate demand) to drop from $500 to $450. Since businesses are still producing $500 worth of bread, however, aggregate demand ($450) is now less than aggregate supply ($500).

of their income by stashing it away in their homes. In that case, $50 will flow out of the circular flow and cause an imbalance in aggregate demand and aggregate supply, as Figure 11–4 illustrates.

The saving arrow on the right shows an outflow of $50 from the circular flow. This outflow causes consumption to fall from $500 to $450. As a result, aggregate demand (consumption) is now only $450, while aggregate supply is still $500. Because of the inequality of aggregate demand and aggregate supply, a circular flow of $500 cannot be sustained. The inequality of aggregate demand and aggregate supply can be eliminated, however, if the *outflow* of consumer saving is matched by an equal *inflow* of nonconsumer spending. This inflow can occur because of the way people save.

Most people don't save by keeping money in their homes. Instead, they deposit their savings in a bank or some other financial institution where their money is safer and where it can earn interest. If banks must pay interest on the funds deposited with them, however, they will want to put those funds to work in order to earn money.

Banks do this when they loan money to consumers who want to buy cars, furniture, or homes. If we take all the money that consumers save and deposit at banks, and subtract all the money that banks loan to other consumers, we obtain a number called *net consumer saving.* For example, suppose consumers in Trigo save $75, which they deposit in their local banks. The banks then loan $25 to other consumers, so net consumer saving is $50 ($75 − $25). This is the saving shown on the circular flow map above.

How do banks use the net saving of consumers to earn money? They loan this money to businesses for investment in new capital goods. In Chapter 1, we have explained that capital goods are resources, such as buildings, machines, and tools, used by businesses to produce goods and services. **Investment** is the production of these kinds of resources.

Most people would probably say that investment is putting money into a savings account, buying a share of stock on the stock market, purchasing gold, or buying some kind of financial asset. This is one way of defining investment, but it is not the definition we are using here. When we say *investment,* we mean the production of new capital goods, not the personal or financial investments most people have in mind. Financial investment is a mere swapping of ownership of resources that already exist. In contrast, "real" investment is the production of ad-

The equipment in this bakery illustrates the capital goods used to produce the goods and services we want. Investment occurs when these capital goods are produced.

ditional resources that a nation can use to produce goods and services.

> **Investment:** The production of new capital goods.

If businesses borrow and invest the $50 of saving deposited at Trigo's banks, they will put this money back into the circular flow. Saving, an *outflow* of money, will then be balanced by investment, an *inflow* of money. If the outflow of saving is exactly equal to the inflow of investment, then aggregate demand and aggregate supply will be balanced, as Figure 11–5 shows.

Figure 11–5 shows that businesses are producing $500 worth of goods and generating $500 of income. Consumers are spending $450 of this income and saving the other $50. That's why the top loop shows $450 of consumption (C), while the middle loop shows $50 of saving (S) being deposited at the bank. Businesses borrow the $50 from the bank and invest it in new equip-

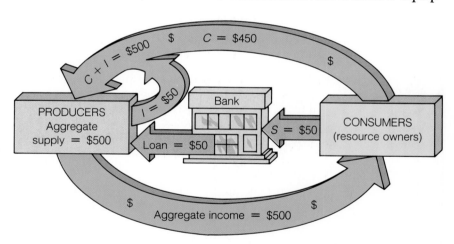

Figure 11–5 Trigo's Circular Flow with an Outflow of Saving and an Inflow of Investment

Because businesses produce $500 worth of goods, they also generate $500 of income for resource owners in the bottom loop. Consumers save $50 of this income in the bank and spend the other $450 as consumption in the top loop. The bank loans the $50 to businesses, which invest the $50 in new capital goods. Consequently, business investment puts back into the circular flow the $50 of saving that consumers took out. Aggregate demand now consists of $450 of consumption and $50 of investment. Aggregate demand totals $500, which is equal to the $500 of aggregate supply produced by businesses. Because investment equals saving, therefore, aggregate demand and aggregate supply are again equal.

Saving

Suppose consumers in our nation save a lot more of their incomes. Will this increased saving help or hurt our economy?

Noneconomic Way of Thinking

If consumers save more of their incomes, they will buy fewer cars, houses, appliances, and other goods and services. As a result, aggregate demand will drop, so a recession will occur. Increased saving by consumers harms our economy because that means less spending, less production, and less income.

Economic Way of Thinking

It's true that greater saving by consumers means less consumer spending, but this fact doesn't necessarily mean less aggregate demand. That's because consumers put their saving in banks, which then try to lend the saving to businesses for new investments in plants and equipment. If the investment spending by businesses equals the saving of consumers, then the amount leaving the circular flow through saving is offset by the amount put back in as investment. Total spending is not reduced, therefore, because businesses end up spending the income that consumers save.

Over time, greater saving and investment benefit us because the larger amount of investment means more capital goods for our nation. More capital goods then enable us to produce more goods and services.

Questions

1. Suppose consumers spend more, not less. What will happen to saving and investment?

2. Why do banks try to lend the money they have available? If they have less to lend, what will happen to the cost of borrowing?

3. If banks have less money to lend, what will happen to the amount of capital goods in our nation? What will happen to economic growth?

ment and other capital goods. As a result, $50 of investment (I) is put back into the circular flow. Aggregate demand, which now consists of consumption ($450) and investment ($50), is shown as $C + I = \$500$ on the left side of the top loop.

Because the outflow of saving ($50) is equal to the inflow of investment ($50), there is a continuous flow of $500 of money around the circular flow of Trigo's economy. Moreover, aggregate demand (C + I) is equal to aggregate supply, so the circular flow remains constant at $500 per day. But bread is no longer the only good produced. Some businesses also manufacture the $50 worth of capital goods that other businesses purchase each day. Although $500 worth of goods is still produced, bread now accounts for $450 of that production and capital goods account for the remaining $50. *Total* spending and *total* income are unchanged, but the kinds of goods produced and the activities by which people earn their incomes have both been affected.

A Ride on a Roller Coaster

Aggregate demand and aggregate supply are equal only when businesses want to invest the same amount that consumers (income earners) want to save. But the investment plans of businesses can be very different from the saving plans of consumers. If investment and saving are unequal, therefore, aggregate demand and aggregate supply will also be unequal.

Suppose, for example, that Trigo's consumers suddenly decide to cut their consumption expenditures by an additional $50 in order to raise their saving. Consumption will fall to $400, and saving will rise to $100. Although consumers are now putting $100 of saving into the bank, businesses still want to borrow and invest only $50. As a result, aggregate demand falls to $450 (C + I = $400 + $50). Since $500 worth of goods is being produced, however, aggregate demand will be $50 less than aggregate supply. This means at current prices producers can't sell everything they are producing. Because aggregate demand and aggregate supply aren't equal, something is going to happen.

One possibility is that the reduced demand for goods, services, labor, and other resources will cause *prices and wages* to

These new rails at the Bethlehem Steel Corporation illustrate the production of an important capital good that will be purchased and used by railroads in the United States. When railroads make these purchases, they are investing and thereby adding to the nation's aggregate demand. The use of the new rails will then enable our nation to produce more railroad services in future years.

fall. The new, lower equilibrium levels of prices and wages will eventually balance the demands and supplies of individual items throughout the economy. Another possibility is that the reduced demand for goods, services, labor, and other resources will cause *production and employment* to fall. Unemployment will rise, and that increase illustrates the *weak-demand unemployment* explained in the previous chapter.

If aggregate demand is less than aggregate supply, the circular flow can slow down and cause production, employment, prices, and wages to fall. On the other hand, if aggregate demand is above aggregate supply, the circular flow can speed up and cause production, employment, prices, and wages to rise. If the balance between aggregate demand and aggregate supply is continually disturbed, therefore, the economy will go up and down as if it were riding a roller coaster.

The saving and investment plans described above help to explain why aggregate demand and aggregate supply can be unequal. If people change the amount they want to save or if businesses change the amount they want to invest, then aggregate demand can rise or fall. On the other hand, factors can affect the willingness or ability of businesses to supply goods and services. For example, bad weather can reduce the availability of wheat and cause Trigo's aggregate supply to fall. In either case, aggregate demand and aggregate supply will be thrown out of balance, causing the entire economy to rise or fall as it tries to bring them back to equality.

Ideally, aggregate demand and aggregate supply should grow at the same rate over time, so that their continued equality will result in a smoothly growing economy. In reality, aggregate demand and aggregate supply are often unequal, causing the economy to rise and fall. The resulting fluctuations in a market economy's aggregate supply and aggregate income are often called **business cycles.** Business cycles occur repeatedly—though at irregular and unpredictable intervals—and are characterized by the four phases of *peak, recession, trough,* and *recovery* shown in Figure 11–6.

Business cycles: The fluctuations in a market economy's aggregate supply and aggregate income.

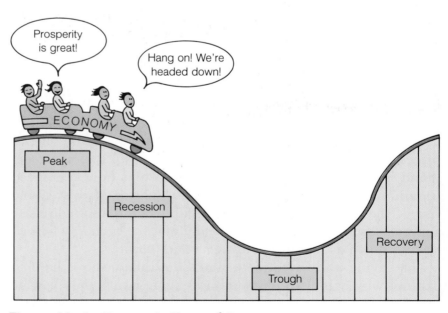

Figure 11–6 Economic Ups and Downs

Changes in aggregate demand and aggregate supply can produce fluctuations in an economy's circular flow. But how can the speed of the circular flow be measured? If a gauge could be put on the economy the way a speedometer is put on an automobile, then the amount of money moving around the circular flow during a given time could be measured. This number would represent the money value of all the goods and services produced in the nation during a particular time.

Economists have invented an economic gauge, called *GNP*, which stands for **gross national product.** In this instance, the word *gross* means aggregate, so that GNP is the aggregate amount of goods and services produced in a nation during a particular time.

That's a simple definition—too simple, in fact, because it ignores two important things. First, GNP usually includes only those goods and services produced for the marketplace. Because most of those things produced and consumed at home cannot be accurately measured, they are not counted as part of GNP. Second, the prices of only certain kinds of goods and services are counted. For example, consider what goes into the production of a loaf of bread sold at the supermarket for $1.50. Suppose a farmer grows wheat and sells it to a miller for 30 cents. The miller uses the wheat to produce flour which he sells to a baker for 60 cents. The baker produces a loaf of bread and sells it to the supermarket for $1.20, and the supermarket then sells the bread for $1.50. Production has obviously occurred, but how much should the GNP gauge show?

If we add the prices of the products sold by each producer, we get the sum of $3.60. This number does not accurately measure production, however, because it counts products more than once. The price of the miller's flour already includes the price of the farmer's wheat, for example, so if we add them together, we end up counting the wheat twice.

The supermarket's price of $1.50 already includes the value of all the intermediate goods produced by the farmer, the miller, and the baker. The GNP gauge would thus count only the price of the bread that is paid by the final consumer at the supermarket. That's why GNP measures only *final* goods and ser-

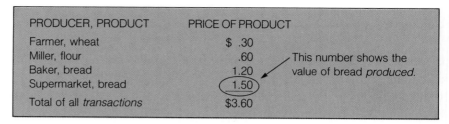

Figure 11–7 The GNP in a Loaf of Bread

In order to produce a loaf of bread, a farmer produces and sells 30 cents worth of wheat. A miller buys the wheat and then sells 60 cents worth of flour. The flour is purchased by a baker and then sold as a loaf of bread to a supermarket for $1.20. The supermarket then sells the loaf of bread to a shopper for $1.50. The value of all *transactions* is $3.60, but this sum is not the value of the production that should be added to GNP. Since the $1.50 sale of the supermarket's bread already includes the value of production added by each of the previous three producers, $1.50 represents the total value of *production* that should be added to GNP.

vices, which are those things that have reached their final stage of production. Prices of *intermediate* products, such as wheat and flour, which will be made into other products, are already included in the prices of these final goods and services. Accordingly, **gross national product** is the sum of all prices of final goods and services produced for the marketplace in a nation during a particular time.

> **Gross national product (GNP):** The sum of all prices of final goods and services produced for the marketplace in a nation during a particular time.

The GNP of the imaginary economy of Trigo was only $500. The GNP of the United States is much greater, as the following number for 1986 shows:

$4,200,000,000,000.00

This number is four trillion two hundred billion dollars, which we will round off to $4 trillion. Because 4 trillion is an enormous number, it is difficult to comprehend. Imagine stacking $1,000 bills until you have $4 trillion in a pile. The pile will literally be out of this world because it will be more than 250 miles high. Or suppose you can spend $1 million a day for the rest of your life. How long will it take you to spend $4 trillion?

When measuring the value of production in our economy, we do not add the values of all transactions. Doing so would count products more than once. The value of wheat this farm sells to millers ends up being counted in the bread and other final products we purchase as consumers.

Unless you find a way to live an unusually long time, you won't come close to spending that much money. Indeed, you will have to live more than 10,000 years to spend all the money.

Our country's GNP is a big number, and it has grown even larger since 1986. The large size of our economy's GNP is one reason why we used the imaginary economy of Trigo instead to illustrate the circular flow. In that example, Trigo's GNP of $500 is purchased by consumers (consumption) and by business (investment). In the U.S. economy, consumption accounts for about 66 percent of all expenditures made to buy our nation's GNP. Investment expenditures account for about 16 percent. Most of the remaining expenditures are those made by federal, state, and local governments. In Chapter 8, we have pointed out that government purchases (of goods and services) account for approximately 20 percent of gross national production (GNP). Government purchases must thus be added to consumption and investment purchases in order to measure the size of our country's GNP.

Imports and exports must also be counted. Some goods and services purchased by consumers, businesses, and government are imported. Since they have been produced abroad, they should not be included as part of our nation's production. Imported goods and services are thus subtracted from the sum of consumer, business, and government expenditures. Similarly, some goods and services we produce are exported and, thus, not included in consumer, business, and government purchases. As a result, exports are added.

The GNP gauge totals up the expenditures for final goods and services made by consumers, businesses, and government, and then adds exports and subtract imports. Figure 11–8 shows the result for 1986.

Using the GNP Gauge

A problem arises when we use the GNP gauge over a period of many years. This problem is **inflation,** which is an increase in the price level. During any year some prices fall, some remain constant, and some rise. When most prices rise, the average of all these prices—the price level—goes up.

> **Inflation:** An increase in the price level.

Again, take the economy of Trigo as an example. If businesses produce 500 loaves of bread today and the price of each loaf is

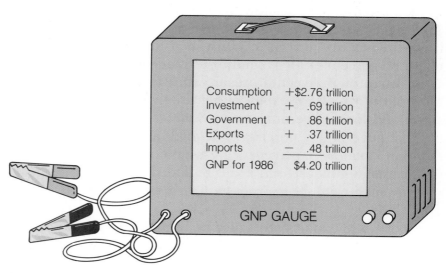

Consumption	+$2.76 trillion
Investment	+ .69 trillion
Government	+ .86 trillion
Exports	+ .37 trillion
Imports	− .48 trillion
GNP for 1986	$4.20 trillion

GNP GAUGE

Figure 11–8 The GNP Gauge of the U.S. Economy, 1986

Money prices do not sit still, as the reduced prices of these suits demonstrate. During inflation, however, most money prices rise. When we count the value of all items produced during inflation, therefore, our measure of production is bloated by higher prices.

$1, then Trigo's GNP gauge will show a GNP of $500 (500 × $1). But suppose the price of bread rises to $2 tomorrow, even though businesses still produce 500 loaves of bread. In this case, the GNP gauge will show a GNP of $1,000 (500 × $2). According to the gauge, Trigo's aggregate production has doubled from $500 to $1,000. Although more *money* is moving around the circular flow, bread production hasn't really increased. Inflation only makes it seem as though production has gone up.

Fortunately, the problem can be solved by putting an adapter on the GNP gauge to take inflation out of the GNP number. This adapter, called the *GNP deflator,* takes inflation out of the GNP numbers; then yearly changes in these numbers reflect *real* changes in production, not inflation. The result is **real GNP,** which is gross national product adjusted for inflation.

Real GNP: Gross national product adjusted for inflation.

Real GNP eliminates the problem of yearly price changes by using the price level of a given (base) year to measure the GNPs of all other years. For example, the base year for the GNP deflator is 1982. By applying the deflator to the GNP of 1970, we replace the 1970 prices that measured the GNP in that year with the higher price level of 1982. Similarly, the deflator uses the price level of 1982 to measure the GNP of any other year. As a result, each year's real GNP is measured in terms of the prices that existed in the base year of 1982.

By examining the changes in *real* GNP from year to year, you can see what is really happening to the production of goods and services in our nation. Figure 11–9 presents real GNP for the United States from 1960 to 1986. Since the deflator has already been applied, the graph presents each year's GNP in terms of the prices of the base year of 1982. Real GNP has risen in most years during this period. However, 1970, 1975, and 1982 are exceptions because real GNP declined during these years. These were years of **recession,** which is defined as a decrease in real GNP for at least one-half of a year.

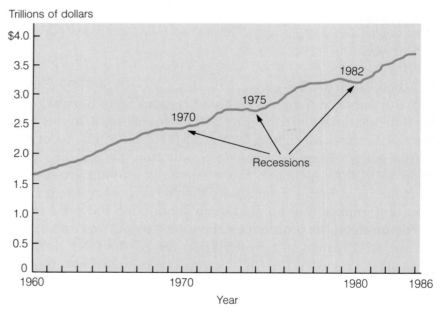

Figure 11–9   Real GNP for the U.S. Economy, 1960–1986 (Base Year = 1982)

Real GNP is gross national product adjusted for inflation. Each year's GNP is measured using the prices of the base year of 1982. Between 1960 and 1986, real GNP has generally increased. The chart's climb to the right demonstrates that increase. The years 1970, 1975, and 1982 were exceptions. During those years real GNP declined for at least one-half of the year. Therefore, these were years of recession.

Source: Economic Report of the President (Washington, D.C.: U.S. Government Printing Office, 1987), 246.

> **Recession:** A decrease in real GNP for at least one-half of a year.

The Growth of Real GNP

If our incomes are to rise, then real GNP must grow. This is because aggregate income cannot rise unless aggregate supply also increases. The growth of real GNP thus means that aggregate income, aggregate supply, and aggregate demand are rising.

One way in which real GNP can grow is by having *more people join the labor force.* More workers mean more production, so real GNP goes up. A rising labor force has been an important source of our economy's growth over the last couple of decades. In particular, many women have joined the labor force and have caused our nation's real GNP to expand.

Real GNP can grow also when there is an *increase in the productivity of labor.* By producing more goods and services per hour, workers can also earn more income per hour. Greater productivity is necessary, therefore, if each member of the labor force is to earn a higher income.

What increases the productivity of work and raises real GNP? One important determinant is the amount of income a nation *saves and invests in new capital goods.* For example, Figure 11–5 has shown the outflow of saving and the inflow of investment. If consumers save more of their income and if businesses borrow and invest that larger amount of saving, there will be more and better capital goods for people to use in their work. The greater amount of technologically improved capital goods will increase workers' productivity and raise real GNP.

It's no secret that the Japanese economy has been growing more rapidly than other economies have because it saves and invests a much larger proportion of its income than do most other nations. But the circular flow map also shows that in order to save and invest a larger fraction of aggregate income, we must reduce the fraction of income we use for consumption. In other words, if real GNP is to grow, so that more can be consumed tomorrow, we must be willing to sacrifice some con-

(text continues on page 313)

The Economic Way of Thinking

Real Incomes

When Mike's father was in high school, he earned $30 a week at a part-time job. Aren't most high school students who have part-time jobs better off today?

Noneconomic Way of Thinking

Thirty dollars a week is hardly any money at all. I don't see how Mike's father could have maintained his car, supported his hobbies, and gone out with his friends. Today's students who work part-time are certainly better off.

Economic Way of Thinking

Prices are a lot higher today than they were when Mike's father was in high school. Because inflation has pushed prices and wages up so much over the years, $30 buys a lot less today than it did years ago. In order to compare living standards between these two times, we must deflate today's incomes into real terms. For example, if prices have tripled since Mike's father was in high school, then someone who is now earning $90 per week will have the same real income that Mike's dad did. Only by earning more than three times what Mike's father earned, will a student today have a higher real income.

Questions

1. Last year Mary received a pay raise of 5 percent. Since that time, prices have increased by 10 percent. What has happened to the real buying power of Mary's pay?

2. Some labor unions have contracts with employers that call for workers' pay to rise with the rate of inflation. What is the effect of these contracts on the real buying power of workers' wages?

3. In Mexico and other nations, workers sometimes receive annual pay increases of between 50 and 100 percent. Are these workers necessarily getting richer?

Real GNP will grow if more people join the labor force and begin producing goods and services. These workers demonstrate that many women have joined the labor force and have contributed to the growth of our nation's real production.

Real GNP will also grow if existing workers become more productive. An important cause of rising productivity has been the increased availability of better capital goods, such as these computers.

The Economic Engine That Could

Why has Japan's economy grown so rapidly? Between 1967 and 1985, the Japanese economy grew about twice as fast as the economies of other industrialized nations. Is there some secret to this extraordinary growth that we could import along with the many goods we purchase from Japan?

The answer might be right in front of our noses. Many factors are responsible for a nation's economic growth, but one especially important element is the amount of income a nation saves and invests in new productive capital goods. If individuals can work with more and better machines, tools, and other capital goods, they can produce more goods and services per hour of work. Consequently, aggregate supply can grow. Saving and investment are important because they provide the new capital goods that enable the supply of goods and services to rise. The more a nation saves and invests, therefore, the faster it can expect to grow.

It is no secret that Japan has been saving and investing a much larger proportion of its gross national product than have other nations. While Japan saved and invested almost one-third of its GNP during the 1960s and 1970s, the United States set aside less than one-fifth of its GNP for investment.

Although the growth of the U.S. economy has not measured up to Japan's in recent years, our nation's economic growth in this century has been remarkable by historical standards. For example, in 1929 gross national product totaled $103.9 billion. By 1985, GNP had grown to $3,998 billion. This increase is extraordinary because in 1985 GNP was more than thirty-eight times what it was in 1929.

This growth does not reflect the real increase in our production of goods and services, however, because the price level changed significantly during this period. Indeed, in 1986 the price level was almost eight times higher than it was in 1929. Consequently, much of the increase in gross national product reflects higher prices, not an increase in the production of goods and services. When GNP is adjusted for inflation, however, the effects of price changes are eliminated. The adjusted numbers, called real GNP, show actual changes in the production of goods and services over the years. Figure A shows the growth of real GNP between 1929 and 1985.

One of the reasons for this growth is the fact that our nation's resources have increased over the decades. For example, as land has been developed or added during this century, our natural resources have increased.

Figure A   Real GNP, 1929–1985 (Base year = 1982)

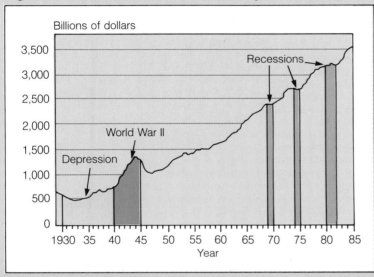

Source: U.S. Department of Commerce, Bureau of Economic Analysis. *Survey of Current Business.* (September 1986): 66, no. 9, p. 66.

And as our population has grown, more workers have been added to the production of goods and services.

But a more important reason for the growth of real GNP has been our nation's saving and investment. As Americans have saved a portion of their incomes and as banks and businesses have channeled this savings into productive investments, workers have obtained more and better capital goods for use in their work. As our country's labor force has produced more goods per hour of work, real GNP has risen.

Figure B shows that between 1929 and 1985 our economy saved and invested an average of about 15 percent of its gross national product. But this average is deceiving because it hides the wide variation in the proportion of GNP invested. Notice that during the Great Depression of the 1930s the relative size of investment sank. Although the economy attempted in 1936 and 1937 to regain some of its lost vigor, investment remained weak. Moreover, during World War II, the proportion of GNP going to investment fell to about 5 percent. That's because the enormous quantity of our nation's scarce re-

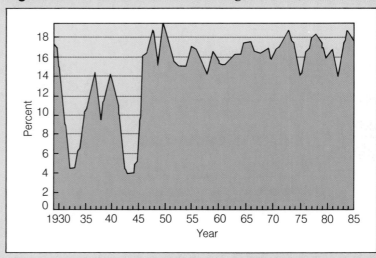

Figure B Investment as a Percentage of GNP, 1929–1985

Source: U.S. Department of Commerce, Bureau of Economic Analysis, *Survey of Current Business*, p. 66.

sources used for the war left considerably fewer resources for investment.

After the depression of the 1930s and the war of the 1940s, therefore, workers had fewer capital goods than they would otherwise have had if the nation's investment had not slowed. As a result, labor productivity did not rise as quickly, and many goods and services that would otherwise have been produced were not supplied. All those goods and services that consumers never got to enjoy represented an important cost that Americans continued to pay long after the Depression and the war had ended.

Saving and investment are a powerful engine that drives our nation's economy forward. Without either one or without the ability to channel savings into investment, we could not come close to the average standard of living we enjoy today.

Figure C shows how saving and investment have generally increased the amount of capital goods that the average worker has had available. From 1930 to the end of World War II in 1945, however, the amount of capital goods per worker fell. It fell during the 1930s because the bottom fell out of investment spending. It fell during the war because resources were diverted from invest-

Figure C Real Capital per Worker, 1925–1981

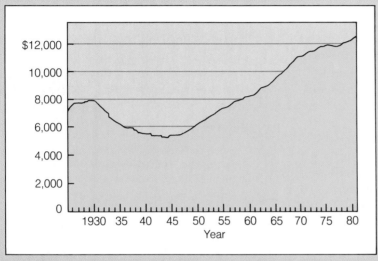

Source: U.S. Department of Commerce, Bureau of Economic Analysis, *Survey of Current Business*, p. 59; U.S. Department of Commerce, Bureau of the Census, *Statistics of the United States, Colonial Times to 1970*, p. 126; *Economic Report of the President*, 1987, p. 288.

ment to fight the war. Moreover, if you look at the mid-1970s, you can see a temporary halt to the growth of capital per worker. One of the reasons for this slowdown was the rapid increase in the labor force at that time, due primarily to the entry of women and teen-agers into the labor force. Even though new investment was being made, the number of people joining the labor force rose so rapidly that the amount of capital per worker remained rather steady.

Although saving and investment have helped propel the economy forward over the years, our nation's economic growth has not been smooth. Instead, it has been punctuated by the ups and downs known as the business cycle. You can see these ups and downs by looking at the bumpy path followed by real GNP in Figure A. These fluctuations illustrate times when saving and investment have been out of balance. For example, when investment plummeted during the 1930s, more income leaked out of the nation's circular flow through saving than was put back in as investment. As a result, aggregate demand fell below aggregate supply, and the economy contracted. Although the scale of Figure A masks the severity of the economic collapse, real GNP declined by almost 30 percent between 1929 and 1933. If a collapse of the same proportion occurred today, it would mean the production of goods and services would drop by more than $1 trillion.

Saving and investment are certainly important to our country's economy. Not only do they allow the nation's productive capacity to grow over the years, but also they help to determine the extent to which we use our productive capacity in any given year.

Most of us want some economic growth in order to obtain more of the goods and services we want. But economic growth requires some saving and investment, and saving and investment mean sacrificing some current consumption. How much current consumption do you think we should give up in order to produce and consume more tomorrow?

References

Economic Report of the President. Washington, D.C.: U.S. Government Printing Office, January 1987.

U.S. Department of the Census, *Statistics of the United States. Colonial Times to 1970.* Washington, D.C.: U.S. Government Printing Office, 1986.

U.S. Department of Commerce, Bureau of Economic Analysis. *Survey of Current Business*, Vol. 66.

sumption of goods and services today. By doing so, we permit scarce resources to be transferred from the production of consumer goods to the production of capital goods.

Saving and investment are important causes of an economy's growth. Without saving, there is no income to invest. Without investment, the growth of real production is unlikely. On the other hand, if planned saving and investment are not equal, aggregate demand and aggregate supply are not balanced. As a result, the circular flow expands or contracts, and the economy moves through some phase of the business cycle.

Most of us don't think about how the savings of consumers are channeled into the productive investments of business. But the improvement of our living standard over time certainly depends on this process. So, too, does the current state of our economy depend on savings being put to work as investment. Lending and borrowing are thus very important functions because they are part of the process that directs an economy's saving into investment. If everyone took Shakespeare's advice and neither borrowed nor lent money, then a good part of our savings would not be put to work as investment. We would all be a lot poorer as a result.

There are undoubtedly times when individuals would have been better off if they had not borrowed or lent money. But, fortunately, most of us save our money by lending it to banks and other financial institutions. Those businesses that borrow and invest the money then put our savings to work.

Chapter Summary

1. *Aggregate demand* is the total of all demands for goods and services in our economy. *Aggregate supply* is the total of all supplies of goods and services in our economy. When aggregate supply and aggregate demand are unequal, the economy adjusts in order to balance them.

2. The circular flow of money shows that production, income, and spending are all interconnected: aggregate demand leads to aggregate supply, aggregate supply leads to aggregate income, and aggregate income leads back to aggregate demand.

3. If no one spends the money saved by consumers, then aggregate demand will be less than aggregate supply. But

most consumer saving is deposited in financial institutions, such as banks, which then lend some of the saving to other consumers. If we subtract from total consumer saving the amount lent to other consumers, we obtain *net consumer saving*. Banks earn money on net consumer saving by loaning this money to businesses for *investment*, which is defined as the production of new capital goods, not personal or financial investment. If businesses borrow and invest all net consumer saving, then aggregate demand and aggregate supply are equal.

4. If net consumer saving exceeds investment, then aggregate supply will be greater than aggregate demand. A balance between the two can be restored by a decrease in wages and prices or by a decrease in production and employment. These adjustments cause the economy to rise and fall, and the resulting economic fluctuations are called *business cycles*.

5. *Gross national product (GNP)* is the sum of all prices of final goods and services produced for the marketplace in a nation during a particular time. Those items not produced for the market are not included in GNP. Prices of intermediate products are not directly counted because their values are indirectly included in the prices of final products.

6. GNP consists of the total of consumption, investment, government purchases, and exports, minus imports. *Inflation*, which is an increase in the price level, must be taken out of the GNP number by the *GNP deflator* in order to obtain *real GNP*.

7. Aggregate income cannot grow unless aggregate supply increases. As a result, real GNP growth means that aggregate income, aggregate supply, and aggregate demand are all rising. Real GNP can grow when the number of workers increases or when existing workers become more productive. If consumer saving is channeled into business investment, workers can become more productive because they will have more and better capital goods to use in their work. Real GNP can then grow.

8. Increased consumer saving is possible if consumers are willing to consume less of their total income now so that more production and consumption can occur in the future. As a result, the growth of our standard of living depends on the diversion of consumer saving to business investment, an important function performed by financial institutions.

1. What is meant by the terms *aggregate demand* and *aggregate supply?*

2. What is the relationship among aggregate demand, aggregate supply, and aggregate income?

3. What is meant by the term *net consumer saving,* and how do banks use the net saving of consumers to earn money?

4. How does an economist define *investment?* How does this definition differ from the everyday use of the term?

5. Can aggregate demand and aggregate supply be unequal? Explain.

6. What is *gross national product,* and why is it an important gauge?

7. What is *real gross national product?* How, if at all, does it relate to inflation and recession?

8. Why does real gross national product have to grow in order for our incomes to rise?

9. Describe two factors responsible for the growth of real gross national product.

Discussion Questions

1. If aggregate demand is less than aggregate supply, what could happen to production, prices, wages, and employment? Why?

2. What factors cause real gross national product to grow? Explain why they cause this growth.

3. Defend or attack the following argument: The trouble with our nation is that everyone thinks about today, not tomorrow. We would be better off if we saved a lot more of our incomes.

Activities

1. In the circular flow map below, aggregate demand and aggregate supply are equal.

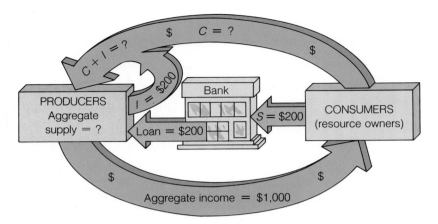

Examine the circular flow, and then answer the following questions:

(a) Compute the missing values for aggregate supply, consumption, and aggregate demand.

(b) Now assume that saving doubles, so that consumers are saving $400 instead of $200. If business investment remains unchanged, will aggregate demand and aggregate supply still be equal? If not, what will their values be?

(c) Go back to part a and assume that businesses double their borrowing and investment from $200 to $400. Also assume that saving and consumption are unchanged. (Banks can lend more than consumers currently save because they can lend money deposited in the past and they can also create new money.) Will aggregate demand and aggregate supply still be equal? If not, what will their values be?

2. Write a paragraph explaining how production is connected to income, how income is connected to spending, and how spending is connected back to production.

3. Draw a circular flow diagram and show the relationship among aggregate demand, aggregate supply, and aggregate income.

4. Defend or attack the following statement: Without investment, our living standard is unlikely to grow.

Additional Readings

Hazlitt, Henry. *Ecomomics in One Lesson*. New York: Arlington House, 1979. Chapter 24.

Heilbroner, Robert L., and Thurow, Lester C. *The Economic Problem*. Englewood Cliffs, N.J.: Prentice-Hall, 1984. Chapters 9–14.

Kendrick, John W. "National Income and Product Accounts." In *International Encyclopedia of the Social Sciences*. London: Macmillan, 1968.

U.S. Department of Commerce, Bureau of Economic Analysis. *Survey of Current Business*. Various monthly issues.

Why do most payments for goods represent the transfer of bank debt?

Money and Banks

■ Student's Goals ■

1. Explain how the difficulties of barter exchange are resolved by a money economy.

2. Explain why our banking system is called a *fractional reserve system.*

3. Explain how and why banks make loans.

4. Describe how the banking system creates new checking account money when someone makes a deposit of currency or coin.

5. Describe some of the banking difficulties of the last century that led to the creation of the Federal Reserve System.

6. Describe the important parts and functions of the Federal Reserve System.

Smokable Money

Despite the fact that cigarette smoking is dangerous to one's health, cigarettes became a source of economic health for the Romanian economy.[1] This strange situation occurred when the government of Romania set many prices below their equilibrium levels. Because these low prices created shortages, consumers were unable to buy much of what they demanded with the official Romanian currency, the leu (pronounced loo).

As the official money lost much of its usefulness, Romanians ignored it and began to *barter*. *Barter* occurs when people exchange goods and services with one another without the use of money. In a Romanian farmers' market, apples were traded for peppers, cauliflowers for beets, and turnips for garlic.

But barter is usually a very difficult way to trade. An apple seller might want to buy peppers, but a pepper seller might not want to buy apples. It's much easier if the apple seller can receive money from a buyer and then use this money to purchase peppers from someone else. Imagine the difficulty of using barter in our nation. If you worked at a fast-food restaurant, you might be paid in hamburgers or French fries. When you wanted to buy gasoline, you would have to find a gasoline seller willing to accept your hamburgers or fries, which by then could be cold and stale.

Barter is also complicated because it requires that the price of each item be given in terms of every other good. If you are selling apples, you will have to give the price in terms of oranges, peppers, hamburgers, gasoline, and every other item that someone might want to trade for your apples. With 500 other goods in the farmers' market in Romania, an apple will have 500 different prices.

No wonder people want to use some kind of money when trading with one another. Then each item has only one price—the money price—and that single money price makes selling and shopping a lot easier. Moreover, instead of barter—in which you might have to find a gasoline seller who would accept hamburgers as payment—people can use nonperishable money, which is readily accepted in exchange.

Because money makes it much easier for people to buy from

[1]Roger Thurow, "In Romania Smoking A Kent Cigarette Is Like Burning Money," *Wall Street Journal*, January 3, 1986.

Because of government price controls, barter began to replace money exchanges at this Romanian farmers' market. Why is barter a costly means of exchanging goods and services?

and sell to one another, a substitute money evolved in Romania, as its official money lost much of its usefulness. No one passed a law or issued a decree. It just happened that cigarettes—Kent cigarettes—became the unofficial, smokable money of Romania.

The prices of many goods and services were then expressed in terms of Kent cigarettes. Kent prices were not government-controlled, however, so they could rise to their equilibrium levels in order to balance the amounts demanded and supplied. At unofficial Kent prices, therefore, there were no shortages of consumer goods. Instead, with Kents to spend, Romanians found adequate supplies and quality merchandise—without the long lines they often encountered when they shopped with the leu. Romanians had invented a new money and, by so doing, were better able to exchange goods and services with one another.

Money: What It Is and What It Does

Cigarettes are one of many commodities that have been used as money throughout history. Tobacco, beads, copper, gold, cattle, silver, olive oil, and feathers have served as money. When you hear someone say that a hard-working person is "worth his or her salt," it is because the Romans used salt to pay their sailors. And when you hear someone complain about having "to shell out" so much money to buy something, it is because shells have been used as money. On the small South Pacific island of Yap, large stones up to 12 feet across are now used as money. These stones, which have holes through their middles and can be moved with tree trunks, are certainly unlike the coin and currency (paper money) we carry with us.

In most nations today, coin and currency are more convenient, so they have replaced commodity moneys, such as boulders, beads, salt, and shells. Unlike large rocks, currency and coin are easy to carry around. They don't run away as cattle often would. They don't spoil, break, or rot the way eggs would if we tried to use them as money. Furthermore, by using good engraving processes, coin and currency can be made difficult to counterfeit.

The fact that so many different things have served as money throughout history tells us that money can be whatever accomplishes its tasks. The important point in defining money is not

This pan of gold illustrates only one of the commodities that have been used as money throughout history. What characteristics of gold have made it a popular form of money throughout the ages? Is gold now one of the items we use as money?

how big it is, what it looks like, how heavy it is, or what shape it has. Whatever the particular object might be, the important point is that it performs the three tasks of money.

Medium of Exchange

Money's most important task is to serve as a *medium of exchange.* To understand the meaning of this task, think about barter, mentioned at the beginning of this chapter. Suppose you want to buy a bathing suit but all you have to offer in exchange are some apples you have grown. No doubt, you will quickly discover that sellers are unwilling to accept the apples in exchange for a bathing suit.

The use of barter would make buying a bathing suit or anything else very difficult because it requires that each seller be willing to accept as payment the good or service offered by the buyer. Since this outcome isn't very likely, everyone would have to spend a lot of time and resources trying to exchange with one another.

Now suppose you can sell your apples for little pieces of paper, called *dollars*, that are generally accepted as payment for goods and services. You will accept these pieces of paper because you know they will be accepted, in turn, by others as payment for the bathing suit or whatever else you want. Instead of trying to trade your apples directly for a bathing suit, you first sell your apples to many different people from whom you accept dollars. Then you trade the dollars for the bathing suit. By acting as a middle good, therefore, the dollars are the *medium* by which the sale of your apples can be easily channeled into the purchase of a swimsuit. That's why money is called a medium of exchange.

Measure of Prices

A second function of money is to serve as a *measure of prices.* At the beginning of the chapter you saw that in the absence of money a single item would have many different prices. For example, without money we would have to express the price of a television in terms of so many radios or pounds of corn or heads of lettuce or some other item. With millions of alternative goods and services available in the marketplace, each item would have millions of prices, instead of the single money price consumers now find. As a result, consumers would find it much more difficult to be informed shoppers.

Store of Buying Power

A third task of money is to serve as a *store of buying power* over time. If there were no money, you would have to keep your buying power in the form of specific goods, such as eggs, goldfish, or cassette tapes that you could later trade for items you want. But eggs eventually spoil, goldfish eventually die, and tapes eventually wear out or become unpopular. On the other hand, money lasts forever and can be a lot easier to trade than a goldfish or some other commodity. There are obviously many ways in which people can store buying power over time, but holding money is certainly a very convenient method of doing so.

Checking Up On Money

Money is whatever people widely use as a medium of exchange, a measure of prices, and a store of buying power.

> **Money:** Whatever people widely use as a medium of exchange, a measure of prices, and a store of buying power.

By performing these three tasks, money makes it easier for us to trade with one another. That's why various forms of money have evolved throughout history. The use of Kent cigarettes as money in Romania certainly illustrates this point. Because Kents were easy to carry and difficult to counterfeit, they served as a convenient medium of exchange. They were also a useful measure of prices because the number of cigarettes could be easily varied to express high or low prices. Moreover, Kent cigarettes were a useful store of value because their supply was limited and they were fairly durable.

We know cigarettes are not money in our nation, but many people do have difficulty identifying all the items that comprise our nation's money supply. Coins and currency are certainly included, but they represent only about 25 percent of the nation's money supply. If it seems logical to include gold, houses, stocks, and bonds, remember these items are not generally accepted as a means of paying for goods and services. If they're not generally accepted as a medium of exchange, they shouldn't be included as part of the stock of money. Nor should credit cards be included because they represent loans. For example, someone who purchases a stereo with a credit card receives a loan that must later be paid with money.

When making payments, most people use checks, not coin or currency (see Figure 12–1). Suppose Sam Eatwell goes to Local Grocery and writes a check for $50, which the store deposits in its bank. Sam gets the groceries, and the grocery store gets. . .

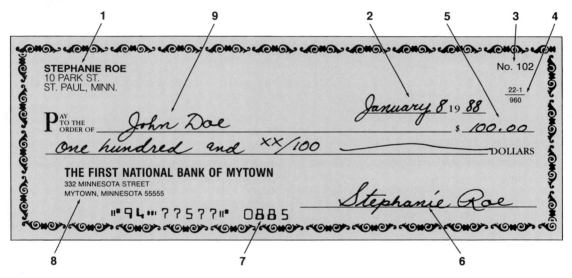

Figure 12–1 The Elements of a Check

1. The name and address of the person (or organization) who writes the check.
2. The date the check is written.
3. The check number used by the check writer to keep track of the checks written.
4. The routing number that identifies the bank on which the check is drawn.
5. The amount of the check is written here in numbers. On the next line below, the same amount is written in words. The amount of cents, however, is written as a fraction with 100 as the denominator. For example, if the check had been written for $100.08, then the fraction would show 08/100 instead of xx/100.
6. The person writing the check is called the drawer. This is the drawer's signature.
7. These magnetic numbers identify the check writer's account number at the bank. These numbers assure that the money will be withdrawn from the proper account at the bank.
8. The name and address of the bank on which the check is drawn.
9. The person (or organization) to whom the check writer wants the bank to transfer money.

What does the grocery store get? Something has certainly been transferred from Sam Eatwell's checking account at his bank to the grocery store's checking account at its bank. But coin and currency aren't moved from Sam's account to the market's account, so what does the store now have $50 more of in its checking account?

The answer is numbers. When Sam Eatwell writes a $50 check on his bank and gives it to the grocery store, $50 of numbers are subtracted from Sam's checking account and then added to the store's checking account. In fact, checks aren't even necessary to make this transfer of numbers because it can be done electronically with computers. Supermarkets and other retail stores do this by providing computers that quickly transfer numbers from the shoppers' checking accounts to the stores' bank accounts. The numbers are still called *checking deposits*, however, and they represent about 75 percent of the nation's money supply. If you add up all the checking deposits, coin, and currency in the country, you will then have calculated the nation's total stock of money. These are the dollars we use as a medium of exchange, a measure of prices, and a store of value.

Creating Money

The stock of money in our nation has grown considerably over the years. Some of this growth has been due to increases in the amount of coin and currency in circulation. But since most of our nation's money supply consists of checking deposits, increases in these deposits have been the most important source of new money in our nation.

Most checking deposits are held at commercial banks. Until the 1980s, commercial banks were the only institutions that could legally keep checking deposits. Since that time, there have been important changes in our banking system. As a result, other institutions, such as savings and loans and credit unions, now also keep deposits on which people write checks. We want to keep our discussion of money and banks clear and simple, however, so we will ignore the differences among these various kinds of financial institutions. Instead, we will call them all *banks,* and we will refer to all the checking deposits they hold as *bank money.*

The Economic Way of Thinking

Credit Cards

Many people use credit cards when they purchase goods and services. For example, when they take vacations they often take along their checkbooks, some cash, and some credit cards. Are these credit cards "plastic money?"

Noneconomic Way of Thinking

It's obvious that credit cards are money. You can use them just like cash or checks to pay hotel bills, to buy gas, or to purchase other goods and services.

Economic Way of Thinking

It is true that you can buy gas, lodging, and other things with a credit card. But some time after using a credit card, usually about 30 days, you receive a bill from the credit card company. You must pay the bill with money, which means you must send cash or a check. Because the cash or the check, not the credit card, is accepted as a means of payment, the credit card is not money. The credit card is only a way of delaying payment by incurring a debt, for which you must eventually pay money.

Questions

1. What situations would cause you to favor using a credit card instead of a check or currency?

2. What do you gain by delaying payment through a credit card purchase? (*Hint:* Does the rate of interest affect your incentive to delay a payment?)

3. If someone steals your credit card, have they stolen any of your money? If the stolen card is used to make a purchase, who is the victim?

Checking Accounts Are Bank Debts

Checking account money is bank debt. If you deposit a $50 bill in your checking account at your bank, you are loaning the bank $50 of currency that you can get back whenever you want. Because the bank owes you $50, your deposit is the bank's debt. But most people do not ask the bank to return the currency they deposit. Instead, by writing checks to pay for their purchases, they transfer their deposits to others who willingly accept them as a means of payment.

Since deposits are actually banks' debts, people are using bank debt as money. For example, if you write a $50 check to buy new clothes, you give the clothing store $50 of bank debt in exchange for the clothes. The store can then ask the bank for $50 in currency if it so desires, but it will probably write its own checks and thereby use the deposit to help pay its expenses. In this way, the $50 of bank debt can be transferred from person to person as they buy and sell goods and services.

The checking accounts we use to buy and sell goods and services represent debts of Bank of America and other banks. The bank owes a depositor an amount of currency equal to the amount deposited. But rather than withdrawing currency when making purchases, most people transfer their bank deposits to others, who accept the bank's debt as a means of payment.

Checking Accounts and Reserves

When people hold checking account money, they often think that banks must have an equal amount of currency or coin on reserve in their vaults. But banks are not "full of money" in the sense that they have a dollar of currency or coin on reserve in their vaults for every dollar of checking account money (bank debt). Because people with checking accounts do not generally demand cash, banks keep on reserve only a fraction of the money deposited with them. No wonder our banking system is often referred to as a *fractional reserve system*. Only a fraction of a bank's deposits need be kept on reserve as an inventory of funds in case people decide on a given day to withdraw more cash than they deposit. After setting aside a fraction of deposits as a reserve, a bank uses the remaining funds to make new loans, the interest payments on which provide the bank with its income.

As an example, look at Figure 12–2. Suppose someone gives you $1,000 of currency, which you quickly deposit at Dry Gulch Bank. You now have $1,000 of new checking account money at the bank, and the bank has $1,000 of new debt because it now owes you that much money. But Dry Gulch Bank's reserves also have increased by $1,000 because it has that much more currency in its vault. However, the bank doesn't have to keep the entire $1,000 of currency on reserve in its vault. Instead, assume that banks generally keep only 20 percent of their deposits on reserve. After keeping $200 in reserves, therefore, Dry Gulch Bank will loan the other $800 in order to earn interest on the money. Suppose it loans the money to Joe's Auto Parts. Dry Gulch Bank makes the loan by taking $800 from its reserves and putting it into the store's checking account.

From the point of view of Dry Gulch Bank, it is merely loaning out money you have deposited; it is not creating new money. But what is true for an individual bank is not true for the banking system as a whole. When all banks are considered together, they certainly do create money.

You can understand how the banking system creates money by following the events that occur after Dry Gulch Bank makes the $800 loan. Joe's Auto Parts spends the $800 by writing a check to Ace Construction Co. for remodeling work. Ace Construction then deposits the money at Sun Bank where it has an account. Notice, however, that the deposit of $800 represents

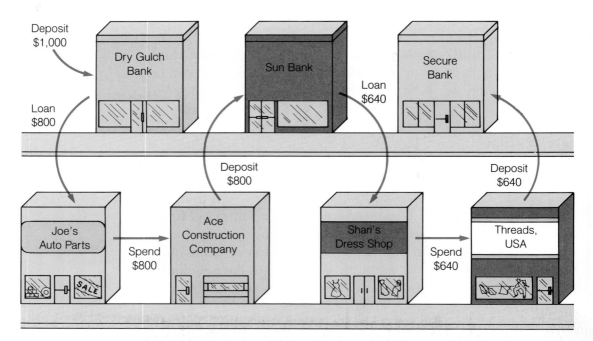

Figure 12–2 How the Banking System Creates Money

After you deposit the $1,000 bill at Dry Gulch Bank, the bank keeps 20 percent or $200 on reserve and loans the other $800 to Joe's Auto Parts by putting $800 in Joe's checking account. Joe's Auto Parts spends the money at Ace Construction Company, which then deposits the money at its bank, Sun Bank. Sun Bank then keeps 20 percent or $160 on reserve and lends the remaining $640 to Shari's Dress Shop. Shari's Dress Shop then spends the money at Threads, USA, which deposits the money at its bank, Secure Bank. As a result of these transactions, total bank deposits (checking account money) have increased by $2,440 ($1,000 + $800 + $640).

new checking account money in the banking system. Thus, the amount of checking account money in the country has increased.

The new $800 deposit at Sun Bank increases its reserves by $800 and, thereby, enables the bank to make a new loan, just as your original deposit of $1,000 at Dry Gulch Bank enabled it to make a new loan. After keeping on reserve only 20 percent of $800 or $160, Sun Bank loans the remaining $640 ($800 − $160) to Shari's Dress Shop. Shari's Dress Shop then spends the money to buy new clothes from Threads, USA, after which Threads, USA deposits the money at Secure Bank where it has an account. The $640 deposit at Secure Bank represents another new deposit in the nation's banking system. Once again, the amount of checking account money in the nation has increased.

Secure Bank can then keep on reserve a fraction of its new deposit and loan the rest in order to earn interest, just as the other banks did. Consequently, the process of new loans and new deposits continues to ripple throughout the banking system.

But notice what has already happened to the total amount of checking account deposits or bank money in the economy. Dry Gulch Bank has a new deposit of $1,000; Sun Bank has a new deposit of $800; and Secure Bank has a new deposit of $640. All these new deposits total $2,440, which means that the amount of checking account money in the nation has increased by $2,440.

New Checking Deposits

Dry Gulch Bank	$1,000
Sun Bank	$ 800
Secure Bank	+ $ 640
Total new checking account money at the three banks	$2,440

Although each bank correctly claims that it is only lending the money of its depositors, the banking system as a whole is actually creating new checking account money. Moreover, the money creation started by your original $1,000 deposit still has a way to go because other banks down the line will continue to receive new deposits and make new loans. But each new deposit will become progressively smaller, as the three deposits at Dry Gulch Bank, Sun Bank, and Secure Bank demonstrate. As a result, the formation of new deposits eventually stops. If we follow this process along and then add up *all* new deposits at *all* banks in the same way we have done for the three banks above, we will find a total increase in checking account money that is considerably larger than the original $1,000 you deposited.[2]

---

[2]Mathematically, this process of expansion is a series of infinite terms that decline progressively and have a total value approaching $5,000. Since we assume banks can lend 80 percent of their deposits, they can expand the supply of bank money as follows: ($1,000) + ($1,000 × 80%) + ($800 × 80%) + ($640 × 80%) + . . . = $5,000. A shortcut method of calculating the total of $5,000 takes the original $1,000 deposit and multiplies it by the ratio 1/reserve rate, where the reserve rate is the 20 percent each bank keeps on reserve:

(a) $\dfrac{1}{\text{reserve rate}} = \dfrac{1}{20\%} = \dfrac{1}{20/100} = \dfrac{100}{20} = 5$

(b) $\dfrac{1}{\text{reserve rate}} \times \$1,000 = 5 \times \$1,000 = \$5,000$

As you can see, reserves are a powerful part of our nation's banking system. If banks can somehow obtain more reserves, they will want to make more loans in order to earn interest. In so doing, they will create more money. New bank reserves are, thus, the fuel that enables the banking system to create more money. As the next chapter will show, the relationship between bank reserves and money creation enables us to expand or contract the amount of bank money in our economy.

The Evolution of Banking in the United States

Our acceptance and use of bank money is an extraordinary development. Think how different checking deposits are from commodities, such as shells, cattle, and gold, that have been used as money throughout history. When we make and accept payments with bank money, we are not transferring commodities from one to another. Instead, we are using bank debts, which are numbers recorded at banks. These numbers are not backed by gold, precious metals, or any other commodity. They are backed by our faith that we can use these numbers to purchase the goods and services we demand.

The confidence people have today in banks and bank money should not be taken for granted. Indeed, this confidence developed gradually during the evolution of our nation's banking system.

State Banks

Our country's first bank, the Bank of North America, was formed in Philadelphia, Pennsylvania, in 1781. As new banks were created in the following years, they were required to obtain corporate charters from the states in which they resided. By 1820, the number of these state banks had grown substantially.

These early banks often failed, however, because they issued currency and bank notes that they promised to exchange for gold and silver on demand. But because the banks often did not have enough gold and silver in reserve, they could not make good on these promises.

The Economic Way of Thinking

The Backing of Money

Is it true that in order to be worth something money must be backed by gold or some other precious metal?

Noneconomic Way of Thinking

Our paper money is backed by all the gold that our government has stored at Fort Knox near Louisville, Kentucky. Our paper money has value only because we know that whenever we want, we can exchange it for a given amount of this gold. If our paper money were not backed by all this gold, it would be worthless.

Economic Way of Thinking

Our paper money is not backed by gold or any other precious metal. That's because our government will not sell gold or other precious metals to citizens whenever they want to convert their paper money into these metals. Instead, our paper money is called *fiat money*, which means that the government, by command or fiat, declares that it is money. Our money has value only because we generally accept it as payment. What really backs our money, therefore, is everyone's confidence that it will be accepted in exchange for goods and services.

Questions

1. Would a period of hyperinflation—rapidly accelerating price increases—affect your willingness to accept money as a means of payment?

2. If you possess money in an economy experiencing hyperinflation, what will you want to do with the money? Why?

3. Why is foreign currency not acceptable as a means of payment in the United States?

The First Bank of the United States

The weakness of state banks led Alexander Hamilton, the first U.S. Secretary of the Treasury, to create a plan for the first United States Bank. The first Bank of the United States was established in 1791, with its central office in Philadelphia and with other branches scattered throughout the states. It had a twenty-year charter, which was to expire in 1811.

The funds to start this bank came from shares of stock bought by the U.S. government and private citizens. The bank issued paper money, accepted deposits, made loans for which it charged interest, and regulated the lending of state banks. For various reasons the charter of the first Bank of the United States was allowed to expire. One of those reasons was that some states thought the bank was growing too powerful and was severely limiting the actions of the state banks.

The Second Bank of the United States

In 1816, the second Bank of the United States was established, also with a twenty-year charter. The funds for this bank were provided by the federal government, states, and private individuals. It performed many of the same tasks as the first bank, including regulating the amount of bank notes that could be issued by the state banks. Andrew Jackson, who became president in 1832, was determined to block renewal of the second bank's charter in 1836. His opposition was based on a deep distrust of banks and a feeling that the second bank favored the interests of citizens in the East over those of citizens in the West. As a result, President Jackson vetoed a bill to renew its charter.

State and National Banking

After 1836, when the charter of the Second Bank of the United States was not renewed, state banks became increasingly important, an importance that lasted until the Civil War. Unfortunately, these banks often issued bank notes (paper money) that were not backed by adequate reserves.

During this time, the nation's money supply fluctuated wildly. It increased greatly during the early 1830s, and then decreased

The First Bank of the United States, on Third Street, Philadelphia, Pennsylvania.
Created by a 20-year charter in 1791, the controversial bank was an attempt to
establish a sound banking system in the United States.

severely in the late 1830s and the 1840s.[3] Many more state
banks were established during this time, but many of them
failed.

Because of the periodic financial panics and numerous bank
failures that occurred between 1830 and 1860, Congress passed
a new banking law, called the National Banking Act, in 1863.
Although state bank charters remained legal, this act established a new banking system of nationally chartered banks. By
placing a 10-percent tax on state bank notes in 1864, the federal
government forced most state banks to stop issuing paper money.
It also forced many banks to join the national banking system
by swapping their state charters for federal ones.

Although the National Banking Act provided more stability
for the banking system, it did not create a true central bank
that would provide a flexible money supply to meet the frequent surges in cash withdrawals.

Cash shortages often occurred in the banking system during
the latter part of the nineteenth century and the early part of

[3]Barry W. Poulson, *Economic History of the United States* (New York: Macmillan, 1981), 341.

(text continues on page 340)

Banking on Panic

By lunchtime everyone at school was talking about the bank panic. Tina was noticeably shaken when she heard the bad news. For the last two years, she had been saving her part-time earnings at a local bank. Now, she thought her savings were gone, thanks to panicky depositors.

The bank panic stemmed from the world debt crisis that had seemed far away and unimportant until now. When the developing nations that had borrowed tens of billions of dollars from U.S. banks suddenly announced their inability or un-willingness to pay another penny of their foreign debts, nervous depositors across the country began withdrawing funds from their bank accounts. These depositors worried that the banks would not have enough money to satisfy their customers' withdrawals if banks suddenly lost the billions of dollars of foreign loans they had made. As more depositors went to their banks to withdraw funds, nervousness spread quickly. Soon, anxious withdrawal requests by some depositors had turned into frenzied demands by all. But since banks keep only a fraction of their deposits on reserve, their cupboards of reserves were soon bare. Tina's savings were gone. Gone also was the college education her savings were to help finance.

Fortunately, the story is fiction. But what would happen if many indebted nations suddenly cancelled their loans to U.S. banks? In 1987, for example, borrowers in the Philippines and in Latin America owed some $85 billion to banks in the United States. This sum exceeded the total amount that bank owners (stockholders) had invested in U.S. banks. Therefore, if these nations suddenly cancelled their debts, the investment of bank owners would be too small to absorb the entire loss to the banking system. In that case, depositors, such as Tina, might also bear the loss by losing some or all of the money they had deposited. This would occur if nervous depositors began rushing to banks to withdraw their money. And because they would demand more cash than banks hold in reserve, many banks would have to close their doors.

In 1986, Brazil, which owed more than $100 billion to banks in the United States and in other Western nations, stopped making some of the interest payments due on its enormous foreign debt. But few people expected Brazil and other troubled debtors to refuse to pay all of their debts. That drastic action would be too costly for indebted nations because they would not be able to borrow more money in the future. And without the ability to borrow in the future, many nations would not get funds to invest in their economy's development.

Still, the continuing inability of many nations to repay their foreign debts convinced U.S. bankers that their foreign loans would not be completely repaid. In 1987, therefore, many banks in the United States began recognizing these unpaid debts as losses. In order to cushion depositors from these losses, banks began to transfer some of their revenues into special reserves, called *loan-loss reserves*. Because these transfers were often greater than profits, banks reported substantial losses for that year. Figure A shows how many banks in the United States suffered huge losses in 1987.

One of the purposes of building these loan-loss reserves was to bolster people's confidence in holding bank money. The Federal Deposit Insurance Corporation (FDIC), which insures each bank account for a maximum of $100,000, also shores up individuals' confidence in bank money. Before the FDIC was created in 1934, however, this insurance did not exist.

Without any insurance, depositors

Figure A Losses of Banks in the United States During Second Quarter of 1987

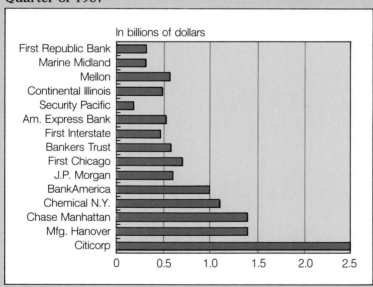

Source: Adapted from Schmitt, Richard B. and Hill, G. Christian, "Banks to Post Record $10 Billion Loss," *The Wall Street Journal*, July 20, 1987, 2.

Figure B Money Supply of United States, 1928–33

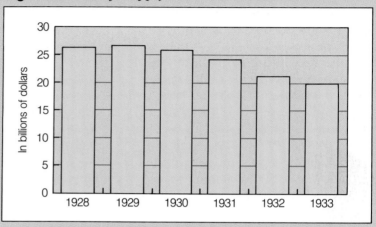

Source: Adapted from *Historical Statistics of the United States, Colonial Times to 1970*, U.S. Department of Commerce, Bureau of the Census, Washington, D.C.: U.S. Government Printing Office, 1975, 992.

became nervous late in 1930 when a New York commercial bank, known as the Bank of the United States, collapsed. Their nervousness was understandable. Not long before—on Black Friday, October 29, 1929—Americans had experienced the frightening crash of the New York Stock Market. The crash reflected the onset of a recession that continued throughout 1930. When the Bank of United States failed at the end of that year, many worried depositors across the country withdrew currency from their checking accounts. Faced with sudden, unusually large withdrawals, many banks failed because their fractional reserves were inadequate. In 1929, for example, only 656 banks

with total deposits of $231 million closed their doors. But in 1931, more than 2,000 banks with total deposits of more than $1.5 billion suspended their operations.

Fear fed fear as depositors panicked and rushed to withdraw their funds. In a frantic attempt to meet customers' demands, banks added to their reserves by calling in loans and by refusing to relend money obtained from loan repayment. With fewer loans being made throughout the banking system, the amount of checking account money plummeted. Consequently, the banking system reeled from an event that was exactly the opposite of the money creation process explained in this chapter. Look at Figure B, and you can see how the money supply decreased from 1928 to 1933.

In the next chapter, you will learn about the measures government can use to prevent a similar collapse of the money supply today. You will also see that the government did not use these measures at the onset of the Great Depression in the 1930s.

References

Baim, Dean; Dickneider, William; and Kaplan, David. "Third World Debt." *Contemporary Economic Issues* vol. 3, no. 4 (Winter 1984).

Vedder, Richard K. *The American Economy in Historical Perspective*. Belmont Calif.: Wadsworth Publishing Co., 1976. 373–82.

the twentieth century. These shortages occurred because the amount of currency could not be quickly increased. This was particularly true in farming areas, where surges in cash holdings were demanded from time to time in order to plant new crops.

Another problem that occurred under the national banking system was the pyramiding of bank reserves.[4] The reserves of small, rural banks were often held in medium-sized city banks, the reserves of which were then deposited in big banks in a few large cities, such as New York. Often, rural banks called for more money from medium-sized banks, and, in turn, these banks called for funds from the very large city banks. As a result, money shortages in rural areas would wind their way up the banking pyramid and, thereby, promote widespread panics. These panics, the most serious of which occurred in 1873, 1884, 1903, and 1907, increased the call for legislation that would create a central bank with the power to change the money supply. The result was the Federal Reserve Act of 1913, which established the *Federal Reserve System*.

The Federal Reserve System

The Federal Reserve System has four important parts.

1. District Banks   There are twelve Federal Reserve banks, one for each of twelve Federal Reserve districts into which the United States is divided. Each of these twelve Federal Reserve banks is owned by the commercial banks in the district that belong to the system.

These commercial banks obtain important services from the district Federal Reserve banks. For example, district banks hold the reserves of commercial member banks. Although banks keep some of their reserves as vault cash, most reserves are actually deposited at the Federal Reserve banks.

Another important function of the Federal Reserve banks is to issue Federal Reserve notes, the paper money we carry. Still another service is to clear the checks of commercial banks. When people write checks, money must be taken out of particular accounts in some banks and added to different accounts

[4]Martin Bronfenbrenner, Werner Sichel, and Wayland Gardner, *Economics* (Boston: Houghton Mifflin 1984), 228.

at other banks. This process is called *check clearing*, and it assures that money is transferred from the account of the check writer to the account of the person receiving the check.

A fourth important service of the district banks is to make loans to the member banks within its district. This task relates to one of the major reasons for the passage of the Federal Reserve Act. By making these loans, a district bank can help its member banks through periods of financial hardship. In this way, bank failures and bank panics are reduced, and public confidence in the banking system is maintained.

2. The Board of Governors A second important part of the Federal Reserve System is the Board of Governors. This board has seven members, each of whom is appointed for a 14-year term by the President of the United States and confirmed by the Senate. Every two years, the term of one of the board members ends. This staggering of terms is intended to free the board from political influence. The President also has the power to appoint a chairperson of the board every four years.

Among the powers of the Board of Governors is the supervision of the twelve district banks, including the appointment and removal of their officers. More important, however, is the power to determine the amount of checking deposits that commercial banks must keep on reserve. Also important is the board's ability to set the discount rate. The discount rate, which will be explained in more detail in the next chapter, is the interest rate commercial banks must pay to borrow reserves from the Federal Reserve banks. These powers of the Board of Governors are especially important because they affect the amount of loans and bank money that commercial banks can create. For example, suppose the Board of Governors tells commercial banks they must keep a larger proportion of their deposits on reserve. In that case, commercial banks would not be able to make as many loans and so would not create as much money.

3. The Federal Open Market Committee Another vital part of the Federal Reserve System is the Federal Open Market Committee. This committee has twelve members, seven of whom are the members of the Board of Governors. The other five members are either presidents or vice-presidents of five of the twelve district banks. The president of the New York Federal Reserve Bank is always a member of the committee because this bank buys and sells huge quantities of U.S. government bonds. The next chapter will explain why these purchases and sales of government bonds are the primary means by which the Federal Reserve System controls the nation's money supply.

4. Member banks The commercial banks that are members of the Federal Reserve System are also important. Not all commercial banks can become members of the system because each member bank must have sufficient capital to meet the requirements of the Board of Governors. These capital requirements are based on the assets and liabilities of the member bank and on the population of the town or city in which it is located. Member banks must also follow all the rules and regulations of the Federal Reserve System. To see that they do, auditors from the district banks periodically examine the financial records of the member banks.

The Federal Reserve Act has certainly had a big impact on our nation's banking system. Since the passage of the act in 1913, however, there have been other important changes in our banking system. During the Great Depression of the 1930s, for example, many banks began to fail as panicky depositors rushed to withdraw their funds. In order to increase people's confidence in banks, Congress passed legislation during the 1930s that would insure customers' bank deposits. As a result, the Federal Deposit Insurance Corporation (FDIC) now insures deposits up to $100,000 at commercial banks. Similarly, the Federal Savings and Loan Insurance Corporation (FSLIC) insures deposits up to $100,000 at savings institutions.

Another change in our banking system occurred as many commercial banks left the Federal Reserve System. These banks felt that they could obtain many of the advantages of being a member—such as loans, currency, and money transfer services—through their relationships with other banks that were members. Since they could obtain these services and not be bound by membership requirements, many banks chose to leave the system.

The Depository Institutions Deregulation and Monetary Control Act was passed in 1980 to slow the decline in the number of member banks in the Federal Reserve System. This law created uniform reserve requirements for all banks, savings and loans associations, and other financial institutions. It also required all banks and financial institutions to pay the same charges for the services of the Federal Reserve System. One of the purposes of this act was to reinforce the Federal Reserve System's control over our nation's banking system. This control is essential if the Federal Reserve System is to fulfill its mission of controlling the country's money supply. How the Federal Reserve System changes the money supply and how these changes affect the economy are the subjects of the next chapter.

Chapter Summary

1. *Barter* is the exchange of goods and services without the use of money. Barter is a difficult system because it requires that each trader want what the other is selling. It is also difficult because the price of each good must be given in terms of all other goods. Money is easier to use because it is nonperishable and is easily accepted by everyone.

2. Many commodities have been used as money throughout history, but now most nations, for convenience, use paper currency and coins. *Money* is defined by the tasks it accomplishes: it serves as a medium of exchange, a measure of prices, and a store of buying power.

3. Coin and currency represent about 25 percent of our nation's money supply. Stocks, bonds, and gold are not money because they are not usually accepted as payment for goods and services. Credit cards are not money either, but they do enable their users to obtain loans that must be paid off with money in the future. Instead of using coin and currency to pay for goods and services, most people use checks. When one person writes a check to another, coin and currency are not physically moved from one bank account to another. Rather, banks subtract *numbers* from the check writer's account and add *numbers* to the check depositor's account. By adding all the checking deposits, currency, and coin, we are able to calculate the nation's total money supply.

4. The most important cause of the growth of our money supply has been increases in checking deposits, most of which are held at banks (although credit unions and other financial institutions now also hold them). Checking deposits are actually bank debt because they represent currency that banks

owe to their depositors. When people write and accept checks as they buy and sell, this bank debt travels from person to person.

5. Banks do not have a dollar of currency and coin for every dollar of checking account money or bank debt. Instead, banks keep only a fraction of their deposits on reserve and use the remaining deposits to make loans, the interest payments on which provide banks with their income. Because banks keep only part of their deposits on reserve, our banking system is known as a *fractional reserve system.*

6. Because only a fraction of deposits is kept on reserve, the banking system is able to create new checking account money when it receives new reserves. A bank obtains new reserves whenever someone makes a deposit of currency. A bank does not have to keep a dollar on reserve for every dollar of checking account deposits. After keeping only a fraction of the new reserves, therefore, the bank loans the remaining reserves. When the borrower spends the money, the recipient deposits it in a second bank. Since the deposit in the second bank represents new checking account money in the banking system, money has been created. The second bank can then keep only a portion of the new deposit as a reserve and use the remainder to make yet another new loan. When the new borrower spends the loan and the recipient deposits it in a third bank, this new deposit represents still another addition to the nation's supply of bank money. As this process of new loans and new deposits continues, it results in a final increase in bank money that exceeds the original deposit of currency.

7. The evolution of our modern banking system began with state banks in 1781. These banks often failed because they did not have enough gold and silver to redeem the currency and bank notes they issued. The evolution continued with the establishment of the first and second Banks of the United States in 1791 and 1816, respectively. The National Banking Act, passed in 1863, established nationally chartered banks. Because the banking system still lacked a central bank, however, it continued to confront problems that often resulted in bank panics. Consequently, the Federal Reserve System was created in 1913.

8. The Federal Reserve System has four important parts: the twelve Federal Reserve district banks; the seven-member

Board of Governors, which sets the amount of reserves to be held by banks; the twelve-member Federal Open Market Committee; and the member banks.

9. The failure of many banks during the Great Depression of the 1930s resulted in legislation creating the Federal Deposit Insurance Corporation (FDIC) and the Federal Savings and Loan Insurance Corporation (FSLIC), both of which insure depositors' funds. In 1980, the Depository Institutions Deregulation and Monetary Control Act was passed to reinforce the Federal Reserve System's control over the banking system.

Review Questions

1. What is *barter*, and what are the difficulties of barter exchange?
2. What is *money*, and what are its functions?
3. Our banking system is a *fractional reserve system*. Explain the meaning of this term.
4. Why do banks make loans? What do they use to make these loans?
5. Explain how a deposit of coin or currency in a bank enables the banking system to create new checking account money.
6. Describe some of the problems of state banking and the National Banking Act during the last century that led to the formation of the Federal Reserve System in 1913.
7. What are the four parts of the Federal Reserve System?
8. What are the major functions of the Federal Reserve banks?
9. What important power does the Board of Governors of the Federal Reserve System have? Why is this power important?

Discussion Questions

1. World history demonstrates the evolution of various kinds of money. Give two reasons why people have generally preferred to use money when exchanging goods and services.

How are these two reasons demonstrated by the Romanians' use of Kent cigarettes as money?

2. Explain what a bank does with the coin and currency that people deposit in it. Why does the bank do this?

3. Does a bank have in its vault a dollar of currency or coin for every dollar of checking account money that people have on deposit? If not, how can the bank survive?

4. Why was the Federal Reserve Act passed, and what kind of a banking system did it create?

5. **Individual A:** "Bankers are heartless when they take over the farms and other property of borrowers who cannot repay their loans."

   Individual B: "In order to protect the earnings of hard-working depositors, bankers sometimes must make tough decisions to assure that borrowers pay off their loans."

   With whom do you agree? Why?

Activities

1. Arrange with the manager to visit your local bank. Ask what it is that people transfer from one to another when they use their checking accounts to buy goods and services. Also determine in what form the bank holds its reserves. Does the bank illustrate a system of fractional reserves? Why don't the bank's depositors get nervous if the bank loans the money deposited instead of keeping it in the vault? Write a brief paper about the answers you obtain, and then compare your answers with those of your classmates.

2. Write a story explaining why Romanians use Kent cigarettes, rather than eggs, as money.

3. Suppose that banks keep 10 percent of their checking accounts on reserve and loan the remaining 90 percent. Trace through the money creation that could occur at Banks A, B, and C as a result of the following events. Use the summary below to record these events. What is the total amount of *new* checking account money at these three banks?

   (a) Annie Brown deposits $1,000 of currency at Bank A.

   (b) Bank A uses the new deposit to make a loan to Harold's Hamburgers.

(c) Harold's Hamburgers spends the borrowed money to buy new chairs from Local Furniture Company.

(d) Local Furniture Company deposits the money in Bank B.

(e) Bank B uses the new deposit to make a loan to Incredible Creatures Pet Store.

(f) Incredible Creatures spends the money at Susan's Veterinary Hospital for the care of some pets.

(g) Susan's Veterinary Hospital deposits the money in Bank C.

Bank	New Deposit	New Loan
Bank A	_____	_____
Bank B	_____	_____
Bank C	_____	_____

Additional Readings

Heilbroner, Robert L., and Galbraith, James K. *The Economic Problem*. Revised 8th ed. Englewood Cliffs, N.J.: Prentice-Hall, 1987. Chapter 20.

Heyne, Paul. *The Economic Way of Thinking*. 5th ed. Chicago: Science Research Associates, 1987. 393–407.

Levi, Maurice. *Thinking Economically*. New York: Basic Books, 1985. Chapter 11.

Miller, Roger Leroy, and Shannon, Russell. *The Economics of Macro Issues*. St. Paul: West, 1986. Chapter 23.

How is oil in an automobile engine similar to money in our economic system?

Monetary Policy and Fiscal Policy

■ Student's Goals ■

1. Define and give examples of *inflation*.

2. Describe three ways in which the Federal Reserve System attempts to influence aggregate demand.

3. Describe three ways in which the government uses fiscal policy to influence aggregate demand.

4. Distinguish between a *budget deficit* and the *national debt*.

5. Compare and contrast the views of Keynesian economists, monetarist economists, and supply-side economists.

Money and Inflation

Even Trivial Pursuit fanatics wouldn't guess one of Bolivia's biggest imports in 1984. After wheat and mining equipment, money was the third largest import of this small South American nation of about 6 million people. Tons of paper money, ordered from printers in West Germany and Britain, arrived by the planeload to satisfy the government's desire to spend. Indeed, newly printed money accounted for about four out of every five pesos spent by the Bolivian government in the early 1980s. Economists weren't surprised when Bolivia ended up with the highest inflation rate in the world. In 1984, prices soared higher than Bolivia's two-mile-high capital of La Paz when they increased by 2,700 percent.

Chapter 11 has explained that inflation is an increase in the price level. During any year, some prices fall, some remain constant, and some rise. When most prices rise, the average of all these prices—the *price level*—goes up. When the price level goes up, you can purchase fewer goods and services with a given amount of money than you used to be able to purchase. That's why inflation, which is defined as an increase in the price level, is also thought of as a decline in the buying power of money.

Because of Bolivia's high rate of inflation, the buying power of its money dropped sharply. But another, more astonishing example of rapid inflation occurred in Germany after World War I. During this time, Germany's money supply soared. In 1923, the money stock in Germany was 15 million times what it had been ten years earlier. You can imagine what happened to prices. During the worst year, 1923, the level of wholesale prices skyrocketed. By the end of the year, the price level was billions of times higher than it was in 1922. If our country experienced the same explosive inflation, called *hyperinflation*, you would need billions of dollars next year in order to buy what now costs you only $1.

Instances of hyperinflation are rare, but they do show how the creation of too much money can lead to inflation. This doesn't mean that a rapidly increasing money supply is the only cause of inflation. Factors that affect an economy's ability to supply goods and services can also affect the rate of inflation. When the amount of oil available around the world declined in the 1970s, our ability to supply goods and services was tem-

At two miles above sea level, La Paz, Bolivia is the highest capital in the world. In 1984, it also experienced a record-high rate of inflation, for prices soared by 2,700 percent. The reason for the enormous inflation was the Bolivian government's printing and spending of new money.

porarily weakened. As the aggregate supply of goods and services fell below the aggregate demand for them, the price level jumped. As a result, the rate of inflation in our nation was temporarily higher.

Anything that affects either aggregate demand or aggregate supply can affect the price level and, thus, influence the rate of inflation. But if relatively high rates of inflation persist year after year, you can bet that the money supply has been rising rapidly.

Money Doesn't Grow on Trees

The money supply is important, not only because of its ability to affect the rate of inflation but also because of other reasons that will be discussed in this chapter. The Federal Reserve System (the Fed) has an important mission, therefore, because its central task is to control the money supply. Some years ago a chairman of the Fed joked that most Americans thought the

Federal Reserve was a national forest. Even today, few people know what the Federal Reserve System is or what it does. But everyone knows that money doesn't grow on trees—even trees in a national forest.

Although the Federal Reserve System does not grow money, it does take particular actions to control the size of our country's money supply. What the Federal Reserve System does to increase or decrease the money supply is known as **monetary policy.**

> **Monetary policy:** What the Federal Reserve System does to increase or decrease the nation's money supply.

The Goals of Monetary Policy

Monetary policy is an attempt to reduce economic fluctuations, so that an economy can grow without the extreme ups and downs of the business cycle that have been presented in Chapter 11. As a result, the major goals of monetary policy are stable prices, full employment, and economic growth. In an attempt to achieve one or more of these goals, monetary policy alters the level of aggregate demand, which has also been explained in Chapter 11. For example, see Figure 13–1. During inflation, aggregate demand is greater than the aggregate supply of goods and services, so the Federal Reserve System might reduce the money supply in order to shrink aggregate demand. On the other hand, during recession, aggregate demand is less than the aggregate supply of goods and services, so the Federal Reserve System might increase the money supply in order to raise aggregate demand.

The Federal Reserve System could take these actions because it knows the money supply is an important determinant of aggregate demand. The reason for this relationship is easy to understand. Any particular dollar, by being spent over and over, can finance a lot more than $1 of spending. For example, suppose the total stock of money in an economy is $200. Each of these dollars will be spent more than once during the year,

Money Creation

Wouldn't our nation be better off if the Federal Reserve System printed some extra money and gave it to poor Americans in order to eliminate their poverty?

Noneconomic Way of Thinking

What makes a country wealthy is how much money its people have to spend. By printing more money, the government will create more purchasing power and make the country richer.

Economic Way of Thinking

It is true that more money makes a person richer. But if lots of money is printed and given to many people, the nation as a whole will not be richer. All the extra money will cause people to bid up prices as they demand more goods and services. If more money "chases" the same quantity of goods and services, the result is higher prices, not greater wealth. Our nation's economic well-being is determined by the amount of goods and services we produce, not by the number of dollars we have to spend.

Questions

1. If a rapidly and persistently growing money supply causes the rate of inflation to soar, will the country be harmed? Explain.

2. If the government prints some more money to spend on things it wants, does the government now have greater purchasing power? Does anyone now have less?

3. How would you measure a nation's economic well-being?

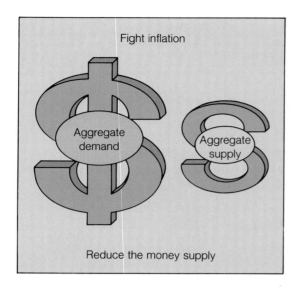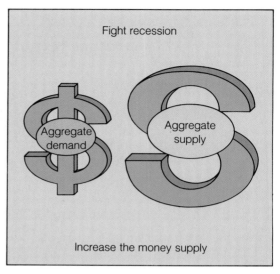

Figure 13–1 How the Federal Reserve System Can Use Monetary Policy to Fight Inflation and Recession

During inflation, aggregate demand is greater than aggregate supply. As a countermeasure, the Federal Reserve System can reduce the money supply in order to shrink aggregate demand. Exactly the opposite occurs during recession. Aggregate demand is less than aggregate supply, so the Federal Reserve System can increase the money supply in order to raise aggregate demand.

so total spending (aggregate demand) is going to be more than $200. If during the year each of these dollars is spent an average of five times, then aggregate demand is $1,000 (5 × $200). Over the year, therefore, total spending in our economy is determined by multiplying the supply of money by the average number of times this money supply is spent.

$$\begin{array}{ccc} \text{Aggregate} & \text{money} & \text{average number of times} \\ \text{demand} = & \text{supply} \times & \text{the money supply is spent} \\ \$1,000 = & \$200 \times & 5 \end{array}$$

By changing the money supply, the Federal Reserve System can alter aggregate demand and thereby increase or decrease the circular flow of the economy. As a result, the Fed can affect GNP, incomes, employment, prices, and wages.

However, monetary policy does not let the Federal Reserve System steer the economy the way a steering wheel let's you drive a car. In the first place, the number of times the money supply is spent does not always stay the same. If the Fed doubles the money supply in the equation above, aggregate demand

An automobile's engine will not run properly without sufficient oil. Without any oil, the engine would quickly stop running. Money is to our economy what oil is to an automobile's engine. Money "lubricates" exchange by allowing people to trade with one another. Without the use of money, our economy would also stop running.

will rise to $2,000 *if* the number of times the money supply is spent remains at five. But if this number rises or falls, doubling the money supply will have a different effect on aggregate demand. Try a few numbers for yourself, and you'll see how a given change in the money supply can produce different changes in aggregate demand.

Another, more important problem with monetary policy is the fact that its effects on the economy are delayed. Some time must pass before enough data can be obtained in order to recognize that the economy has turned up or down. Then, after a corrective monetary policy has been implemented, more time must pass before this policy visibly affects the economy. Imagine if every time you turned the steering wheel on your car, the car didn't turn until sometime later. This delayed reaction would certainly make driving a lot more difficult. So, too, does the delayed reaction of monetary policy make the Federal Reserve System's job much more difficult—and this difficulty has produced much controversy among economists.

Some economists believe the difficulty can be overcome and the Fed can do a reasonable job of smoothing out the business

An automobile engine doesn't look like an economy, and oil certainly doesn't look like money. But there *are* similarities. Without the lubrication of oil, the engine would grind to a halt. Similarly, without the lubrication of money, much of our economic activity would also grind to a halt.

cycle by steering our economy to greater stability. Others believe the job is too difficult, especially because of the inevitable delay between the time the money supply goes up or down and the time monetary policy affects the economy. For instance, suppose the Fed reduces the money supply because it is concerned about inflation. By the time this policy affects the economy, inflation might have disappeared, and the economy might have turned down. As a result, the earlier monetary policy, which has reduced the money supply will only worsen the current downturn in the economy.

This situation is one reason why some economists believe that the Federal Reserve System's efforts to smooth out the economy's growth path only worsen its fluctuations. These economists, often called *monetarists*, believe that economic stability is best achieved by letting the money supply increase by a small, constant rate year after year.

How the Fed Controls the Money Supply

Although there is debate about how the Fed ought to conduct its monetary policy, no one disputes the fact that the Federal Reserve System can increase or decrease the money supply. Because most of the country's money consists of checking deposits, the Fed controls the money supply by regulating the amount of checking deposit money in our nation. That's why the Fed's influence on bank reserves is so important. By directly controlling the amount of banks' reserves, the Fed indirectly controls the amount of checking deposit money in our banking system. As the last chapter has pointed out, banks have an incentive to make as many loans as their reserves permit. If reserves somehow rise above the required fraction of deposits, banks will have excess reserves. They will then use these excess reserves to make more loans in order to earn more interest. When banks make more loans, however, they also create more money.

The Federal Reserve System has three ways of altering our banking system's reserves in order to control the money supply: buying and selling government bonds, changing the discount rate of interest, and changing the legal reserve rate. Each of these methods will be discussed below.

Open Market Operations

This method of controlling the money supply is particularly important because it is the tool most often used by the Fed to conduct its monetary policy. We mentioned this method briefly in the last chapter when we identified the Federal Open Market Committee. The purchase or sale of government bonds by the Federal Reserve System's Open Market Committee is the primary method used to control the money supply.

Perhaps when you read this paragraph you wondered what government bonds were. The explanation is not difficult. Suppose you borrow $10 from someone and give that person an IOU in return. Similarly, a government bond is an IOU issued by the government when it borrows money from individuals and businesses. Think of all these bonds as IOUs the government has issued in the past and has not yet paid back. Since the bonds pay a yearly premium called *interest*, many individuals and businesses like to own them. In fact, people trade government bonds with one another, just as they trade used cars. Accordingly, the bond market is a market in which people buy or sell government bonds which, like used cars, were first sold sometime in the past. The Open Market Committee of the Federal Reserve System is one of the buyers and sellers of these government bonds.

By buying or selling government bonds, the Open Market Committee changes the reserves of our banking system. Because the committee buys and sells bonds in the open market, therefore, this method of conducting monetary policy is called *open market operations*. Here's how it works.

Suppose the Fed's Open Market Committee decides to increase banks' reserves in order to raise the nation's money supply. In order to achieve this objective, the committee will buy bonds in the open market from any organization or individual willing to sell them. Since the Fed cannot force the public to sell bonds, it must offer a price high enough to encourage bond owners to sell them.

To simplify our explanation of monetary policy, suppose the Open Market Committee purchases bonds from commercial banks. The committee will pay for this purchase by giving the banks new reserves. Most bank reserves are actually deposits at the Federal Reserve System's district banks, not cash held in the individual banks' vaults. These reserves, deposited at the Fed, are not coin, currency, gold, silver, or any other commodity. Instead, they are numbers that commercial banks have in their reserve accounts at the Fed, just as individual's have numbers in their checking accounts at commercial banks.

The Federal Reserve Board meets in Washington, D.C. to consider the nation's monetary policy. This picture shows Paul Volcker, who was chairman of the Federal Reserve Board from 1979 to 1987. Who currently heads the Fed?

Vaults, such as this one, hold only a small part of the reserves of commercial banks. Most bank reserves are held as deposits at the Federal Reserve. Those reserves are not currency or gold or any other commodity. They are numbers recorded under the commercial bank's name at the Federal Reserve.

When the Fed's Open Market Committee purchases government bonds from the banks, therefore, it pays the banks by adding numbers to the banks' reserves. Banks can then use these new reserves to make new loans. And as they make new loans, they create new checking account money, as the last chapter has described.

If the Open Market Committee sells, rather than buys, government bonds, then the opposite will occur. Banks will lose reserves, so they will decrease the amount of loans they make. As a result, the amount of checking deposit money in the nation will fall.

The Discount Rate

Although open market operations are the most important method of conducting monetary policy, the Federal Reserve System can also change the *discount rate of interest*. The discount rate is the interest rate that commercial banks must pay if they borrow reserves from the Federal Reserve System. If the Fed lowers the discount rate, the banks' cost of borrowing reserves from the Fed is reduced. When the cost is lower, banks will want to borrow more reserves and then use the additional reserves to make more loans and create more money. On the other hand, if the Federal Reserve System raises the discount rate, banks will pay more to borrow reserves from the Fed. Therefore, banks will borrow fewer reserves and will create less money. Changes in this rate are treated as major stories in the daily news.

The Legal Reserve Rate

The third, and last, way by which the Federal Reserve System can conduct its monetary policy is by changing the *legal reserve rate*. This rate indicates the fraction of checking deposits that a bank must legally hold on reserve. Suppose the Federal Reserve System reduces the fraction of checking deposits that banks have to keep on reserve. In this case, banks could use more of their reserves to make loans. When making the new loans, however, the banking system is creating new money, as the last chapter has described. On the other hand, suppose the Federal Reserve System increases the legal reserve rate. Banks will then have to keep a larger fraction of their deposits on reserve. As a result, the banking system will use the repayment of existing loans to build up their reserves instead of lending them out to new borrowers. As the banking system's total loans diminish, therefore, the amount of checking account money will contract through a series of events exactly the reverse of those that occur when money is created.

The legal reserve rate, the discount rate, and open market operations are the three methods by which the Federal Reserve System can control the nation's money supply. However, that control is not exercised directly over the money supply. The Federal Reserve System can alter the supply of money only indirectly by changing the reserves (or deposit-reserve rate) of the banking system.

Fiscal Policy

Monetary policy is not the only way in which the federal government tries to alter aggregate demand and, thereby influence production, prices, wages, and employment. The government also uses **fiscal policy,** which is a change in federal spending or taxes in order to influence aggregate demand.

Fiscal policy: A change in federal spending or taxes in order to influence aggregate demand.

Suppose the government increases its expenditures for space exploration, military security, national parks, or other final goods and services. As Chapter 11 has pointed out, government expenditures for final goods and services are added to those of consumers and businesses to obtain total spending. Therefore, increased government spending for space exploration and other final goods and services will *directly* increase the nation's aggregate demand.

But direct purchases of final goods and services represent only about one-third of all federal expenditures. Chapter 8 has pointed out, for example, that the federal government also makes substantial transfer payments, such as Social Security pay-

Fiscal policy often begins with a President's proposal, and it is implemented through the U.S. Treasury Department of the Executive branch. But it must wind its way up and down Capitol Hill, where Congress enacts policies relating to government spending and taxes.

ments to retired citizens, that are not direct purchases of goods and services. If the government increases these transfer payments, citizens will have more income, and they can purchase more goods and services. In this way, the federal government tries to change aggregate demand *indirectly* by altering citizens' incomes in an effort to change their expenditures for goods and services.

Similarly, the federal government can also change the taxes it collects from citizens and businesses in an attempt to modify their purchases of goods and services. By reducing its tax collections, for instance, the government can let us keep more of our incomes. With more after-tax income to spend, we can increase our purchases and thereby raise aggregate demand.

Fiscal policy is the responsibility of Congress and the Department of the Treasury (which is part of the executive branch). Congress decides how many taxes will be collected and how much revenue will be spent, but it is the Treasury that actually implements these directives by collecting and spending the funds. On the other hand, monetary policy is the responsibility of the Federal Reserve System, which, though politically independent, is still the creation of Congress.

Fiscal policy, like monetary policy, is a method by which the federal government tries to bring greater stability to the economy. For example, during inflation, aggregate demand exceeds aggregate supply, so the federal government can reduce its expenditures or raise its taxes in order to decrease aggregate demand (see Figure 13–2). On the other hand, if aggregate demand falls below aggregate supply, the circular flow will slow down and a recession can occur. Consequently, the government might increase its expenditures or reduce its tax collections in order to stimulate aggregate demand.

To some extent, these changes in government spending and taxes occur automatically whenever the economy moves up or down. During a recession, less income and less employment cause welfare and unemployment expenditures to rise and tax revenues to fall. These changes are called *automatic stabilizers* because they do not require specific action by Congress to set them in motion when the economy expands or contracts.

Fiscal policy attempts to promote economic stability by trying to steer the economy away from inflation and recession. But there are delays when turning the fiscal policy steering wheel that resemble those of monetary policy. For example, time must pass before enough data are available to recognize that the

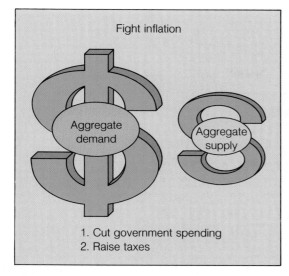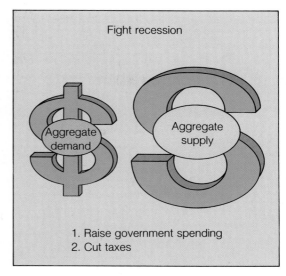

Figure 13—2 How the Government Can Use Fiscal Policy to Fight Inflation and Recession

During inflation, aggregate demand is greater than aggregate supply. As a countermeasure, the government can raise its taxes and reduce its expenditures. Exactly the opposite occurs during recession. Aggregate demand is less than aggregate supply, so the government can raise its spending and reduce its taxes.

economy has turned up or down. In addition, except for the automatic stabilizers, Congress requires time to propose and pass changes in federal taxes and spending. Moreover, once these changes are made, more time must pass before the economy is affected. Given all these delays, fiscal policy probably requires even more time than does monetary policy to affect aggregate demand.

Because of these delays, economists disagree about government's ability to use fiscal policy to steer the economy to greater stability. Many who believe in the government's ability to smooth out the economy base their thinking on the ideas of the late John M. Keynes, a famous economist (whose last name rhymes with rains). During the Great Depression of the 1930s, Keynes forcefully recommended that the government use fiscal policy to promote economic recovery. Following his recommendation, *Keynesian economists* today believe that fiscal policy can be used to reduce the economy's fluctuations.

Other economists disagree because they believe the delays of fiscal policy produce the same problems as the delays of

(text continues on page 368)

Economic Pains and John Maynard Keynes

Benjamin Franklin wrote, "In this world nothing is certain but death and taxes." Perhaps he should also have included recessions. The National Bureau of Economic Research has identified 30 recessions in the United States economy since 1854. But there has also been an equal number of expansions. Fortunately, the expansions have generally been stronger than the contractions, so our economy has grown substantially over the years.

In the early 1980s, our economy experienced one of the worst downturns since the Great Depression of the 1930s. In 1981 and 1882, real gross national product plunged, causing unemployment to soar above 10 percent for the first time since the 1930s. But the recession did not mysteriously appear like a meteor in the night sky. In fact, the government's economic policies helped produce it.

The momentum began during the latter half of the 1970s, when rapid money growth in our nation created the worst inflationary binge of the century. As the rate of inflation rose above 10 percent in 1979, 1980, and 1981, Americans worried about their economic well-being. In order to reduce inflation, the Federal Reserve Board decreased the nation's money supply growth. Because of the delayed effects of monetary policy,

however, the lower rate of money creation could not quickly reduce inflation. In addition, many argued that our economy had become "intoxicated" on big yearly doses of money creation. They claimed that Americans must pass through a painful period of "withdrawal" before the inflationary effects of past money creation could be cleansed from our economic system. "Withdrawal" meant a recession, in which aggregate income drops and unemployment rises.

Before the rapid pace of inflation had slowed, therefore, the lower growth of our money supply produced a severe recession. But after passing through a trying period in which prices and unemployment soared simultaneously, the economy began to recover in December of 1982. As the economy continued to grow over the following years, inflation dropped and remained well below the double-digit rates of the late 1970s and early 1980s. The unemployment rate also dropped, reaching 6 percent of the labor force in 1987.

The recession of the early 1980s—and the money-induced expansion that preceded it—underscores a controversial question about the causes of recessions and expansions in our economy. When are economic fluctuations the result of instability in

our market economy, and when are they the result of inappropriate monetary and fiscal policies?

Consider the Great Depression of the 1930s as an example. Until that time, Americans widely believed their economy would automatically pull itself out of a recession. True, recessions had occurred many times in the past, and they were sometimes severe; but most people thought the economy would recover best on its own. Then came the Great Depression, whose misery and hardship challenged this optimistic perception. Many began to see this economic tragedy as proof that a market economy is essentially unstable: it can collapse and remain depressed unless the government's economic policies rescue it.

Why might a market economy remain depressed? One individual thought he knew the answer. He did not grow up in an ordinary environment. His father was a noted writer about political economy and a teacher at the University in Cambridge, England. His mother was mayor of that city. After graduating from Cambridge, he took the British Civil Service exam and received his worst grade in economics. His explanation for the low mark was that "I evidently knew more about Economics than my examiners."

John Maynard Keynes was not known for his modesty. While writing *The General Theory of Employment, Interest, and Money* during the turmoil of the Depression in 1935, Keynes wrote to the British author George Bernard Shaw: "I believe myself to be writing a book on economic theory which will largely revolutionize—not, I suppose, at once but in the course of the next ten years—the way the world thinks about economic problems."

Keynes was bright, imaginative, and well-educated. And, as he prophesied to Shaw, he was also influential. Keynes described why he thought the market economies of Britain, the United States, and other nations would not recover on their own during the economic disaster of the 1930s. His explanation centered on an imbalance between saving and investment in the circular flows of market economies. Gloomy expectations had taken hold of business managers, said Keynes, so they were unwilling to borrow and invest all the money consumers were saving. With so much income saved, not spent, aggregate demand fell below the aggregate supply of goods and services. To rid themselves of the excess supplies, continued Keynes, businesses reduced production. As businesses produced less output,

Now and Then—Continued

however, consumers received less income. And with less income, consumers cut their spending another notch.

Keynes argued that in order to break out of this cycle of depression, the government should use fiscal policy by borrowing and spending the savings that gloomy business managers were refusing to borrow and invest. But if government borrows and spends, the result is deficit spending. Consequently, Keynes challenged the popular view at that time that a deficit in the government's budget should be avoided. In fact, during the early years of the Depression in 1932, Franklin Roosevelt campaigned on the Democratic Party platform to cut government

spending and balance the federal budget.

There is no doubt that the stock market crash of October, 1929, focused attention on a gap that had opened up between saving and investment. This gap weakened aggregate demand and caused a recession in 1930. Examine Table A, and you will see that in 1930 real investment spending declined by about $42 billion, a decrease of about 30 percent. In the face of this decline, the government did not follow the advice that Keynes was to offer when his book, *The General Theory*, was published in 1936. Total government expenditures did increase slightly in1930, rising from $94.2 billion to $103.3 billion. But this increase did

Table A   Key Economic Indicators, 1929–33

Year	Real[a] GNP	Real Investment	Real Government Expenditures[b]	Money Supply
1929	$709.6 billion	$139.2 billion	$ 94.2 billion	$26.6 billion
1930	642.8	97.5	103.3	25.8
1931	588.1	60.1	106.8	24.1
1932	509.2	22.6	102.2	21.1
1933	498.5	22.7	98.5	19.9

[a] Real GNP, investment, and government expenditures are in 1982 dollars.
[b] Government expenditures represent the total of federal, state, and local expenditures for goods and services.

Source: Real GNP, investment, and government expenditures are from *Survey of Current Business,* U.S. Department of Commerce, Vol. 66, No. 9, Washington D.C., U.S. Government Printing Office, September 1986, 66. Money supply numbers are from *Historical Statistics of the United States, Colonial Times to 1970,* U.S. Department of Commerce, Bureau of the Census, Washington, D.C.: U.S Government Printing Office, 1975, 992.

not compensate for the large drop in investment spending. Moreover, the Federal Reserve Board followed a hands-off policy during this year, because it failed to pump new reserves into the banking system in order to shore up the money supply. As a result, the money supply dropped.

In the following year of 1931, fiscal policy provided a mild stimulus to the economy as government expenditures increased by a little more than $3 billion. Monetary policy, however, moved in the opposite direction, as the Federal Reserve Board again failed to provide new reserves for the banking system. Hindsight now tells us that the Fed's failure to provide these reserves at this critical time was disastrous. The confidence of bank depositors was plunging, but the Federal Reserve Board did not provide the new reserves banks needed to restore confidence by meeting the increasing withdrawals of depositors. Instead, depositors rushed to banks to withdraw their money, bank failures mushroomed, and the money supply tumbled.

In 1932, the situation worsened. Once again, the Federal Reserve failed to provide new reserves to the banking system, and the money supply plunged from $24.1 billion to $21.1 billion, a decline of more than 12 percent. Like an individual rolling a snowball down a steep hill, the Federal Reserve Board unwittingly pushed the economy downhill. Furthermore, Table A demonstrates that government spending dropped during 1932, meaning that both fiscal and monetary policies were moving in the opposite direction of that required to counteract a declining economy. Not until the 1940s, when government spending for World War II awakened aggregate demand, did the economy begin to climb back up the steep hill from which it had tumbled.

References

Keynes, John Maynard. *The General Theory of Employment, Interest, and Money.* New York: Harcourt, Brace, & World, Inc., 1936.

Friedman, Milton and Friedman, Rose. *Free to Choose: A Personal Statement.* New York: Harcourt Brace Jovanovich, 1980, Ch. 3.

monetary policy. For instance, suppose the government increases its spending and reduces its taxes because it is concerned about recession. By the time this policy affects the economy, recession might have disappeared and the economy might be experiencing inflation. As a result, the earlier fiscal policy, which is now stimulating aggregate demand, will only worsen the economy's current inflation. Unlike Keynesians, therefore, these economists believe that attempts to use fiscal policy to smooth out the economy are more likely to produce more and bigger fluctuations in the nation's economy.

Deficits

The federal government's expenditures and taxes are seldom balanced. One reason relates to the automatic stabilizers. If the economy enters a recession, taxes can fall below spending because there is less income in the economy to tax. Spending can also rise above taxes because welfare, unemployment, and other expenditures go up during a recession. On the other hand, when the economy is growing rapidly, expenditures for welfare and unemployment fall, while tax revenues rise. In that case, taxes can be greater than spending.

But the automatic stabilizers are not the only reason why government spending and taxes might not be balanced. Another, more important reason relates to the spending and tax plans adopted by Congress. Congress can vote either to spend more than it taxes or to tax more than it spends. Whatever the cause for the imbalance, the total of all federal expenditures seldom equals the total of all federal taxes. When federal taxes fall short of federal expenditures, the result is a **federal budget deficit.**

> **Federal budget deficit:**   The amount by which federal taxes fall short of federal expenditures.

On the other hand, federal taxes might total more than federal spending. When this occurs, the result is a **federal budget surplus,** which is defined as the amount by which federal taxes exceed federal expenditures.

> **Federal budget surplus:** The amount by which federal taxes exceed federal expenditures.

The federal budget has been in deficit in every year since 1970. Indeed, as Figure 13–3 shows, the deficit has generally increased as a percentage of gross national product during this time.

The deficits in each of these years meant that the federal government continually spent more than it received in taxes. In 1986, federal expenditures totaled $990 billion, but tax revenues equaled $769 billion. In that year the deficit came to $221 billion ($990 billion − $769 billion).

How Deficits Are Financed

In order to spend more than it receives in taxes, the government must borrow from the public. It accomplishes this borrowing when the Department of the Treasury sells new debt instru-

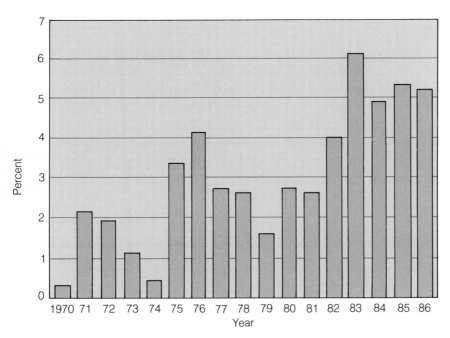

Figure 13–3 Federal Deficits as a Percentage of GNP, 1970–1986

Source: Economic Report of the President, 1987, pp. 224, 331. Deficits are for the fiscal year, which begins October 1.

ments, consisting of Treasury bills, notes, and bonds. These instruments differ mainly in the amount of time for which the government can borrow the money. For example, money borrowed by selling bonds doesn't have to be paid back for many years, but money borrowed by selling bills is usually paid back in a few months. When the Treasury sells bonds, notes, and bills, therefore, it borrows from private businesses, individuals, and foreigners by giving them IOUs.

If a deficit is substantial, the government borrows large amounts of the nation's available credit. Less credit might then be left for businesses to borrow and invest in the new plants and equipment that make our work more productive. Because substantial Treasury borrowing might "crowd out" private borrowing for investment, the Federal Reserve System might decide to increase the banking system's reserves; then banks could create more money by making new loans. By following this course of action, the Federal Reserve System would *monetize the deficit*. In other words, the Federal Reserve System would be creating new money in order to enable the government to spend more than it receives in taxes. Although an extreme example, Bolivia's rapid money creation, described at the beginning of this chapter, illustrates the monetizing of deficits.

If large deficits persist and if the Federal Reserve System continues to monetize them, the nation's money supply can grow too rapidly. The result could then be increased inflation. On the other hand, if the Federal Reserve System does nothing to help the federal government finance its deficit, private investment spending can drop if the government borrows credit that would otherwise be available for business investment.

Deficits and Debt

Although budget deficits are often confused with the national debt, there is a big difference between the two. The deficit shows how much the government borrows in a given year to finance the spending it cannot pay for with current tax revenues. The national (or public) debt is much bigger, however, because in addition to the amount borrowed this year by the government, it also includes all past borrowings that have not yet been repaid. Accordingly, the **national debt** is the total amount borrowed over the years by the federal government and not yet paid back.

> **National debt:** The total amount borrowed over the years by the federal government and not yet paid back.

In 1986, the budget deficit was $221 billion, but the national debt was $2.1 trillion. When the government has a budget deficit, it adds this amount of current borrowing to the national debt. When it has a budget surplus, however, the government pays off some of its past debt. As a result, budget deficits make the national debt grow, and budget surpluses make it shrink.

Because there have been budget deficits in every year since 1970, the national debt has grown. Until the 1980s, however, the national debt grew about as fast as our gross national product, so the debt remained about 35 percent of GNP. Because of the large budget deficits during the first half of the 1980s, however, the public debt grew faster than our gross national product. As a result, Figure 13–4 shows that the national debt as a percentage of GNP began to rise in the 1980s.

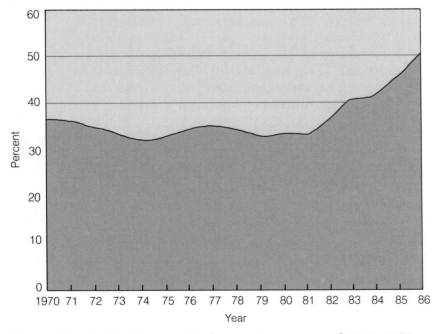

Figure 13–4 The National Debt as a Percentage of GNP, 1970–1986

Source: Economic Report of the President, 1987, pp. 224, 340.

The National Debt

The federal government has incurred an enormous amount of debt over the years. Doesn't this mean that future generations will bear a big burden when it comes time to pay off the debt?

Noneconomic Way of Thinking

The national debt is over $2 trillion and growing. Maybe the debt will never be paid off. Maybe future borrowing will be used to pay off past borrowing, so that the size of the debt will remain the same. Even if this occurs, interest must still be paid on the balance, and that means an enormous burden on the future generations that will be taxed to pay this interest.

Economic Way of Thinking

Although future interest payments on the national debt might be very large, there is another side to these payments. This other side can be seen by recognizing that most of the national debt is owned by people in our country. When future interest payments are made on the debt, therefore, Americans who own these government IOUs will receive these payments as income. There are problems when the government adds to its debt by spending more than it receives in taxes, but a heavier burden on future generations of taxpayers is not one of them.

Questions

1. Would the national debt be a burden on future generations of U.S. citizens if it were held by foreigners? Why or why not?

2. In what sense is running up the national debt similar to running up a debt on a credit card? In what sense is it different?

3. If the national debt rises because the government borrows to expand and improve the country's system of ports and roads, will future generations of Americans be better off than if the money is used to finance the current consumption of goods and services? Why or why not?

Aggregate Demand or Aggregate Supply?

Monetary and fiscal policies both represent attempts to change aggregate demand, so it is not surprising that they have many of the same effects. Because of these similar effects, one policy depends on the other—and this interdependence makes the formulation of monetary policy or fiscal policy more difficult. In addition, the delays with which each policy affects the economy make it difficult to decide what a particular monetary or fiscal policy should be trying to accomplish.

It's not surprising, therefore, that monetary and fiscal policies can be difficult to evaluate. Indeed, many people have difficulty just telling the difference between these two policies. For example, it was reported that John Kennedy, before becoming President, was able to tell the difference only by remembering that the chairman of the Federal Reserve System was William McChesney Martin, Jr. The chairman's name started with M, and that letter stood for monetary policy. To keep these two policies clear in your own mind, just remember the simple equation presented earlier in this chapter:

| Aggregate demand | = | Money supply | × | Average number of times the money supply is spent |

Monetary policy affects this — Fiscal policy affects this

Monetary policy is an attempt to affect aggregate demand by changing the money supply. Fiscal policy is an attempt to affect aggregate demand by increasing or decreasing the average number of times a given money supply is spent during the year. In an effort to raise aggregate demand, for example, the Federal Reserve System can increase the money supply. On the other hand, if fiscal policy is to raise aggregate demand, budget deficits will be used in an effort to increase the number of times the nation's money is spent. Despite their differences, however, both policies represent an effort by the government to influence aggregate demand. By raising or lowering aggregate demand, these policies attempt to control GNP, incomes, employment, prices, and wages.

Besides influencing aggregate demand, monetary and fiscal policies can also directly affect aggregate supply over a period of time. This is because they can influence the ability and willingness of producers to supply goods and services. If monetary policy encourages a sound banking system and promotes price stability, then we will feel more secure in saving or investing our wealth. Moreover, if fiscal policy yields tax rates that do not take excessive amounts of our income, then we will be more willing to save, invest, and produce.

If the goods and services we all want are to be supplied, therefore, producers must have the incentives to provide them. Economists have always agreed on the importance of these incentives, but in recent years there has been renewed interest in the ways by which government can increase production incentives. This renewed interest has been popularized as *supply-side economics.*

Supply-side economics emphasizes the long-term effects of monetary and fiscal policies on aggregate supply. In particular, it stresses the effects of marginal tax rates on individuals' willingness to save, to invest, and to work. A *marginal tax rate* refers to the amount of an extra dollar of income that you would pay as tax. According to the discussion of *thinking at the margin,* presented in Chapter 1, the additional dollar is the dollar at the margin. If your marginal tax rate is 28 percent, for example, then you will pay 28 cents of additional tax when you receive an additional dollar of income.

Because the marginal tax rate is the fraction of an additional dollar that would be paid in tax, its magnitude can alter your incentives to earn additional income by contributing to the production of goods and services. Because the tax rate rises as income rises, at a higher income level you keep less of an extra dollar of income. The result might be that you have less incentive to earn the higher income by helping to produce goods and services and more incentive to discover legal ways of avoiding taxes on your existing income. At a lower marginal rate, however, you keep more of an extra dollar of income. You might then have more incentive to earn additional income and less incentive to find legal ways of avoiding taxes. If lower tax rates create more incentive to earn income, therefore, workers, businesses, and investors might divert resources from activities that save taxes to activities that produce goods and services. As a result, the nation's aggregate production and aggregate income will increase.

These thoughts greatly influenced Congress in 1986 when it passed an important tax reform bill that lowered many individuals' marginal tax rates. As this book is written, it is too early to evaluate the consequences of this important law. But one of its objectives was to encourage Americans to shift their resources from uses that avoid taxes to uses that produce goods and services. Whether or not it will accomplish this long-term objective remains to be seen. There is no doubt, however, that the law illustrates an effort to bolster the supply side of our economy.

Chapter Summary

1. *Inflation* is an increase in the price level or a decline in the buying power of money. Any factor that influences aggregate demand or aggregate supply can affect the rate of inflation. If high rates of inflation last for some years, or if there is a hyperinflation, the cause is usually a rapidly increasing money supply.

2. *Monetary policy*, which is controlled by the Federal Reserve System, is what the Fed does to increase or decrease the nation's money supply. Monetary policy attempts to reduce economic fluctuations. Its goals are stable prices, full employment, and economic growth, which it attempts to achieve through changes in aggregate demand.

3. Total spending or aggregate demand is determined by multiplying the supply of money by the average number of times that supply is spent. By increasing the money supply and, thereby, changing aggregate demand, the Federal Reserve System can change GNP, incomes, employment, prices, and wages.

4. Monetary policy runs into difficulty because the number of times the money supply is spent can vary, so that a specific change in the money supply can produce very different changes in aggregate demand, and because the economic effects of that policy are delayed. As a result of these difficulties, *monetarist economists* believe that economic stability can be best achieved by allowing the money supply to grow by a small, constant rate each year. Other economists disagree and advocate that the Fed should ac-

tively pursue monetary policy and attempt to reduce business cycles.

5. The Fed can increase or decrease the money supply, which is essentially checking deposits, by changing the amount of banks' reserves. Government bonds are IOUs issued by the government, and the Fed can change the amount of reserves in the banking system by buying those bonds from the banks. This increases banks' reserves beyond the fraction of deposits required. The excess reserves allow them to make new loans, and these new loans create new checking account money. If the Fed sells government bonds to the banks, then the banks will make fewer loans and checking deposit money decreases.

6. The Fed can also alter bank reserves by increasing or decreasing (a) the *discount rate of interest,* which is the interest rate commercial banks must pay if they borrow reserves from the Federal Reserve System, or (b) the *legal reserve rate,* which indicates the fraction of checking deposits that banks must legally hold on reserve. Changing either of these rates causes the money supply to rise or fall.

7. The federal government can also use fiscal policy to alter aggregate demand. *Fiscal policy* is an intentional change in federal spending or taxes in order to influence aggregate demand. The federal government *directly* alters demand by changing its spending for final goods and services. It *indirectly* alters aggregate demand by making transfer payments and also by reducing or increasing taxes.

8. A *federal budget deficit* is the amount by which federal taxes fall short of federal expenditures; a *federal budget surplus* is the amount by which federal taxes exceed federal expenditures. Unplanned deficits often occur when the economy slides into a recession. During a recession, federal spending very often increases, and federal taxes decrease. Planned deficits or surpluses, unlike unplanned deficits or surpluses, represent fiscal policy—intentional changes in federal spending or taxing.

9. Fiscal policy, like monetary policy, suffers from delays, such as the time it takes to legislate changes in federal taxes. Economists, noting these delays, disagree about the usefulness of fiscal policy in stabilizing the economy. Those

economists who favor fiscal policy are called *Keynesian economists* because they base their ideas on those of the late economist John M. Keynes; other economists believe fiscal policy accentuates economic fluctuations.

10. The federal budget has been in deficit each year since 1970. The government might finance these deficits by borrowing from the public by selling bonds. When deficits are large, this borrowing might capture much of the nation's available credit. The Federal Reserve System, noting the scarcity of credit for productive investment, might create more credit by increasing bank reserves; then the banks can make more credit available through increased loans. This process, called *monetizing the deficit*, might lead to rapid increases in the money supply and equally rapid increases in inflation.

11. The *national debt* is the total amount borrowed over the years by the federal government and not yet paid back. It is much larger than the federal budget deficit, which shows what the government borrows in a specific year when federal spending is greater than federal tax revenues. Budget deficits increase the public debt; budget surpluses decrease it.

12. Monetary and fiscal policies are highly interdependent, and, therefore, they are hard to evaluate and easy to confuse. A simple way of not confusing them is to remember that monetary policy influences aggregate demand by changing the money supply; fiscal policy influences aggregate demand by increasing or decreasing the average number of times a given money supply is spent during the year.

13. Monetary and fiscal policies can also change aggregate supply over time by either positively or negatively influencing individuals' ability and willingness to earn income by producing goods and services. Recently, there has been increased interest in the ways government can increase the incentive to save, invest, and produce. This renewed interest has been popularized as *supply-side economics*, so called because it emphasizes the important effect of marginal tax rates on individuals' incentives to save, invest, and work.

Review Questions

1. What is *inflation,* and how does it relate to a nation's money supply?
2. What is *monetary policy,* and what are its goals?
3. What is the major shortcoming of monetary policy in promoting economic stability? Explain.
4. How does the Open Market Committee of the Federal Reserve System control the nation's money supply? Explain.
5. What is the *discount rate of interest,* and how does it relate to monetary policy?
6. How does the Federal Reserve System use the legal reserve rate to control the nation's money supply?
7. What is *fiscal policy?* Describe three ways in which the government tries to use fiscal policy to influence aggregate demand.
8. Define a *federal budget deficit* and a *federal budget surplus.* How are federal budget deficits financed?
9. What is the difference between *budget deficits* and the *national debt?*
10. What is the difference between the ways in which monetary policy and fiscal policy influence aggregate demand?

Discussion Questions

1. Identify the goals of monetary policy, and explain how the Federal Reserve System can use monetary policy in an effort to reach these goals. What difficulties does it face in doing so?
2. Identify the goals of fiscal policy, and explain how the federal government can use fiscal policy in an effort to reach these goals. What difficulties does it face in doing so?
3. Are there any differences between the *national debt* and *budget deficits?* If so, what are they?
4. If you are trying to raise aggregate demand, what fiscal and monetary policies should you use? Why?

5. Do you think the government's use of monetary and fiscal policies over the years has made our economy more or less stable? Why?

1. Draw a cartoon or cartoon strip that illustrates the meaning of inflation.

2. Write an essay defending or attacking the following statement: When changing the legal reserve rate, the Federal Reserve System *indirectly* alters the supply of money.

3. Write an essay describing the views of monetarist, Keynesian, and supply-side economists. In the last paragraph, explain why you agree or disagree with each of these views.

4. The following data show our nation's GNP and the federal government's expenditures and tax revenues for different years. Calculate the percentage of GNP that expenditures and tax revenues each represent for these years. Based on your calculations, would you say that changes in expenditures or tax revenues were more responsible for the development of large budget deficits in the 1980s? Why?

Year	GNP	Federal Expenditures	Federal Tax Revenues
1960	$ 515 billion	$ 92 billion	$ 92 billion
1965	705	118	117
1970	1,015	196	193
1975	1,598	332	279
1980	2,732	591	517
1985	3,998	946	734

Additional Readings

Carson, Robert B. *Macroeconomic Issues Today: Alternative Approaches.* 4th ed. New York: St. Martin's Press, 1987. 54–70.

Fleisher, Belton M.; Ray, Edward J.; and Kniesner, Thomas J. *Principles of Economics*. Dubuque, Iowa: Wm. C. Brown, 1987. Chapter 27.

Friedman, Milton. "The Case for Overhauling the Federal Reserve." In *Annual Editions: Economics 86/87*, edited by Rueben Seisinger and Glen Beeson. Guilford, Conn.: Dushkin, 1986. 163–70.

International Economics

Would we strengthen our economy if we did not purchase foreign goods and services?

International Trade

■ Student's Goals ■

1. Explain the benefits of trade in terms of specialization and comparative advantage.

2. Distinguish between a *balance of trade* and a *balance on current account* in terms of international trade.

3. Explain how and why the balance of payments must always balance.

4. Demonstrate how a nation's exchange rate is affected by its currency's demand and supply in world currency markets.

5. Give at least two arguments each in favor of and against a policy of protectionism.

Wheels of Trade

Reginald Giles knows that replacing a hubcap can be difficult and expensive because he makes a living for his family of seven children by locating and selling hubcaps.[1] Giles became self-employed some years ago when his old Cadillac hit a pothole and lost two hubcaps. After stopping to recover them and discovering many other hubcaps scattered nearby, he recognized the potential for a new business.

Giles operates his used hubcap business in an old, baby-blue school bus that he often parks near a busy intersection. Close to 1,000 hubcaps dating back to 1965 are stuffed into Giles's baby-blue bus. "If I've touched it, I'll remember where it is," says Giles. Indeed, when a woman drove up in a Ford Thunderbird one day, Giles was ready with the missing hubcap before she had gotten out of her car. For a price of $25 the woman happily bought it, and Giles gladly sold it.

The exchange of a hubcap for $25 demonstrates the ability of trade to create benefits for both buyers and sellers. The gain of one person is *not* the loss of the other. Giles gains because he values the $25 more than the hubcap. The woman in the Thunderbird also benefits because she values the hubcap more than the $25 she paid for it. This benefit occurs both when existing things are traded—at swap meets, garage sales, used hubcap businesses, and the like—and when newly produced goods and services are traded.

Trade and Production

Trade allows us to concentrate on producing particular new goods and services. Without trade, each of us would have to produce everything we want to consume. We would have to grow our own food, make our own clothes, create our own entertainment, produce our own health care, and so on. As a result, we would be unable to produce many of the goods and services we now enjoy.

With trade, however, people can concentrate on those tasks they understand. **Specialization,** which is the concentration of

[1] Michael Days, "For Reginald Giles, Potholes Aren't Bad, They're a Blessing," *Wall Street Journal*, May 13, 1985.

The buying and selling of used hubcaps illustrates how a buyer and a seller both gain from trade. The buyer obtains a hubcap valued more than the price paid, and the seller obtains money valued more than the hubcap given up. The gain of one is *not* the loss of the other.

one's work on a particular good or service, enables people to produce those goods and services for which their opportunity costs are lower than are those of other people. Then they can sell their products and use the money they receive to buy the goods and services that other people produce at lower costs. As specialization continues, the production of more and more items shifts from high-cost to low-cost producers; as a result, more goods and services can be supplied with the same quantity of resources. By specializing and trading with one another, individuals become wealthier. They can produce and consume more than if each tries to be self-sufficient.

> **Specialization:** The concentration of one's work on a particular good or service.

Specialization and Comparative Advantage

The same principle applies to trade among people of different nations. A nation is wealthier if its citizens specialize in those products they can make at lower cost and then produce enough to sell both at home and abroad. Citizens can then use the money from their foreign sales to buy goods that individuals in other countries can produce at lower cost. For example, Colombia has a clear advantage over the United States in producing coffee, and Honduras is naturally superior in growing bananas. Our weather is not suitable for these crops, so it makes sense for us to buy coffee from Columbia and bananas from Honduras instead of trying to grow them ourselves. Meanwhile, Colombia and Honduras can use the money they receive from their sales of coffee and bananas to purchase items from us that we can produce more cheaply than they can.[2]

Choosing which products to trade internationally is not always as obvious as it is with coffee and bananas. Although a nation benefits by specializing in those goods and services it can produce at lower cost, what happens if a particular nation can produce *every* product with fewer resources? Should that nation make everything for itself? The correct answer is *no*, but the reasons for this answer require some explanation. By the end of this section you will see why a country that can produce every product with fewer resources will still be better off if it specializes and trades. You will understand why a nation with an *absolute advantage* in producing everything will still gain by specializing in those goods in which it has a *comparative advantage*.

Although absolute advantage and comparative advantage are new terms, the ideas are familiar. For example, when George Herman "Babe" Ruth began playing for the New York Yankees, he was thought to be the best hitter and the best pitcher on the team. That is, Babe Ruth had an absolute advantage in both hitting and pitching. The coaches would have liked him to do both, but pitchers can't play every day because their arms need a rest after pitching. The coaches decided that Babe should not pitch because they believed the opportunity cost of using him as a pitcher was too high.

There were two reasons for this conclusion. In the first place, although other members of the team were fine pitchers, no one could touch Babe at hitting. In the second place, even if Babe's arm held up well enough for him to pitch every fifth game, he

[2]We speak of nations as though they were people in order to make our explanation simpler. We are still talking about individuals; however, now the individuals live in different countries.

The Economic Way of Thinking

The Reasons for Trade

In the nineteenth century the United States exported grain and many other agricultural products and imported manufactured goods. Why did the United States trade in this way with other nations?

Noneconomic Way of Thinking

In the nineteenth century the United States became an exporter of grain and other farm products because it had a surplus of these items. In return, it imported many manufactured goods because it had a shortage of these products. It's clear that international trade depends on the existence of surpluses and shortages.

Economic Way of Thinking

The United States became an exporter of agricultural products because it had a comparative advantage in these items. Farmers could have sold all their output in the U.S. market, but they found it more profitable to sell some output overseas at higher prices. Countries that had much higher opportunity costs of producing farm products willingly paid the higher prices to U.S. farmers. Although these nations lacked a comparative advantage in farm goods, they had a comparative advantage in manufactured products. The result was that the United States specialized in farm goods and traded them for the manufactured goods in which foreigners specialized. The United States did not have a shortage of manufactured goods. Instead, it purchased these goods from other nations because these countries could produce them at lower opportunity costs.

Questions

1. What factors contributed to the comparative advantage of the United States in agriculture during the nineteenth century?
2. If there had been shortages of manufactured goods in the United States during the nineteenth century, what would have happened to their prices?
3. In what items do you think the United States now has a comparative advantage? Why might comparative advantage change over time?

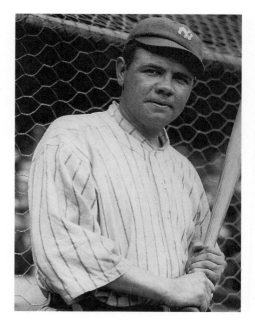

When "Babe" Ruth played for the New York Yankees, he was the best pitcher and best hitter on the team. In economic terms, Babe had an absolute advantage in both hitting and pitching. But his comparative advantage was in hitting. So Babe specialized in this activity instead of pitching and thereby missing many games while his tired arm rested.

would still warm the bench during the other four games. The opportunity cost of Babe's pitching was the hitting the team would sacrifice during the games when Babe was not allowed to play. Even though Babe was the best pitcher, the team sacrificed more hits and home runs by his pitching than it did when other teammates pitched. Because Babe had a comparative advantage in hitting, therefore, the coaches ended up with a more successful team by having Babe specialize in hitting.

This example illustrates the difference between absolute advantage and comparative advantage. An **absolute advantage** is the ability of a producer to provide a good or service with *fewer resources* than do other producers. For example, with fewer times at bat Babe Ruth could produce the same number of hits or home runs as any other teammate. In contrast, a **comparative advantage** is the ability of a producer to provide a good or service at a *lower opportunity cost* than do other producers. In other words, a comparative advantage is the ability to produce a good or service with a smaller sacrifice, not of resources but of some other good or service. Compared with other teammates who knew how to pitch, Babe Ruth would have sacrificed more hits and home runs if he pitched, so the opportunity cost of his pitching was higher than that of other pitchers on the team. His comparative advantage was, therefore, in hitting, not pitching.

> **Absolute advantage:** The ability of a producer to provide a good or service with fewer *resources* than do other producers.
>
> **Comparative advantage:** The ability of a producer to provide a good or service at a *lower opportunity cost* than do other producers.

Consider another example. Suppose a high school drama club is planning a school play. If the play is to be successful, it must have good directing and good acting. Carol is the best director and the best actor in the club, which means she has an absolute advantage in both acting and directing. Still, she can't do both because each job requires full-time effort. What if other members of the club are almost as good at acting as Carol but have no ability to direct? In this case, Carol's directing ability stands out. If her talents are used at acting, therefore, the club will incur a higher opportunity cost because it will lose Carol's valuable directing. Carol is a superior actor and director, but her comparative advantage is in directing, not acting.

Each of these examples illustrates a case in which a particular supplier can produce more of either good with a given input of resources. But the degree of the supplier's superiority is greater in one good than in the other. In other words, the supplier has an absolute advantage in producing both goods but a comparative advantage in producing only one.

How Nations Gain from Trade

Comparative advantage works much the same way with nations. Imagine there are only two nations in the world, Morofit and Lesofit. Morofit is very efficient and can produce both food and clothes with fewer resources than can Lesofit. Accordingly, Morofit has an absolute advantage in the production of both food and clothes, and so decides that it will not benefit by trading with Lesofit. Let's evaluate the wisdom of this decision by looking at some actual production figures for each nation.

In the food category we will focus on their production of peanut butter. For clothing, we will look at their production data for cotton T-shirts. Table 14–1 summarizes the work time required by each nation to produce one jar of peanut butter and one cotton T-shirt.

Without specialization and trade, the two nations require a total of fifteen hours to produce two jars of peanut butter and two T-shirts. Because Morofit requires fewer hours than Lesofit to produce either a jar of peanut butter or a T-shirt, it has an absolute advantage in the production of both items. But Lesofit, in an effort to persuade Morofit to begin trading, claims to have a lower opportunity cost of making T-shirts. That is, Lesofit (which has an absolute *dis*advantage in each good) claims to have a comparative advantage in producing T-shirts and wants to specialize in their production in order to obtain its peanut butter through trade.

Morofit doesn't see how Lesofit can be relatively better at either item and is, therefore, reluctant to trade. But Morofit is making a costly mistake. In order to see why, Morofit must stop thinking of the *number of hours* required to produce a T-shirt and think instead of the *number of jars of peanut butter* that are sacrificed in order to make a T-shirt. In the time required to make one T-shirt, Lesofit sacrifices the production of only a half of a jar of peanut butter. But Morofit sacrifices two jars of peanut butter in order to make a T-shirt. Thus, Lesofit has a

Table 14–1 Production Figures (Before Specialization and Trade)

Morofit		Lesofit	
1 jar of peanut butter	1 hour	1 jar of peanut butter	8 hours
1 T-shirt	2 hours	1 T-shirt	4 hours
Total time	3 hours	Total time	12 hours

Morofit has an absolute advantage in the production of both peanut butter and T-shirts because it requires less time to produce either good. In the absence of international trade, Morofit must spend three hours to obtain one jar of peanut butter and one T-shirt, and Lesofit must spend twelve hours to obtain one unit of each good. Together, both nations spend a total of fifteen hours to produce two jars of peanut butter and two T-shirts.

These satin coats for sale in New York City illustrate how we gain from international trade. By specializing in products where we have a comparative advantage and selling them to foreigners for products in which they have a comparative advantage, we (and they) obtain products at lower opportunity costs.

lower opportunity cost, giving it a comparative advantage in shirt production.[3]

When Morofit finally agrees to trade, Lesofit is happy because it doesn't have to make peanut butter anymore. By making one less jar of peanut butter, Lesofit can save eight hours of work time. Lesofit requires only four of those hours to produce an extra T-shirt, which it can offer to Morofit in exchange for a jar of peanut butter. Lesofit still ends up with one T-shirt and one jar of peanut butter, but it saves four hours of work time because it now works eight hours instead of twelve.

Morofit is also happy about the trade. By giving up the production of one T-shirt, it saves two hours. Only one of these hours is needed to make an additional jar of peanut butter, which it can exchange for one T-shirt. Morofit also ends up with both a jar of peanut butter and a T-shirt, as before, but it has saved an hour of work time by specializing and trading with Lesofit. Table 14–2 summarizes the results of speciali-

[3]Similarly, Morofit has a lower opportunity cost of producing peanut butter. For each jar produced, it sacrifices the production of one-half T-shirt, while Lesofit forfeits two T-shirts for each jar of peanut butter it produces.

Comparative Advantage

Successful managers of rock groups know how to assign roles to the group's members for maximum effectiveness. Should a good manager have a member play the drums because that member is the best drummer in the band?

Noneconomic Way of Thinking

It's obvious that the group will be most effective if each spot in the band is filled by the member who does it best. If Kathy is the best drummer in the group, then she should play the drums.

Economic Way of Thinking

Just because one member of a rock group is the best at a particular role doesn't necessarily mean that this person should fill that spot. Kathy may be the best drummer, for example, but she may also be the best vocalist. If no one compares to her as a vocalist, but Sam is quite adequate as a drummer, then the manager should have Kathy sing and Sam play the drums.

In this case, Kathy has an absolute advantage as both a vocalist and a drummer, but her comparative advantage is in singing. Using Kathy as a drummer will be too costly for the group because it will have to forego her more highly prized singing abilities. Similarly, countries should specialize in the production of goods and services in which they have a comparative advantage.

Questions

1. What is the opportunity cost of having Kathy play the drums when she can also sing?
2. If a lawyer can type his letters faster and more accurately than any secretary he can hire, should he type his own letters?
3. When does it make sense for a busy executive to delegate tasks to others who cannot do them as well?

Table 14–2 Production Figures (After Specialization and Trade)

Morofit		Lesofit	
1 jar of peanut butter for itself	1 hour	1 T-shirt for itself	4 hours
1 jar of peanut butter for Lesofit	1 hour	1 T-shirt for Morofit	4 hours
Total time	2 hours	Total time	8 hours

If Morofit produces Lesofit's jar of peanut butter and if Lesofit produces Morofit's T-shirt, both nations gain. Morofit still gets a jar of peanut butter and a T-shirt but works two hours instead of three. Lesofit also gets a jar of peanut butter and a T-shirt but works eight hours instead of 12. As a result, the nations together produce two jars of peanut butter and two T-shirts by working a total of ten hours—a total saving of five hours, which they can use for greater production or for leisure time.

zation and trade, which enable each country to reduce its work time in obtaining a jar of peanut butter and a T-shirt.

These two nations are certainly better off after the trade. Altogether, they have saved a total of five hours of work time, which they can use for leisure or for the production of more goods. International trade pays, therefore, because it allows nations to specialize according to comparative advantage. Furthermore, comparative advantage allows us to understand why trade can occur even between more productive economies and less productive ones. Both types of economies will benefit because specialization transfers the production of a particular good, such as peanut butter, from producers with high opportunity costs to producers with low opportunity costs. In this way, the same amount of an item can be produced with a smaller sacrifice of other goods and services. Because nations end up with more goods and services, they are wealthier than they would be without trade.

Imports, Exports, and the Balance of Payments

The gains of specialization are the motivation for international trade. In order to obtain these gains, a nation buys and sells abroad. As a result, payments go back and forth between a nation and its trading partners. The bookkeeping record of all the international transactions a country makes during a year is called the **balance of payments.**

> **Balance of payments:** The bookkeeping record of all the international transactions a country makes during a year.

One measure of a nation's balance of payments is the *balance of trade*, which shows only the goods (not the services) a country buys and sells abroad. A deficit in the balance of trade means a country is importing more goods than it is exporting; a surplus means it is exporting more goods than it is importing.

The *current account balance* is a broader measure of a country's international trade. In addition to goods, the balance on current account includes services, which is comprised of transportation, travel, insurance, international interest and dividends, and other services. The current account also includes gifts, pensions, aid, and other international payments made by the individuals and government in our nation. Figure 14–1 shows the United States current account balance and balance of trade between 1970 and 1986.

For most years from 1970 to 1986 the balance of trade line is below the horizontal axis of the graph. That's because our nation had a deficit in its balance of trade, meaning our country imported more goods than it exported. Until 1982, however, the current account balance was usually above the horizontal axis, meaning it was usually in surplus. How could the balance of trade be in deficit while the current account balance was in surplus? This difference occurred because the balance of trade includes only goods, but the balance on current account includes both goods *and services*. In 1981, our balance of trade was in deficit by $28 billion. But this deficit was more than canceled by our exporting more services than we imported. As a result, our current account balance ended up in surplus by $6.3 billion. After 1982, however, our current account balance also fell deeply into deficit.

This deficit means foreigners were sending us more goods *and* services than we were sending them. How did we pay for the difference? Put simply, we borrowed from foreigners. In order to compensate for a current account balance deficit, a nation must borrow an equal amount from other nations. On

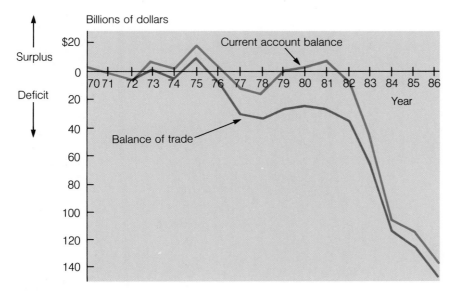

Figure 14–1 The U.S. Balance of Trade and Current Account Balance, 1970–1986

The balance of trade is the difference between exports and imports of goods; services are excluded. The balance on current account includes services and other payments, such as foreign aid and gifts and pensions to individuals abroad. When either the balance of trade or the balance on current account is above the line marked zero, it is in surplus, meaning that exports have exceeded imports. When either measure is below the line, it is in deficit, meaning that imports have exceeded exports.

Source: Economic Report of the President, 1986 (Washington, D.C.: U.S. Government Printing Office, 1986), 366–67; Council of Economic Advisers, *Economic Indicators* (Washington, D.C.: U.S. Government Printing Office, April 1987), 36–7.

the other hand, if a country has a surplus in its current account, it sends more goods and services to foreign countries than foreign countries send back. As a result, the nation must make loans to enable foreigners to pay the difference. A *deficit* in a nation's current account balance is, therefore, balanced by an equal amount of *borrowing*. A *surplus* in a country's current account balance is balanced by an equal amount of *lending*.[4]

This lending or borrowing is included in a nation's balance of payments along with exported and imported goods and ser-

---

[4]The causality does not necessarily run from a current account balance deficit to international borrowing. It can also run the opposite direction because international borrowing can lead to a deficit in the current account balance. In the 1980s, foreigners eagerly made loans to our nation because of the attractive returns they could earn here. As a result, we used the borrowed funds to purchase more goods and services abroad than foreigners purchased from us.

Oil often costs much more to produce in our own nation than it does in other nations, such as Saudi Arabia. Do you think we should produce and consume a barrel of U.S. oil if we can import and consume a barrel of foreign oil at a lower price?

vices. Because the amount of foreign borrowing or lending always equals the deficit or surplus in the current account balance, the total balance of payments must always balance.

As an example, consider Table 14–3, which presents an abridged balance of payments of the United States for 1986. The column labeled *Debits* shows how we provided dollars to foreigners when we bought goods and services from them and when we sent dollars to foreigners as gifts and aid. The column labeled *Credits* shows what foreigners did with these dollars: they used the dollars either to buy goods and services from us or to make net loans to us.

The dollars foreigners obtain from us must be used in some way, so the columns must always balance. That is, the balance of payments must always balance. When the government measures these payments, however, it must rely on the imperfect recordkeeping of individuals and businesses, and, in some cases, it must even estimate the amounts. It's not surprising, therefore, that *measured* payments are not exactly equal. In order to account for this imperfect recordkeeping, the government adds an amount called *statistical discrepancy* to assure the equality of both columns.

Table 14—3 The Balance of Payments of the United States, 1986 (billions of dollars)

	Debits	Credits
Exports of goods		$222
Imports of goods	$370	—
Trade Deficit	$148	
Export of services		$149
Import of services	$127	
Gifts, pensions, foreign aid	$ 15	—
Current Account Deficit	$141	
Net borrowing from foreigners		$114
Statistical discrepancy		$ 27
	–0–	–0–

Source: Council of Economic Advisers, *Economic Indicators,* (Washington, D.C.: U.S. Government Printing Office, April 1987), 36–37.; *International Economic Conditions* (St. Louis; Federal Reserve Bank of St. Louis, April 1987), 6.

The left column, which lists the balance of payments' debits, shows how foreigners obtained dollars from the United States. They obtained these dollars as the United States imported goods and services and as it sent money abroad as gifts, pensions, and foreign aid. The right column, which lists the credits, shows what foreigners did with the dollars they obtained. They used these dollars to buy American goods and services and also to make loans in the United States. Since foreigners must in some way use the dollars they receive, total debits must always equal total credits. As a result, the balance of payments must always balance. The particular transactions comprising these debits and credits are so numerous, however, that some are not recorded and others are recorded inaccurately. As a result, total debits and total credits are never exactly equal in any given year. The difference, called a "statistical discrepancy," was relatively large in 1986.

Exchange Rates

When a nation trades internationally and makes all the transactions shown in its balance of payments, it must exchange its currency for those of other countries. When Americans buy Japanese cars, Americans will have dollars to pay producers in Japan. But Japanese producers want yen to pay their expenses, so the dollars must be traded for yen. On the other hand, suppose an airline in Mexico purchases an airplane from a U.S. manufacturer. The Mexican airline will have pesos to make the purchase, but the U.S. manufacturer will want dollars to pay its expenses. As a result, pesos must be exchanged for dollars.

International currency markets are not unlike the market for apples. In the apple market, demand and supply produce prices, such as the one in this picture.

When our nation trades internationally, therefore, foreigners who want to make purchases here will *demand* dollars in world currency markets. At the same time, Americans who want foreign currencies to make purchases abroad will *supply* dollars in world currency markets. Just as the demand and supply of apples produce a price for apples at supermarkets, the demand and supply of dollars produce a price for the dollar in world currency markets. This price is called the **exchange rate,** which is defined as the price of one country's currency in terms of another nation's currency.

> **Exchange rate:** The price of one country's currency in terms of another nation's currency.

In 1987, for instance, the exchange rate between the dollar and the Mexican peso was about 2,000 pesos to the dollar, which means the price of the dollar was 2,000 pesos. The exchange rate between the dollar and the Japanese yen, however, was approximately 150 yen to the dollar, which means the price of the dollar was 150 yen. These are only two of many exchange rates for the dollar. Because our nation has international transactions with many countries, each of which has a different currency, there are many different exchange rates for the dollar.

The exchange rate for the dollar or for any other nation's currency is determined by the currency's demand and supply in world currency markets. For example, Figure 14–2 illustrates the demand and supply of dollars in relation to Japan's yen. The exchange rate of 150 yen to the dollar represents the equilibrium price of the dollar in terms of the yen. If the exchange rate is above this level, there will be a surplus of dollars (relative to yen) in the world currency market. A shortage of dollars will occur if the exchange rate is below this level.

If foreigners demand more dollars, the dollar's exchange rate will rise. If Americans supply more dollars, the exchange rate will fall. When a country's exchange rate rises or falls, its international trade will be affected. As an example, suppose the dollar's exchange rate rises in terms of all foreign currencies. Because foreigners will have to pay more of their own currencies to obtain a dollar, they will pay more of their own currency to buy our goods and services. For example, if the dollar rises

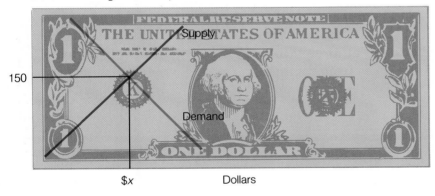

Dollar's exchange rate in Japanese Yen

Supply

150

Demand

$x   Dollars

Figure 14–2 The Demand and Supply of Dollars in Relation to Japanese Yen in the World Currency Market

This graph illustrates the dollar's exchange rate relative to the Japanese yen. Japanese buyers of American goods and services demand dollars in the world currency market. Americans who purchase goods and services from Japan supply dollars. The exchange rate is the price (number of yen) that the Japanese must pay for a dollar or that Americans receive for a dollar. If governments do not control the exchange rate, it will settle at its equilibrium level, which in this graph is 150 yen to the dollar.

In Punta del Este, Uruguay, a *cambio* is a business that buys and sells foreign currencies. Similar sales and purchases around the world are combined into an international market for a nation's currency. In this market, the international supply of and demand for a nation's currency produce a price for that currency.

from 150 yen to 300 yen, then a Japanese importer would pay twice as much for $1 worth of our wheat. As a result, foreigners will buy less from us, causing our exports to fall. On the other hand, the higher exchange rate of the dollar will reduce the *dollar* price of foreign products. We will then buy more goods and services from foreigners, causing our imports to rise.

Protectionism

Changes in exchange rates are not the only factor that can affect a country's international trade. Sometimes a country's comparative advantage can change, and this change will affect trade with other nations. This change has occurred in the United States steel industry. For many years the United States held a comparative advantage in steel production and was, thus, a large exporter of steel. But other countries, such as Japan, West Germany, Mexico, Brazil, and South Korea, have developed newer, more efficient methods of producing steel. Large U.S. integrated steel companies have felt the effects of this change, which has helped make the United States an importer of steel.

American consumers have certainly benefited from this change because lower steel prices have kept down the prices of products made from steel. So, too, have producers and workers gained in those nations that sell us steel. While some have gained, however, our own large integrated steel companies have been in trouble and have asked the government to intervene to protect them from foreign competition. Should our government agree to this industry's request?

The question is difficult to answer. Economists generally point out that in the long run nations are better off if there are no restrictions on trade. But despite the advice of economists, every nation protects its producers to some degree from foreign competition.

All nations now use some form of **protectionism**—among them, tariffs, quotas that limit the quantity of imports or exports, regulations and standards that exclude foreign products, or government subsidies to domestic producers.

> **Protectionism:** A government's use of tariffs, quotas, and other measures to protect particular domestic producers from foreign competition.

All these types of protectionism, and many more, testify to the frequent restriction of free trade by governments all over the world. What are some of the arguments that support this protectionism? In this section we will examine these arguments and then use economic principles to evaluate them.

Protects Infant Industries

This argument justifies protectionism because particular industries are believed to be capable of developing a comparative advantage if they can only get started. By protecting them from harsh international competition, the government gives the infant industry a chance to mature. At first, the nation's consumers will pay high prices for the industry's high-cost products, but prices will decrease when the industry's costs decline. Once developed, the industry can compete successfully on its own, so the temporary protection can be withdrawn.

(text continues on page 406)

Now and Then

Reports About American Manufacturing

Galloping through the dark streets of Massachusetts in 1775, Paul Revere sounded the alarm about the British invasion. Today, many Americans sound a similar alarm, warning that foreign manufacturers are "invading" our economy. They warn that unless we rally, our manufacturing industries will die, leaving us a nation of janitors and fast-food workers.

In the 1980s, the merchandise trade deficit—the gap between imports and exports of goods—soared to record heights. At the same time, reporters sadly recounted the declining production and employment in newsworthy industries like steel. As many mourned the death of manufacturing, however, they pointed to the rise of services. Between 1950 and 1985, more than 90 percent of all new jobs occurred in services, and services accounted for about 70 percent of the increase in national production.

Services is a broad category that has different definitions. One definition divides the economy into three groups: (1) industries producing goods, (2) industries producing services, and (3) industries producing agricultural products. Apart from agriculture, goods-producing industries consist of mining, construction, and manufacturing. (Of this group, manufacturing is the largest; it produces

about three-fourths of all goods.) Services-producing industries consist of everything else: examples are banking, wholesale and retail trade, transportation, and other services like those of doctors, teachers, engineers, accountants, and janitors.

Before you conclude that foreign competition is destroying our nation's manufacturing industries, think of the cable Mark Twain sent from England in 1897 upon hearing a rumor about his ill health: "The reports of my death are greatly exaggerated." Are reports about the death of U.S. manufacturing also exaggerated?

To answer the question, consider some of the fundamental changes that have occurred in the U.S. economy since many years before Twain's cable. Figure A shows that in 1850, almost two-thirds of the labor force worked in agriculture. About 18 percent worked in manufacturing and other goods-producing industries, and an equal percentage worked in services. From 1850 to 1970, the proportions increased for both goods-producing and services-producing industries. The *proportion* of the labor force working on farms (as well as the *total number* of farmers) steadily decreased as advancing productivity enabled fewer farmers to produce substantially more food.

In the 1960s, however, the propor-

Figure A Percentage of All Workers Producing Goods, Services, or Agricultural Products, 1950–1986

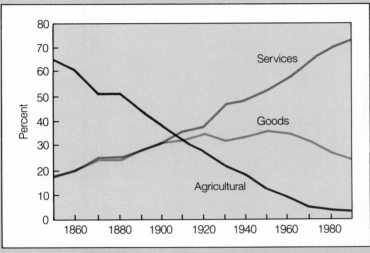

Sources: Adapted and calculated from the following: Urquhart, Michael, "The Employment Shift to Services: Where Did It Come From?" *Monthly Labor Review*, April 1984, 16: *Economic Report of the President* (Washington, D.C.: Government Printing Office, 1987) 280, 290–91.

tion of our labor force employed in the production of goods began to decrease. But a decreasing *proportion* does not necessarily mean a decreasing absolute number of goods-producing workers. For example, Figure B shows that even though total manufacturing employment bounces up and down with the business cycle, it has remained fairly constant over the last few decades. But while the total number of manufacturing workers has remained relatively stable over the years, the number of people employed in services has increased rapidly. This growth of service employment has *not* occurred because workers have been migrating from manufacturing jobs to service jobs. Instead, a growing labor force has provided the new workers for our service industries. In particular, many women entering the labor force have sought jobs in service industries. As employment in services has mushroomed, therefore, the relatively constant number of manufacturing workers has accounted for a declining *percentage* of total employment. As an illustration, imagine that everyone else in your class somehow grows taller overnight but you remain the same size. In the morning, you will be smaller *relative*

Figure B Total Number of Manufacturing Workers, 1950–86

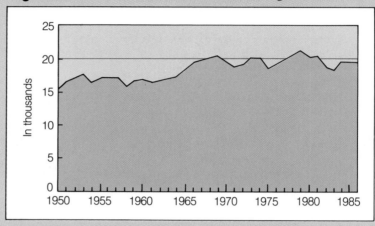

Source: Adapted from *Economic Report of the President* (Washington, D.C.: U.S. Government Printing Office, 1987) 290.

to your classmates, even though you have not shrunk. Similarly, manufacturing employment has become smaller *relative* to total employment because the number of jobs outside of manufacturing has increased rapidly.

Although manufacturing employment has fallen relative to total employment, manufacturing *production* has remained fairly constant relative to total production. This is because labor productivity has grown much faster in manufacturing than in the rest of the economy. Thus, the same number of workers has been able to produce enough additional goods to allow manufacturing production to grow in step with the rest of the economy. Figure C shows how manu-

facturing production has remained fairly constant as a percentage of gross national product at the same time that manufacturing employment has fallen as a percentage of total employment.

It is true that particular industries, such as steel and leather products, have endured much stress in the 1980s. But similar declines have not occurred generally throughout our manufacturing industries. It is also true that our manufacturers have seen their share of the world's total manuacturing production decline since World War II. But this decline is probably due to other nations' economic development, not the sickness of our own producers. As other nations develop and catch up with our

Figure C Manufacturing Employment and Output, 1960–85

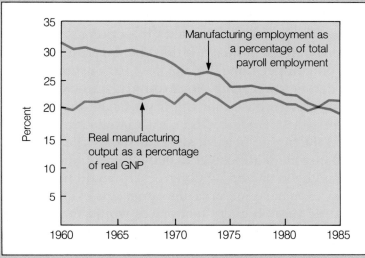

Source: Calculated from *Economic Report of the President,* 1987.

technology and skills, they, too, will probably see their manufacturing sectors overtake their agricultural sectors, just as ours did. Their increasing production of manufactured goods will increase their *share* of world production and decrease our nation's *share*. In a growing world economy, however, our manufacturing output can continue to grow even though we account for a smaller share of the world's total manufacturing production.

Do you think our manufacturing industries are threatened by an invasion of foreign producers, or do you think reports of its death are "greatly exaggerated"?

References

Beeson, Patricia E., and Bryan, Michael F. "The Emerging Service Economy." *Economic Commentary.* Federal Reserve Bank of Cleveland. June 15, 1986.

Kutscher, Ronald E., and Personick, Valerie A. "Deindustrialization and the Shift to Services." *Monthly Labor Review* (June 1986): 3–13.

McUsic, Molly. "U.S. Manufacturing: Any Cause for Alarm?" (New England Economic Review (January/February 1987): 3–16.

Perna, Nicholas S. "The Shift from Manufacturing to Services: A Concerned View." *New England Economic Review* (January/February 1987): 30–37.

Urquhart, Michael. "The Employment Shift to Services: Where Did It Come From?" *Monthly Labor Review* (April 1984): 15–21.

History confirms some cases in which young, protected industries grew up to stand on their own feet. It also confirms many cases of unending infancy, in which government protection continually supported inefficient industries at consumers' expense.

Increases Employment

Many people defend protectionism on the ground that it increases employment. It is true that protectionism can increase employment in those industries that the government insulates from foreign competition. But the cost to consumers for each job saved can be staggering. For example, in the early 1980s a strict quota was proposed for imports of steel into our nation. The Congressional Budget Office estimated that over a five-year period the higher price of steel caused by the quota would cost U.S. consumers almost $190,000 for each job saved. If the proposal had been passed by Congress, it would have been one of the most expensive job creation programs ever enacted.

At the same time, higher steel prices would have raised the production costs and prices of U.S. auto makers and other pro-

Strong emotions surround the effects of international trade on American jobs. Many people incorrectly believe that foreign trade reduces our employment and makes our economy weaker. How would you explain to someone that foreign trade makes us wealthier and does not reduce the level of American employment?

ducers that use steel in their products. Their higher prices would have reduced their sales, causing production and employment to fall in those industries. Indeed, one economist estimated that the import quota would have caused a net reduction in the nation's total employment because more jobs would have been lost in the steel-consuming industries than would have been saved in the steel industry itself.[5]

Even without this direct effect on the employment of other industries, there is no guarantee that protectionism will raise the nation's total employment. Here's why. When consumers in our country purchase larger quantities of protected American products and fewer quantities of imported products, foreigners earn fewer American dollars. With fewer American dollars to spend in our country, foreigners purchase fewer goods and services from us. As a result, our exports decrease, causing employment to fall throughout our export industries. So in order to protect our industries that cannot meet foreign competition, we hurt the industries that can.

Protects Wages from Cheap Foreign Labor

Protectionism is also commonly supported because it is thought to prevent lower foreign wage rates from reducing higher wage rates of domestic workers. Not long ago, a newspaper printed an article about low wages in the Chinese economy. The author claimed there was no way for the free enterprise world to challenge $20-a-month Chinese wages. Within the next ten years, he wrote, Chinese workers would displace huge numbers of workers throughout the western world.

Although this argument seems reasonable, it ignores differences in nations' productivities and the role of exchange rates in comparing countries' wage rates. For example, turn back to this chapter's discussion entitled "How Nations Gain from Trade." The comparison of Morofit and Lesofit has pointed out that Morofit's labor is more productive in all commodities: Morofit requires less labor time to produce peanut butter and T-shirts. Because Morofit's labor is more productive, it earns more money per hour than Lesofit's labor without increasing the item's production cost or price.

[5]Arthur T. Denzau, *American Steel: Responding to Foreign Competition* (St. Louis: Center for the Study of American Business, 1985), 16–17.

Here's why. Morofit's workers require only one hour to produce a jar of peanut butter, but Lesofit's workers require eight hours. Morofit's workers can then earn up to eight times as much per hour without making their production costs or prices higher than those of Lesofit. If Lesofit's workers receive an hourly wage of $1, for instance, the labor cost per jar will be $8 because eight hours are required to produce it. But if Morofit's workers receive a wage of $8 per hour, the labor cost per jar is still $8 because only one hour is required to produce it. In this case, the higher money wage rate in Morofit exactly balances its superior physical productivity, so that labor costs per unit are identical.

Secondly, foreign workers are paid in their own currencies, not dollars. If a Chinese worker receives 10 yuan per hour, is that wage more or less than the $8 earned by an American? It depends on the rate of exchange between the yuan and the dollar. If the dollar is worth ten yuan, then the Chinese wage of 10 yuan will equal $1 (10 yuan/10 yuan). But if the dollar is worth only one yuan, then the wage of ten yuan will equal $10 (10 yuan/1 yuan). Depending on the exchange rate, therefore,

These workers in India receive low wages compared to workers in the United States. Many people incorrectly believe that similar workers around the world threaten the general employment and living standards of our workers. But this belief ignores the fact that lower wages abroad are often neutralized by lower productivity, so that the cost per product is not lower. The belief also ignores the role of exchange rates in converting foreign wage rates into dollars.

the Chinese wage could be either higher or lower than the American wage.

When comparing wage rates among countries, we must consider both the effects of exchange rates and the differences in productivities. American wage rates are generally higher than foreign wage rates because American labor is often more *productive*. When the higher money wage in our country is offset by our edge in physical productivity, our products are not relatively more expensive. But suppose the gap between foreign and American wage rates becomes greater than the gap between worker productivities. In that case, the high money wage in our nation will more than offset our edge in physical productivity. Our products will then be relatively expensive, and our nation will, indeed, experience difficulty competing with cheaper foreign labor.

As our exports fall and our imports rise, however, the dollar's exchange rate will fall in the world currency market.[6] It will then take more dollars to equal a given foreign wage, so the dollar measure of the foreign wage will rise. Foreign wages—measured in dollars—will rise until they once again reflect the difference between foreign and American productivities. Thus, adjustments in the dollar's exchange rate keep American wages competitive with foreign wages.

When countries participate in world trade, therefore, their exchange rates adjust to reflect the general level of their productivity relative to other countries. In this way, nations end up having similar production costs *on average*. Each country will, however, have a comparative advantage in specific industries in which its opportunity costs are lower than those of other countries. Trading internationally allows each nation to profit by specializing in these particular industries. The flip side of this rule is that nations will *not* be able to compete internationally in those industries in which they do *not* have a comparative advantage. International trade exposes the relatively high costs of these industries, causing them to decline. The decline, however, is not the result of "cheap foreign labor."

[6]The dollar's exchange rate will fall because of changes in the demand and supply of dollars in the world currency market. As foreigners purchase fewer American products, they will demand fewer dollars. As Americans purchase more foreign products, they will supply more dollars. The smaller demand and larger supply will create a surplus of dollars. As a result, the price of the dollar will fall in terms of foreign currencies until the demand and supply of dollars are balanced at a new, lower equilibrium exchange rate.

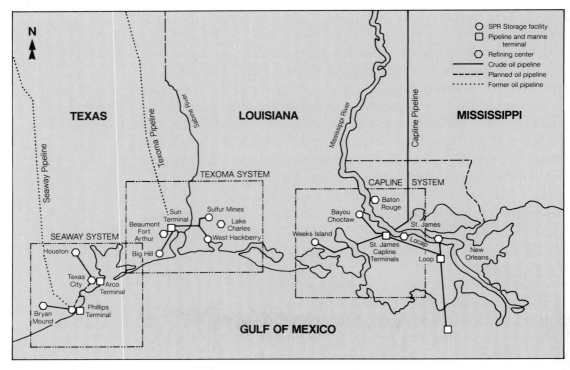

Figure 14-3 The Strategic Petroleum Reserve

In order to insure our nation's security against possible reductions in the world oil supply, the federal government stores vast quantities of oil in the Strategic Petroleum Reserve. This map shows where these storage cites are located in Texas, Louisiana, and Mississippi.

Provides for National Defense

Still another argument in favor of protectionism is that government restrictions on international trade are sometimes necessary for national security. It is often believed, for example, that imports can so weaken a strategic industry (such as oil, (see Figure 14–3), steel, or shipbuilding) that it cannot be counted on in times of war or national emergencies. As a result, protectionism is advocated to secure the nation's defense.

Although this argument has merit, it also has its faults. It is not always easy to identify which products are vital to the nation's defense, and it seems to assume that a long preparation time is available, as in World Wars I and II. Also, one cannot assume that protectionism will necessarily strengthen an industry because it might instead induce inefficiency and leave the industry less competitive over time. Furthermore, other methods, such as building government stockpiles, might better secure the nation's defense without interfering with international trade.

Allows Retaliation

Protectionism is also supported as a method of retaliating against foreign protectionism. When the trade restrictions of other governments deny free trade, it is argued, we should retaliate by increasing the protection of our own producers and workers. If foreign producers are heavily subsidized by their governments, for example, many believe that our government should protect domestic producers who compete with these subsidized foreign businesses.

If foreign governments subsidize their businesses, then comparative advantage might not be the reason for the lower costs and prices of foreign producers. But by reducing prices, the subsidies are a gift from foreigners to consumers in our nation. If our government responds by restricting trade in these subsidized items, it will prevent consumers from taking advantage of this gift. Indeed, protectionism designed to reduce this gift brings to mind the satire written in 1845 by the witty French economist Frederic Bastiat. Pretending to represent candlemakers, he petitioned the French government to pass a law against nature's gift of sunlight. The petition asked the government to pass a law against windows and all other openings through which sunlight might be "imported." Although the law would have benefited candlemakers, it would have caused a greater amount of harm to others. Similarly, retaliation against foreign protectionism benefits some domestic producers, but it causes greater harm to consumers in our nation.

An exception arises, however, if the *threat* of our retaliation causes foreigners to relax, not intensify, their restrictions on trade with us. In that case, increased specialization and trade will serve both us and the nations with whom we trade.

Chapter Summary

1. Trade creates benefits for both buyers and sellers. Trade also allows us to engage in *specialization*, which is the concentration of one's work on a particular good or service.

Specialization makes possible the production of goods and services at lower costs; this results in a greater supply of goods and services for the same amount of resources.

2. A nation also becomes wealthier by specializing in the production of those goods and services for which its opportunity costs are lower and by selling some of that production to other nations. With the money this nation receives from those sales it can buy goods and services made by other nations at lower opportunity costs.

3. *Absolute advantage* is the ability of a producer to provide a good or service with fewer resources than do other producers. *Comparative advantage* is the ability of a producer to provide a good or service at a lower opportunity cost than do other producers. Nations gain by specializing in the production of goods where they have a comparative advantage, and then trading some of what they produce. They gain because each nation winds up with more goods and services.

4. The *balance of payments* is the bookkeeping record of all the international transactions a country makes during a year. One measure of this record is the *balance of trade,* which measures only the goods (not the services) a nation buys and sells, and which can show a deficit or surplus. The *current account balance* shows both goods and services and also includes gifts and foreign aid.

5. A deficit in the balance of trade can be offset by a surplus in the current account balance. A deficit in the current account balance means a nation must borrow from other nations. A surplus in the current account balance means a nation is making loans to other countries. Because deficits in the current account balance are balanced by an equal amount of borrowing, and surpluses are balanced by an equal amount of lending, the total balance of payments must always balance.

6. An *exchange rate* is the price of one country's currency in terms of another nation's currency. Foreigners who purchase American goods demand dollars; Americans who purchase foreign goods supply dollars. This interaction of demand and supply produces a price for dollars. When an exchange rate rises or falls, it affects a nation's international trade.

7. *Protectionism* is a government's use of tariffs, quotas, and other measures to protect particular domestic producers

from foreign competition. Arguments for protectionism include the following: protecting infant industry, increasing employment, protecting wages from cheap foreign labor, providing for national defense, and retaliating against foreign protectionism.

Review Questions

1. What is *specialization,* and why do individuals attempt to specialize?

2. What is the difference between *absolute advantage* and *comparative advantage?* Can a person have both? Explain.

3. Distinguish among the following terms: *balance of payments, balance of trade,* and *current account balance.*

4. What is meant by a *deficit* in the balance in the trade? What is meant by a *surplus* in the balance of trade? Can the balance of trade be in deficit while the current account balance is in surplus? Explain.

5. Explain how a deficit in a country's balance of payments is balanced.

6. Define *debit* and *credit,* and explain how these terms are related to a country's balance of payments.

7. What is an *exchange rate,* and how is the exchange rate for any country's currency affected by the currency's demand and supply in the world currency market?

8. What is *protectionism,* and how can it affect a country's international trade?

9. What are two arguments in favor of protectionism? What are two arguments against protectionism?

Discussion Questions

1. How do nations gain from trade? Can you identify any situations in which nations might lose from trade? Explain briefly.

2. Suppose many countries reduce their purchases from the United States at the same time that the United States begins

buying more products from foreigners. Explain how this event will affect the dollar's exchange rate.

3. The president of a poor, developing nation once remarked that the increasing impoverishment of his nation's people resulted from "the system of international trade and exchange which has grown up over the years . . ." Discuss why you think the leader was right or wrong.

Activities

1. Write a paragraph explaining how the concept of opportunity cost relates to comparative advantage.

2. Write a paragraph in support of or against the following assertion: The total balance of payments must always balance.

3. Go to the library and obtain current data for the dollar's exchange rate. (This can be found in the current issue of *The Wall Street Journal*. The front-page index will direct you to the page for foreign exchange.) You can pick the nations' currencies to which you want to compare the dollar. Then compare these rates to those that existed at some time in the recent past. Write a brief paper in which you describe any changes. Present some possible reasons to explain the changes (or the lack of them).

4. The following data present hypothetical information about the demand and supply of dollars relative to the Mexican peso in the world currency market:

Exchange Rate (Number of Pesos Needed to Buy a Dollar)	Demand for Dollars (Number of Dollars)	Supply of Dollars (Number of Dollars)
1,400	2 billion	14 billion
1,200	4 billion	12 billion
1,000	6 billion	10 billion
800	8 billion	8 billion
600	10 billion	6 billion
400	12 billion	4 billion
200	14 billion	2 billion

(a) Plot the demand and supply of dollars on a piece of graph paper.

(b) What exchange rate would you expect between the dollar and the Mexican peso? Why would the exchange rate not be above this level? Why would it not be below this level?

(c) Suppose the demand for dollars increases by 2 billion at each possible exchange rate. Plot the new demand curve on the graph, and explain the effects on the dollar's exchange rate.

(d) How do you think each of the following persons would feel about the change in the exchange rate: an American buyer of Mexican oil; an American tourist in Mexico; a Mexican buyer of U.S. computers; a Mexican hotel owner in a resort that is popular with U.S. tourists.

Additional Readings

Barron, John M., and Lynch, Gerald G. *Economics*. St. Louis: Times Mirror/Mosby, 1986. 464–75.

Levi, Maurice. *Thinking Economically*. New York: Basic Books, 1985. Chapter 17.

Miller, Roger Leroy, and Shannon, Russell. *The Economics of Macro Issues*. 5th ed. St. Paul: West, 1986. Chapter 29.

Mansfield, Edwin, and Behravesh, Nariman. *Economics USA* New York: W.W. Norton, 1986. 546–62.

What Soviet leader is shown in this picture?

The Economy of the Soviet Union

■ Student's Goals ■

1. Compare and contrast Lenin's economic policy of 1921 and Stalin's economic policy of 1927 in terms of their features and results.

2. Compare and contrast the ways in which the Soviet Union and the United States make the necessary decisions about what, how, and for whom to produce.

3. Compare and contrast the ways in which consumers' incomes are determined in the Soviet Union and the United States.

Markets or Mandates?

No nation has enough resources to satisfy all the wants of every citizen. Instead, every country must cope with scarcity by deciding which wants to meet and which to deny. Chapter 2 has pointed out the kinds of choices that each nation must make about its scarce resources. Not only must it decide *what* goods and services to produce, but also it must decide *how* to produce each item. Similarly, it must decide *for whom* to produce these goods and services.

Although all countries are confronted by these choices, the methods they use to make them vary widely. Chapter 2 has explained that some nations, by allowing and enforcing the property rights of private individuals, have developed market economies. Others, by emphasizing the collective ownership of property, have developed command economies.

Our book has emphasized how a market economy makes the what, how, and for whom choices. Although the economy of the United States is influenced by a mixture of markets and government commands, it honors the private ownership of re-

These citizens of Moscow live in an economy very different from our own. In the Soviet economy, the government owns most resources, so it decides what, how, and for whom to produce.

sources and is directed and coordinated to a great extent by the "invisible hand" of market prices. The Soviet economy is also influenced by a mixture of markets and government commands, but it stresses collective, rather than private ownership of resources. As a result, the Soviet economy is an example of an economy that is directed and coordinated primarily by central planners. This chapter will briefly explain how the Soviet economy copes with scarcity by using central planning to make the choices of what, how, and for whom to produce.

The Adoption of Collective Ownership

When the Russian revolution ended the rule of the Czars in 1917, groups of workers in the industrial centers organized local councils or *soviets* to maintain order and to control food supplies. After a temporary national government under Aleksandr Kerenski failed, Vladimir Ilyitch Lenin and the Bolshevik party (later to become the Communist party) seized control of the government. The workers' councils (soviets) became the local branches of the new government, and the nation officially became known as the Union of Soviet Socialist Republics (USSR or Soviet Union).[1]

Almost immediately the new government began to implement collective ownership. Money and prices were thought to be "capitalistic" and were quickly eliminated, while efforts were made to provide for everyone's basic "needs" without charge. Through a series of government decrees, titles to land and large-scale industry were transferred to the state. The government also took ownership of banks, major factories, railways, and canals.

During the revolution in 1917, many peasants had seized the agricultural land of the large estates where they had been tenants and then had divided it into individual holdings. The decrees of the new government officially transferred title of this

[1]This description of the Soviet economy is based largely on the following sources: William N. Loucks, *Comparative Economic Systems*, 9th ed. (Lanham, Md.: University Press of America, 1985), Chapters 22–28; Hebert Heaton, *Economic History of Europe*, rev. ed. (New York: Harper & Bros., 1984), 464–72; and Robert L. Heilbroner, *The Making of Economic Society*, 7th ed. (Englewood Cliffs, N.J.: Prentice- Hall, 1985).

farmland to the state, but in reality ownership was left in the hands of the peasants.

Because of the revolution, property rights to the nation's major resources were transferred from private individuals to the government. As Chapter 2 has explained, collective ownership of resources tends to produce a centrally planned economy. Thus, it is no wonder the government immediately began to plan the use of the nation's resources. Not only did the central authorities issue orders in an attempt to control the output of industry, but also they requisitioned food and other agricultural products from the peasants who controlled much of the nation's farmland.

These initial efforts at central planning were unsuccessful, especially in agriculture where the government undermined incentives to produce. Incentives diminished because the government took most agricultural products to use as food for industrial workers and as raw materials in factories. Peasants were allowed to keep only a small amount of the agricultural output they produced. Although they were promised some of the factory output in return, the promised industrial goods did not arrive in sufficient quantities. Instead, peasants ended up with only a small amount of their own output and few, if any, of the industrial products they were promised. No matter how hard they worked, peasants were not rewarded with increased amounts of goods from the factory or the farm.

Not surprisingly, peasants became unwilling to give output to the state in return for little more than a recognition that they were contributing to "socialist welfare." Instead, they either produced only what they were allowed to keep for themselves or they illegally traded their output in black markets. As a reaction, the government sent troops into the countryside to punish the peasants and to seize farm output for the cities.

The government's policy was devastating because it greatly diminished the amount of cultivated land and produced famine throughout the nation. By 1920, the peasants were revolting against the government, and industrial output had declined to only a small fraction of what it had been before World War I.

This dismal failure prompted the government to restore some of the nation's market economy under Lenin's New Economic Policy of 1921. This policy consisted mainly of allowing private ownership and personal profit in retail trade, small-scale industry, and agriculture. Of these, the change in agriculture was

The resources on this state farm are mostly owned by the government, which commands the farm to produce a stipulated amount of food.

particularly important. Instead of allowing peasants to keep only a small fixed amount of what they produced, the government kept a fixed amount and allowed peasants to keep whatever was left. This change helped to improve incentives to produce because increases in farm output went to the peasants, not the government.

Following the introduction of the New Economic Policy, the Soviet economy improved. Indeed, by 1926, both agricultural and industrial production had returned to the levels that had existed before World War I. The Soviet leaders must have been happy about the increased production, but they could not have been pleased by the fact that it resulted from methods that emphasized markets. Once output had increased and the nation's survival seemed assured, the government decided that market economy methods could not be tolerated in a society supposedly devoted to the collective ownership of resources. Especially distasteful to the government's leaders was the fact that agriculture, a large and important part of the economy, was still controlled by private individuals.

Therefore, in 1927, Joseph Stalin, who had become head of the Communist party after Lenin's death in 1924, decided to end, in his words, the "pampering" of peasants. His policy was to collectivize the peasants' lands by combining individual plots

Although Vladimir Ilyitch Lenin died in 1924, his pictures can still be seen throughout the Soviet Union. Here, Lenin's picture dominates a street in Moscow.

into large, state-operated farms, which were supervised by local officials of the Communist party. The peasants, who formerly owned the lands, were organized into "brigades" to work the newly formed collective farms.

This change was not accomplished easily. Comparatively wealthy peasants, known as *Kulaks*, resisted the collectivization of their lands by the Communists. Sabotage and fighting occurred as a result. Instead of submitting to collectivization, many peasants slaughtered and consumed their livestock, destroying in the process about one-half of the nation's pigs, two-thirds of its poultry, and about one-third of its sheep, goats, and cattle.

The Communist leaders responded forcefully to the Kulaks' resistance. It has been estimated, for example, that from 1 to 5 million Kulaks were banished, sent to concentration camps, or killed as the Communist party forced the peasants to honor the collective ownership of agricultural resources.

What and How to Produce

In the Soviet economy there is a comprehensive economic plan, the supreme authority of which reaches from the Communist party's leaders down to every factory, farm, mine, and worker in the nation. The plan assigns to enterprises their supplies and capital, and specifies and allocates their output. The state selects the goals to be achieved and then assigns specific tasks to the productive units in the nation in order to achieve these goals.

This is real planning, and it is based on the collective (government) ownership of all natural resources and large-scale industry. Just as market prices solve the problems of what, how, and for whom to produce in an economy that honors the private ownership of resources, government planning solves these problems in the Soviet economy.

In order to make these basic choices in the Soviet Union, the State Planning Commission, called the *Gosplan*, constructs a plan for the entire economy. The Gosplan, which is directly responsible to the Communist party, then directs the planning ministry in each republic in the Soviet Union. Each of these ministries then directs its own regional planning agencies, which, in turn, send the commands down through the hierarchy to individual enterprises and farms. Orders flow from top to bottom, but the orders are not made in a vacuum. Instead, data and requests flow from the bottom up, and this information is then used to help formulate the overall economic plan.

Although central planning covers many different time spans, the most important blueprints for the operation of the economy are probably the Five-Year Plan and the One-Year Plan. In order to carry out the annual industrial plan, for example, the Gosplan constructs a record of the available amounts of approximately one thousand materials used by industry. These data are forwarded to the regional planning agencies, which then ask the industrial enterprises under their jurisdiction to specify the amounts of materials they will need to meet their assigned output quotas. Thus, each region and republic get to estimate how much material they will need to fulfill their established goals. These estimates are passed back up the planning network to the Gosplan, which then divides the available materials among the various republics. Each republic distributes the rights to the materials among its regions, which, in turn, allocate them to their various enterprises.

The enormity of this planning task can be appreciated if you suppose that you are the head planner of the Gosplan. First, you must have a reasonably accurate idea of the types and quantities of resources that will be available for the coming

Consumer Wants

In the U.S. economy, businesses produce goods and services to earn a profit. Does this fact make the U.S. economy more responsive to consumer wants than is the Soviet economy?

Noneconomic Way of Thinking

In the United States, big corporations produce to satisfy their desire for profits, not to satisfy the wants of consumers. In the Soviet Union, the government decides what to produce. In either case, consumers do not direct production. Neither economy is responsive to consumers' wants.

Economic Way of Thinking

It is true that businesses in the United States produce for profit, but profits are necessary for businesses to know which goods and services consumers want. The U.S. economy is based on both profits and losses. When businesses efficiently produce to satisfy consumers' wants, consumers reward them with profits. But when businesses produce inefficiently or do not provide what consumers want, then consumers penalize them with losses. Through the constant push and pull of profits and losses, consumers direct production in the U.S. economy. In the Soviet Union, however, the government makes its production plans without much consideration of profits and losses. Instead, the economy is commanded to meet the objectives of government planners, not consumers. That is why the U.S. economy is more responsive to consumers' wants than is the Soviet economy.

Questions

1. Why doesn't the Soviet government make consumer wants the most important objective of the economy?

2. Why is there consumer freedom in the Soviet Union? Why doesn't this freedom also mean that consumers direct production in the Soviet economy?

period for which you are planning. This is no small problem, but let's assume you somehow obtain this information. Next, you must decide how to divide these resources between the two major types of goods and services: consumer goods, such as food and clothes, and capital goods, such as factories and machines. This, too, is no small problem, but let's assume you divide total resources between these two types of goods in order to satisfy your overall objectives. Your next problem is to decide precisely what kinds of consumer goods and capital goods to produce. Take consumer goods. You have already earmarked some of the nation's available resources for this purpose, but now you must decide what specific consumer goods to produce.

Think for a moment about the possible number and variety of consumer goods. Because the resources you have set aside for the production of consumer goods are scarce, they cannot produce all of the goods that people want. Instead, you must decide which specific goods to produce. Some goods must be given up in order to produce others, so you must decide which wants are most important.

On the assumption that you make this difficult choice, your next task is to determine the specific characteristics of the goods and services you have chosen. If one of the items you have selected is toothbrushes, what kind of toothbrushes should be produced? Should they be long or short? If they should be long, how long? Should they be colored or plain? What kind and what number of bristles should they contain?

Suppose you make these choices and decide to produce a given number of toothbrushes with hog bristles. How many hogs do you need to get the right amount of bristles? What should the hogs be fed? If they are to eat corn, how much land, labor, machinery, and fertilizer should be set aside to produce it? Once the bristles are obtained from the hogs, what should be done with the meat? What resources should be used to process this meat? What about the meat by-products that will result? Should they be thrown away or converted to fertilizer? If they are used for fertilizer, what kinds and what amounts of resources will be required?

Somehow these difficult choices must be made in any economy. But if you multiply them by the enormous number of possible goods and services, you get an idea of the complexity of the task that will face anyone who consciously tries to direct an economy. In comparison, a market economy makes these

In the Soviet economy, long lines are common, such as this one at a government department store. Because government planners, rather than market prices, direct and coordinate the Soviet economy, prices are often set much below their equilibrium levels. As a result, goods and services are frequently rationed by nonprice methods, such as first come, first served.

decisions without the central direction of government. Instead, the choices of many independent individuals are guided by market prices. The result is that the goods and services demanded by consumers are produced and usually made available in the right amount to those who are willing and able to buy them.

In order to deal with the complexity of central planning during the last few years, the Soviet Union has abandoned the practice of starting from scratch when making its annual plans. Instead, by using the previous year as a benchmark, Soviet planners have simplified their task. In addition, the Gosplan now focuses each year on about 50 basic products and industries that are crucial to the achievement of the overall plan's primary objective. Moreover, in the last few years, the Soviet Union has relied much more heavily on market-type strategies to direct its economy. For example, at one time the Communists announced an experiment that freed managers in the shoe and food-processing industries from planned quotas. Instead, the managers were directed to maximize profits. Most of these profits went to the state, but a small part was used as bonuses to reward successful managers.

Although the Soviet Union has copied some techniques of the marketplace, its rewards for successful economic performance are still based largely on the decisions of the planners. In contrast, economic rewards and punishments in the United States are based largely on whether producers succeed or fail at satisfying the demands of consumers.

For Whom to Produce

Soviet citizens, like citizens in the United States, must earn money in order to purchase goods and services. In the United States, incomes depend largely on the benefits that resource owners indirectly produce for consumers when selling their resources to businesses. If you have a larger quantity of resources or more productive resources, you earn more income. With more income you are then able to cast more dollar votes in the goods and services markets. By responding to these dollar votes, suppliers end up producing goods and services for resource owners according to owners' abilities to help producers satisfy the demands of consumers. The Soviet Union is different, however, because consumers' incomes are determined mostly by the state. Here's why.

Both U.S. and Soviet citizens are free to spend their money incomes as they wish on the goods and services that are available. As Chapter 2 has explained, this freedom is called *consumer freedom*. But unlike U.S. consumers, Soviet consumers have little to do with determining the kinds and amounts of consumers goods that are available. Soviet consumers do not have *consumer sovereignty*, therefore, because their spending decisions do not much influence the way resources are used. As a result, by spending or withholding their money, Soviet consumers do not reward or punish producers for their successful or unsuccessful performance.

That is certainly not the way a market economy works. When consumers in a market economy cast more dollar votes for something, producers will tend to supply more of it. On the other hand, when consumers cast fewer dollar votes something, producers will tend to supply less of it. In their search for personal gain, businesses produce what is demanded.

In the Soviet economy, resources are owned by the state, and the government's plan determines what will be produced with those resources. Thus, the government's planning determines the kinds and quantities of consumer goods to be produced. The government also tries to set the money prices of these goods, so that they will be just high enough to absorb what consumers want to spend. If the Soviet planners decide that 5,000 pairs of shoes will be produced, they also try to set the price of shoes at a level that will result in 5,000 pairs' being demanded.

The prices set by the government, however, are often below their equilibrium levels, resulting in widespread shortages of consumer goods in the Soviet Union. But if goods and services are not rationed by prices, then some other rationing method must be used. For example, Chapter 7 has pointed out that first come, first served rationing is an alternative to rationing by price. The long lines that are often found at the Soviet Union's government stores show that first come, first served rationing of consumer goods is common there.

If the Soviet government finds that consumers are spending more than was anticipated for shoes, more shoes are *not* produced. Instead, either the price of shoes is increased in order to soak up the additional money being spent for them, or lines lengthen as first come, first served rationing intensifies. In the Soviet Union, therefore, goods and services are produced to satisfy the objectives of the Communist party, not the preferences of resource owners who have contributed to the satisfaction of consumers' wants. If the Gosplan wants resources to produce steel mills instead of shoes, then it will command that the nation's resources be so used, regardless of how consumers are spending their money. Because the Soviet government determines what will be produced with the nation's resources, consumer sovereignty is not present as it is in market economies. As a result, the Soviet economy produces goods and services for individuals according to their abilities to help government enterprises satisfy the government's plans. This differs from our economy, which mostly produces goods and services for individuals according to their abilities to help businesses satisfy the demands of consumers.

Labor in the Soviet Economy

Soviet workers have some freedom to choose among alternative jobs, but the alternatives themselves are structured by the gov-

Wages

Could a centrally planned economy like that of the Soviet Union pay equal wages to all workers?

Noneconomic Way of Thinking

It can, but it doesn't. Paying equal wages to everyone is the only fair method of dividing up the economic pie that is produced.

Economic Way of Thinking

No economy has ever been able to pay equal wages, regardless of the work that people do. Some work is more important than other work, so incentives must exist in order to assure that enough people will do it. In the Soviet Union, the government decides which work is more important and then sets wage rates to assure than enough people will want to work to meet the goals set by the state's planners. In the U.S. economy, consumers determine which work is more important by means of their money votes in the marketplace. As businesses respond to consumers' money votes, they pay more for the labor that produces more value for consumers. In both economies, however, wage rates are used as a means of directing workers to those tasks that are considered most important.

Questions

1. Suppose you are a government planner in the Soviet Union, and you require more workers to meet this year's planned production of tractors. If you cannot pay higher wages to attract more workers into tractor production, how can you obtain the additional labor?

2. If you obtain the additional workers for tractor production, can that affect the attainment of the economy's other production goals? Why or why not?

ernment's economic planning, not by demand and supply in the marketplace. Since the type of training influences one's occupation, for example, the state can control admissions to schools in order to assure that each type of job has enough workers to meet the state's plans.

The Soviet Union does have labor unions, but their main functions are to increase production and to enforce labor discipline. Strikes are not allowed, and the unions have little or no effect on wages. Although wage rates are set by the state, planners have used a technique of the marketplace to assure that workers have incentives to produce. They have done this by paying workers according to their ability to produce the goods and services specified by the nation's central plan. From highest to lowest, pay rates in the Soviet Union are ranked in approximately the following order:

1. Leading scientists
2. Senior government officials
3. Artists, such as opera and ballet stars
4. Professors of science and medicine
5. Plant managers
6. Engineers
7. Skilled workers
8. Physicians
9. High school teachers
10. Semiskilled workers
11. Unskilled workers

Although workers are free to change jobs, the government does use its power to allocate desirable housing in order to hold workers on particular jobs. By changing jobs, for example, one might be put at the end of the line when housing, much of which is government owned and in short supply, is allocated by the state.

Whether as workers or as consumers, citizens of the Soviet Union are certainly not slaves. They have considerable economic freedom, although it is much less than that enjoyed by American citizens. Neither economy illustrates a pure market economy or a pure command economy because each contains some elements of the other. But the economy of the United States is one in which property is primarily privately owned.

As resources are used by private owners, who make their own decisions in their own interests, income is allocated by the marketplace. Furthermore, economic activity by the U.S. government operates through the market as the government casts its own dollar votes for goods and services and as it uses its taxes and income transfers to influence the dollar votes cast by individuals and businesses.

On the other hand, the Soviet Union is primarily a centrally planned economy, in which property is owned by the state. Resources are used and income is distributed according to the commands of central planners. Those who prefer the way in which a centrally planned economy solves the basic problems of what, how, and for whom to produce tend to believe that individual self-interest should be contained by central authority. Those who prefer the way in which a market economy solves the basic economic problems tend to believe that voluntary trade in open markets will direct individuals' self-interest to the benefit of the community.

Chapter Summary

1. Scarcity compels all nations to decide what, how, and for whom goods and services will be provided. In the United States these choices are made largely through the direction of privately held resources by market prices. In the Soviet Union these choices are made under the direction and control of government planners who channel publicly owned resources.

2. The Russian Revolution ended Czarist rule in 1917. Shortly after that, Lenin and the Bolshevik Party seized control of the government. Russia then became known as the Union of Soviet Socialist Republics (USSR). Property rights to both agricultural and industrial resources were then transferred to the government. Collective ownership of these resources was quickly established, and central planning of the economy was begun.

3. Central planning in agriculture was initially unsuccessful because the peasants who produced agricultural products were allowed to keep very little of their output. After the government realized its policies had produced a serious de-

cline in agricultural output, Lenin's New Economic Policy was instituted in 1921. It permitted some private ownership and personal profit in agriculture; the peasants were allowed to keep all of their output after they met government quotas.

4. Although the New Economic Policy produced significant improvements in the economy's output, the Soviet government was unhappy with having to use market methods, such as private ownership of resources in agriculture. Not long after Lenin's death in 1924, Stalin became the head of the Soviet government. In 1927, Stalin collectivized agriculture, combining privately owned peasants' lands into large collective farms, operated and supervised by the government. This change was fiercely resisted by the wealthier peasants, called *Kulaks*, millions of whom were banished, sent to concentration camps, or killed.

5. The Soviet economy has an overall economic plan, according to which government planners make the choices of what, how, and for whom to produce. This plan is constructed by the State Planning Commission, called the *Gosplan*. The Gosplan directs planning ministries in the republics which, in turn, direct individual businesses.

6. In a market economy, goods and services are produced to satisfy consumers' demands. Those resource owners more able to help businesses satisfy consumers' demands earn more income and can then cast more dollar votes in the goods and services markets. By responding to these money votes, suppliers produce goods and services for individual resource owners according to their abilities to help satisfy the demands of consumers. In the Soviet Union, incomes— and the resulting abilities to buy goods and services—are determined by the government, not by individuals' abilities to satisfy consumers' demands. Consequently, the Soviet economy produces goods and services for individuals according to their abilities to satisfy the government's plans, not the demands of consumers.

7. Soviet citizens have some freedom to choose their jobs, but the alternative jobs and wage rates from which they can choose are determined by the government, not supply and demand. Workers are free to change their jobs, although government allocation of suitable housing influences these changes.

1. What was the effect of the Russian Revolution of 1917 in terms of property rights?

2. Why was central planning unsuccessful immediately after the Russian Revolution of 1917?

3. What was Lenin's New Economic Policy of 1921, and what were its initial effects?

4. How did Joseph Stalin change the Soviet Union's economic policy in 1927? Was the change successful? Explain.

5. What is the role of the Gosplan in determining what is produced in the Soviet economy?

6. Is central planning a simple or a complex process? Explain.

7. How are consumers' incomes determined in the Soviet Union?

8. What is the difference between *consumer freedom* and *consumer sovereignty?* Do consumers in the Soviet Union have consumer freedom and/or consumer sovereignty? Do consumers in the United States have consumer freedom and/or consumer sovereignty? Explain.

9. What is the role of labor unions in the Soviet Union?

Discussion Questions

1. Why was the New Economic Policy introduced in the Soviet Union in 1921? What changes in the Soviet economy resulted from that policy?

2. Explain how the basic economic decisions of what, how, and for whom to produce are made in the Soviet economy.

3. Who owns most of the resources in the Soviet Union? Who owns most of the resources in the United States? Explain how the two different types of resource ownership affect the decision of what to produce in each nation.

4. Explain why you agree or disagree with this statement: Political freedom depends on the existence of private property rights and the economic freedoms they permit in a market economy; when property rights are concentrated in the government, individuals lose their political freedom because they lose their economic freedom.

Activities

1. Write an essay analyzing the following opinion: Whether you live in a planned economy or a market economy, you are still at the mercy of somebody. In a planned economy, you are at the whim of the planners; in a market economy, you are at the whim of the buyers.

2. Interview someone who has recently visited the Soviet Union or go to the library and try to answer the following questions: (a) What is the price of a ticket for a concert (rock or ballet) in the Soviet Union, and what do you think the price of a similar ticket is in the United States? (b) Describe the quality of the restaurant and hotel service in the Soviet Union. Is it better or worse than the typical service you receive in the United States? (Then compare your answers with those of other classmates, and in a class discussion give possible reasons for the results you obtained.)

3. Using supply and demand graphs, show what will probably happen in the long run (a) if U.S. citizens are continuously standing in long lines to buy shoes, and (b) if Soviet citizens are continuously standing in long lines to buy shoes.

Additional Readings

Baumol, William J., and Blinder, Alan J. *Economics: Principles and Policy.* 3d ed. San Diego: Harcourt Brace Jovanovich, 1985, 839–55.

Dolan, Edwin G. *Economics.* 4th ed. Chicago: Dryden, 1986. Chapter 37.

Gurley, John G. *Challengers to Capitalism.* 2d ed. New York: W.W. Norton, 1979, Chapter 4.

Samuelson, Paul A., and Nordhaus, William D. *Economics.* 12th ed. New York: McGraw-Hill, 1985, 771–79.

Appendix
Careers in Economics

Your economics class in high school has provided you with an introduction to this vast field. Assuming that you like what you learned and would like to learn more, what kind of information do you need? Your next step might be to begin asking questions and considering a college major in economics. As well, you might want to find out just what kinds of jobs people in economics do, and what kind of training or education they need. You may also want to consider what opportunities are available in related fields, after majoring in economics.

First Questions

Let's begin by exploring some questions about the kinds of skills the field of economics develops. You might ask yourself:

Do you enjoy analysis and thinking critically about issues and concepts?

Do you enjoy being a problem-solver, using economic information?

Could you enjoy working with details?

How are your writing skills, or your willingness to acquire better writing skills?

Do you have good verbal skills?

Have you read popular books on economics and found them interesting? Do you read the business section of the newspaper?

Do you enjoy working with other people? Could you direct or manage other people's activities on the job? Could you take direction as well as offer advice in a diplomatic way?

If you find yourself answering "yes" to most of the questions above, then perhaps a career in economics or a related field might be a wise choice for you.

Majoring in Economics

Although many students may take a class in economics, there may be few who actually choose to major in it. Even those who are majoring in it may not be planning to become economists or even to do work in economics. Students realize that a degree in economics not only offers excellent training in analysis and concepts, but also that through this training one is prepared to move into other areas of interest. As you launch your career and consider what options are available to you in school and in the job market, remember some important insights from career counselors:

The jobs you see available right now may change in your lifetime. Technology and the way people conduct business may be revolutionized during the course of your work career.

Most people will not work at the same job or in the same field for their entire life. They will change two or three more times, at least.

Employers generally seek people with particular sets of skills and talents, not necessarily highly specific skills alone.

Given the ever-changing nature of work, educational programs offered today may or may not offer the training needed for jobs tomorrow. A degree in economics may be a wise idea, giving you solid grounding in thinking skills and analysis. You may need to specialize and expand your knowledge in a specific position at a later time.

General Skills

A degree in economics can open the door to a vast number of interesting career choices. Consider the variety of skills you would acquire in training in economics: precise analytic training and thinking skills; theoretical background; an ability to handle data; attention to detail; knowledge about banking, business, trade, the economy, and employment trends, to name a few specific areas; ability to communicate clearly; ability to understand and evaluate complex ideas; and general knowledge important to success in many areas.

Education and Options

Various levels of training in economics will offer you various options. Keep in mind that while you may be able to find job satisfaction with positions open at the A.A. or the B.A. levels, more interesting opportunities and choices require advanced degrees. Let's consider some options available at the various levels.

Associate Degree Level Opportunities for positions at the associate degree level may be limited. Some of the possibilities for people with a two-year A.A. degree in economics include manager of a fast-food restaurant or management trainee in a small retail store. Keep in mind that even with the degree, employers may require training on the job.

Bachelor's Degree Level People who choose economics as an undergraduate major may wish to continue work in the field at an advanced level. The bachelor's degree is the first step towards graduate work. Economics majors may enter related fields—fields which also require graduate training—such as law, business, management, public administration, journalism, social welfare, architecture, and urban planning, education, banking, and financial areas like investing, stocks and bonds, or development.

Other economics majors at the bachelor's level, such as economics and business, economics and computing, or economics and international relations, further tailor the types of jobs that might be pursued upon graduation or after graduate school. Even if you choose not to minor in the above-mentioned fields, you should consider taking courses in related fields, to strengthen and diversify your options. Consider courses in statistics, mathematics, education, finance, urban planning, computer programming, technical writing, business, or journalism.

Master's Degree Level The master's degree in economics assumes knowledge equivalent to the bachelor's degree as a prerequisite. The degree is usually a one- or two-year program composed of graduate-level courses and culminating in a major paper, master's examination, or both, depending on the institution. Most master's candidates continue on to the doctoral level program.

Doctoral Degree Level Students at this level usually plan to pursue a career in economics. One should plan on a three- or four-year commitment to fulfill coursework, followed by the writing of a doctoral dissertation. The Ph.D. is a research degree, and doctoral work must demonstrate scholarly ability and analysis. Professional economists, those in position to direct research, recommend policy to governing boards of major businesses or local, state, and federal government. Professors of economics teach, lecture, and do research at the university level. They may serve as consultants or advisors to business and government, preparing reports describing or forecasting general economic conditions; or they may recommend policies related to the production, distribution, and consumption of goods and services. They use statistical methods and standard economic models, skills learned in their graduate-level coursework.

Professional economists contribute greatly to the well-being of the business, academic, and government communities. Obtaining a Ph.D. in economics represents a significant achievement in one's life and would offer the widest variety of choices of jobs in economics.

It is wise to plan early in your academic career if you are interested in doctoral work. You may need to structure classes and focus your work in the direction of research and theory at an early stage, in order to prepare for a doctoral emphasis.

Employment Outlook

Having a solid foundation in economics and majoring in economics at the bachelor's level allows for flexibility in planning a variety of challenging careers. As mentioned earlier, economics graduates go on to careers in related fields as well as on to graduate school in economics. Students interested in law school, business school, education, government, and public administration programs will find economics a good basis for further study. The ability to think, analyze, and communicate concepts in topics such as finance, employment, trade, and banking serve one well in the world of work. Consider further study in economics!

Additional Sources of Information

American Economic Association
1313 21st Avenue, South
Nashville, Tenn. 37212

National Association of Business Economists
28349 Chagrin Blvd., Suite 201
Cleveland, Ohio 44122

American Marketing Association
250 South Wacker Drive
Chicago, Ill. 60606

Joint Council on Economic Education
2 Park Avenue
New York, New York 10016

Glossary

Absolute advantage: The ability of a producer to provide a good or service with fewer resources than do other producers.

Aggregate demand: The total of all demands for goods and services in our economy.

Aggregate income: The total of all incomes in our economy.

Aggregate supply: The total of all supplies of goods and services in our economy.

AFL-CIO (American Federation of Labor-Congress of Industrial Organizations): The largest national labor organization, formed in 1955 by the merger of the AFL and the CIO. The union represents both craft and industrial workers and includes millions of workers in its membership.

Antitrust laws: Laws that were designed to prevent monopolies and promote a competitive market economy.

Balance of payments: The bookkeeping record of all the international transactions a country makes during a year.

Balance of trade: The balance between the amount of goods (not services) our nation buys and sells abroad.

Bank of the United States: The first Bank of the United States was established in 1791 in order to issue paper money, accept deposits, make loans, and regulate the lending of state banks. Its 20-year charter expired in 1811. The second Bank of the United States was established in 1816 for many of the same purposes. Its 20-year charter also was allowed to expire in 1836.

Barter: The exchange of goods and services without the use of money.

Black market: A market in which buyers and sellers trade at prices that exceed the legal limit.

Board of Governors: The group of seven individuals who supervise the operation of the Federal Reserve System. Each member is appointed by the President of the United States and then confirmed by the Senate. A term is for fourteen years, with one term ending every two years.

Business cycles: The fluctuations in a market economy's aggregate supply and aggregate income.

Change in demand: A change in the entire list of amounts that consumers will purchase at all possible prices.

Check clearing: The process of transferring money from the account of the check writer to the account of the person receiving the check.

Checking deposits: The money that individuals and organizations have deposited in their checking accounts at commercial banks and other institutions, such as credit unions, that allow depositors to write checks to spend their deposited money. Checking deposits represent debts of the banks where the money is deposited.

Civilian labor force: All persons at least 16 years of age who are not in the military and who are either employed or unemployed.

Collective bargaining: The process in which a union, as a representative of all its workers, deals with an employer in order to increase wage rates or improve working conditions.

Command economy: An economy in which the government owns the nation's resources and decides what, how, and for whom to produce.

Comparative advantage: The ability of a producer to provide a good or service at a lower opportunity cost than do other producers.

Consumer freedom: The ability of consumers to spend their money on whatever goods and services they choose.

Consumer sovereignty: The ability of consumers to influence the kinds and quantities of goods and services produced.

Consumption: The amount of income that individuals spend to purchase goods and services.

Corporate profits tax: A tax levied directly on the profits of a corporation.

Craft union: A labor union, especially common in the last century, whose membership is limited to workers in a particular craft, such as carpentry.

Credit cards: A means of delaying the payment of money for goods and services. Credit cards are not money.

Current account balance: The balance between the amount of goods and services our nation buys and sells abroad. The balance also includes gifts, pensions, aid, and other international payments made by individuals and government in our nation.

Deflator (GNP Deflator): A statistical gauge that takes inflation out of gross national product figures. The current base year for the deflator is 1982, which means that the gauge expresses the GNP of any year in the prices of 1982.

Demand: A list of the various quantities of an item that someone is willing and able to buy at different possible prices.

Demand for labor: A list of the various quantities of labor that would be bought at different possible wage rates during a particular time.

Discount rate: The rate of interest that commercial banks must pay if they borrow reserves from the Federal Reserve System. The Federal Reserve can change this rate in order to increase or decrease the nation's money supply.

Discrimination: Identifying differences among alternatives in order to make a choice.

Economics: The study of how scarce resources are allocated among alternative uses.

Equilibrium price: The price that balances the amount of a good or service demanded with the amount supplied.

Exchange rate: The price of one country's currency in terms of another nation's currency.

External cost: A cost that remains outside the consideration of those making decisions about the use of resources.

Fair Labor Standards Act: Legislation passed in 1938 which specifies minimum hourly wage rates and prohibits the use of child labor for products sold in interstate commerce.

Federal budget deficit: The amount by which federal taxes fall short of federal expenditures.

Federal budget surplus: The amount by which federal taxes exceed federal expenditures.

Federal Deposit Insurance Corporation (FDIC): A government institution created in 1933 in order to insure checking accounts at commercial banks. Accounts are now insured for amounts up to $100,000.

Federal Reserve System: Established by the Federal Reserve Act of 1913, this system represents our nation's central bank. The major function of the Federal Reserve is to control the nation's money supply.

Federal Savings and Loan Insurance Corporation (FSLIC): A government institution created in 1934 in order to insure savings accounts at savings institutions. Accounts are now insured for amounts up to $100,000.

Final product: A product that has reached its final stage of production.

Fiscal policy: A change in federal spending or taxes in order to influence aggregate demand.

Fractional reserve system: Our banking system. Only a fraction of the money deposited with banks is kept on reserve. The rest is loaned to borrowers who pay interest on the loan and thereby provide banks with their income.

Frictional unemployment: Unemployment that occurs normally as people move from one job to another or as they move into and out of the labor force.

Full employment: The unemployment that remains when there is no weak-demand unemployment.

Going wage: The prevailing wage rate in a particular labor market.

Gompers, Samuel (1850–1924): The first president of the American Federation of labor, who held that office for all but one year between 1886 and 1924.

Gosplan: The state planning commission in the Soviet Union.

Gross national product (GNP): The sum of all prices of final goods and services produced for the marketplace in a nation during a particular time.

Hyperinflation: Unusually rapid or explosive increases in the price level.

Indirect business taxes: Business taxes, such as a sales tax, that are not levied directly on the profits of the business.

Inflation: An increase in the price level.

Intermediate products: Products, such as meat, that businesses use in order to make final products, such as hamburgers.

Investment: The production of new capital goods.

Keynes, John M. (1883–1946):   A famous economist who recommended the use of fiscal policy in order to promote economic recovery during a recession or depression. His most famous book, *The General Theory of Employment, Interest, and Money,* was published during the Great Depression of the 1930s.

Keynesian economists: Those economists who believe that fiscal policy can be used to reduce the fluctuations of a market economy.

Knights of Labor: A national labor organization formed in 1869 and headed by Uriah Smith Stevens. The union declined and disappeared because of bad organization, unsuccessful strikes, and its support of radical and unpopular political changes.

Kulaks: Comparatively wealthy peasants in the Soviet Union who resisted the collectivization of their lands by the Communist party in the last 1920s and early 1930s.

Law of diminishing returns: As more workers share the limited resources of a business, the marginal productivity of labor eventually diminishes.

Legal reserve rate: The fraction of checking deposits that banks must legally hold on reserve. The Federal Reserve system can change this rate in order to increase or decrease the nation's money supply.

Lenin, Vladimir Ilyitch (1870–1924):   Head of the Communist party in the Soviet Union after the revolution in 1917.

Loss: The amount by which the earnings of resources fall short of their opportunity cost.

Marginal productivity of labor: The additional production obtained by hiring one more unit of labor.

Marginal tax rate: The tax rate that applies to the additional (marginal) income that one receives. It is the tax rate paid on the last dollar of income received.

Market: A market exists whenever buyers and sellers trade with one another. A market might or might not have a particular physical location.

Market demand: A list of the total quantities of a good or service that all consumers will buy at different possible prices.

Market supply: A list of the total quantities of a good or service that all producers would sell at different possible prices.

Monetarist economists: Those economists who believe that the Federal Reserve's efforts to use monetary policy to reduce the economy's fluctuations tend instead to increase those fluctuations.

Monetary policy: What the Federal Reserve System does to increase or decrease the nation's money supply.

Monetizing the deficit: The creation of new money in order to provide funds for government spending when that spending exceeds tax revenues.

Money: Whatever people widely use as a medium of exchange, a measure of prices, and a store of buying power.

Money supply: The total of all the public's currency, coin, and checking accounts.

Monopoly: A market in which a single seller or a small group of sellers restricts competition and keeps the price artificially high.

National Banking Act of 1863: Legislation passed by Congress in 1863 in an effort to provide stability to the nation's banking system. The act established a new banking system of nationally chartered banks and forced most state banks to stop issuing paper money.

National debt: The total amount borrowed over the years by the federal government and not yet paid back.

New Economic Policy: An economic policy initiated by Lenin in the Soviet Union in 1921. Under this policy, the government temporarily restored some of the nation's market economy as a response to declining national production.

Open Market Committee: A part of the Federal Reserve System that is responsible for controlling the nation's money supply by buying or selling government bonds in the open market. This committee is composed of the seven members of the Board of Governors of the Federal Reserve plus presidents or vice-presidents from five of the twelve District Federal Reserve Banks.

Open market operations: The purchase and sale of government bonds by the Open Market Committee of the Federal Reserve for the purpose of increasing or decreasing the nation's money supply.

Opportunity cost: The best opportunity given up when a choice is made.

Ownership: The authority or right to determine how resources are used.

Personal taxes: Taxes, such as federal and state income taxes, that are levied directly on individuals.

Price ceiling: A government limit that keeps a price from rising to its equilibrium level.

Price effect: Higher prices cause people to buy less of an item, and lower prices cause them to buy more.

Price effect: Higher prices cause producers to supply more of an item, and lower prices cause them to supply less.

Price elasticity of demand: A measure of the price effect. When the price effect is strong, demand is elastic. When the price effect is weak, demand is inelastic.

Price floor: A government limit that keeps a price from falling to its equilibrium level.

Productivity: The amount of a good or service that a resource can add to production during a given time.

Profit: The amount by which the earnings of resources exceed their opportunity cost.

Progressive tax: A tax that takes a larger percentage of a richer person's income and a smaller percentage of a poorer person's income.

Proportional tax: A tax that takes an equal percentage from both richer and poorer persons.

Protectionism: A government's use of tariffs, quotas, and other measures to protect particular domestic producers from foreign competition.

Public good: A good or service that has the following two characteristics: (1) everyone can consume it at the same time, and (2) those who do not pay for it cannot be prevented from consuming it.

Rationing function: The task of determining how scarce goods and services are divided among those who want them.

Real GNP: Gross national product adjusted for inflation.

Recession: A decrease in real GNP for at least one-half of a year.

Regressive tax: A tax that takes a larger percentage of a poorer person's income and a smaller percentage of a richer person's income.

Reserves: Funds that banks have kept and have not loaned. Some reserves are kept as vault cash, but most are kept as deposits at the Federal Reserve Bank.

Resources: The four basic ingredients used to produce what we want: land, labor, capital, and management.

Saving: The amount of income that individuals do not spend for the consumption of goods and services.

Scarcity: The inability of limited means to satisfy all of everyone's wants.

Seasonal unemployment: Temporary unemployment caused by the normal, seasonal decline in the demand for particular goods and services.

Shortage: The amount by which the quantity demanded of a good or service exceeds the quantity supplied at a particular price.

Social insurance tax: A tax, such as the Social Security tax, that transfers income to retired citizens.

Specialization: The concentration of one's work on a particular good or service.

Stalin, Joseph (1879–1953):   Head of the Communist party in the Soviet Union from the time of Lenin's death in 1924 until his death in 1953.

Structural unemployment: Unemployment that results from a mismatch of (1) workers' skills and the skills required for available jobs or (2) the geographic location of workers and that of the jobs available.

Sunk cost: A cost that was incurred in the past and can no longer be avoided.

Supply: A list of the various quantities of an item that a producer is willing to sell at different possible prices.

Supply-side economists: An emphasis on the long-term effects of monetary and fiscal policies on aggregate supply. Supply-side economists believe that high marginal tax rates reduce a market economy's aggregate supply.

Surplus: The amount by which the quantity supplied of a good or service exceeds the quantity demanded at a particular price.

Thinking at the margin: Comparing the additional (marginal) benefit of a choice with its additional (marginal) cost.

Transfer payments: Government payments to individuals for the purpose of redistributing income.

Unemployment rate: The proportion of the nation's civilian labor force that is not working but is looking for employment. The unemployment rate is calculated as follows:

$$\text{Unemployment rate} = \frac{\text{Number unemployed}}{\text{Number in civilian labor force}}$$

Weak-demand unemployment: Unemployment that results from a drop in the total demand for a nation's goods and services.

Index